**This book is to be returned on or before
the last date stamped below.**

15. JUN. 1992

LATE RETURN WILL INCUR
PENALTY \ FINE

Hypermedia/Hypertext And Object-oriented Databases

UNICOM Applied Information Technology

Each book in the series is based upon papers given at a seminar organized by UNICOM Seminars Ltd. The reports cover subjects at the forefront of information technology, and the contributors are all authorities in the subject on which they are invited to write, either as researchers or as practitioners.

Hypermedia/Hypertext And Object-oriented Databases

UNICOM

APPLIED INFORMATION TECHNOLOGY 8

Edited by **Heather Brown**

Reader in Computer Science, University of Kent at Canterbury

CHAPMAN & HALL

London · New York · Tokyo · Melbourne · Madras

Published by Chapman & Hall, 2–6 Boundary Row, London SE1 8HN

Chapman & Hall, 2–6 Boundary Row, London SE1 8HN, UK

Van Nostrand Reinhold, 115 5th Avenue, New York NY10003, USA

Chapman & Hall Japan, Thomson Publishing Japan, Hirakawacho Nemoto Building, 7F, 1–7–11 Hirakawa-cho, Chiyoda-ku, Tokyo 102, Japan

Chapman & Hall Australia, Thomas Nelson Australia, 102 Dodds Street, South Melbourne, Victoria 3205, Australia

Chapman & Hall India, R. Seshadri, 32 Second Main Road, CIT East, Madras 600 035, India

First edition 1991

© 1991 UNICOM and contributors

Printed and bound in Great Britain by T J Press (Padstow) Ltd, Padstow, Cornwall

ISBN 0 412 39970 9   0 442 31412 4 (USA)

The publisher makes no representation, express or implied, with regard to the accuracy of the information contained in this book and cannot accept any legal responsibility or liability for any errors or omissions that may be made.

A catalogue record for this book is available from the British Library

Library of Congress Cataloging-in Publication available

CONTENTS

CONTRIBUTORS

P. Baird, B. Cronin and
L. Davenport
Department of Information Science
Strathclyde Business School
University of Strathclyde

L. Bottaci and A. Stewart
Department of Computer Science
University of Hull

H. Brown and F. Cole
Computing Laboratory
University of Kent at Canterbury

P. Brown
Computing Laboratory
University of Kent at Canterbury

D. Diaper
Department of Computer Science
Liverpool University

A. Dillon
HUSAT
Loughborough University
Leicester

N. Hammond
Department of Psychology
University of York

G. Kemp and D. Melvin
Department of Computing Science
King's College
University of Aberdeen

J. Nielsen
Technical University of Denmark

C. Plaisant-Schwenn
Human Computer Interaction
Laboratory
The University of Maryland

R. Rada
Department of Computer Science
University of Liverpool

S. Roberts
School of Computer Studies
University of Leeds

J. Spiers
Oracle Corporation UK Ltd
Surrey

I. Williams
Office Workstations Ltd
Edinburgh

H. Wilson
Exmar
AI Ltd
Watford

PREFACE

Many areas of computing may be justifiably described as fast-moving and exciting. When developments in two such areas come together to provide new techniques and make new applications possible it is difficult to pick a single term to describe the result — perhaps 'explosive' is the best. The chapters in this volume come from two fast-moving and exciting areas where there is certainly an explosion of interest and activity at the interface between the two. A single volume cannot cover both areas in great depth, but the chapters presented here offer a good picture of current issues and the current state-of-the-art.

Hypertext is concerned with the presentation of information in a non-sequential fashion. Unlike paper texts, where information is generally expected to be read in a sequential manner, hypertexts allow readers to navigate their own paths through the information. This exploits the interactive nature of the electronic medium and opens up many new possibilities, but demands careful design by the author and a degree of discipline by readers. Typically, the author provides links between related pieces of information in a manner that allows readers to choose which links they wish to explore. Links may be used to direct readers to additional information in much the same way that footnotes and glossaries do in paper texts, or they may provide more direct links between related pieces of information. In either case readers can view the related information simply by pointing to a 'button' or other indication on the screen. Mechanisms are generally provided to allow readers to backtrack to their original position or to follow further links. If the author does not provide an adequate number of links readers are restricted and may find the information less useful and accessible.

Too many links, on the other hand, can lead to the well-known problems of 'spaghetti' information and of readers becoming lost in a maze of links. The author may thus attempt to provide primary routes through the information to guide readers while allowing them to explore side routes at will. A considerable amount of work is under way in the Human Interface community to try to evaluate and understand the way readers absorb information in this new environment.

The distinction between hypertext and hypermedia is not clear cut. Indeed, the two terms are often used interchangeably. Although hypertext strictly refers to textual information, the term is also commonly used to refer to bodies of information containing graphics and images as well. The term hypermedia is generally used to refer to information containing a high proportion of graphics and images, and is almost always used where the information also includes video sequences or any form of animated information. The chapters in this volume, as in the literature in general, do not make a clear distinction between the two terms.

Where the information in a hypertext is both extensive and highly inter-linked, the hypertext system can be regarded as a means of browsing through a database of information. The information in a hypertext is not generally as rigidly structured as in a traditional relational database, but may be similar to the looser structure of information in the developing generation of object-oriented databases. This is the interface area that is causing so much interest. Hypertext practitioners regard object-oriented databases as a convenient means of storing and accessing the information handled by their hypertexts, while database specialists regard hypertext and hypermedia systems as new and friendly front-ends for accessing the information in their databases. The chapters in this volume look at both sides of the interface, though the majority of them concern the user interface and application areas and therefore focus more on the hypertext side.

The chapters are divided into four sections. The first section provides a general introduction and looks at a number of different applications. Readers who are not familiar with hypertext will find a clear introduction to the basic principles and ideas in the first chapter 'Usability Considerations in Introducing Hypertext' by Jakob Nielsen. This chapter sketches the history of hypertext, discusses its advantages and disadvantages compared to paper, and presents an unusual example of a hypertext designed for children. Two chapters providing a good description of more serious hypertext systems are 'An Overview of Hyperties, its User Interface and Data Model' by Catherine Plaisant and 'Hypertext: Dreams and Reality' by Peter Brown. The first of these describes the Hyperties system that was developed at the University of Maryland. A Hyperties database consists of a set of articles, each covering a single topic. Links embedded in the content of articles provide readers with an easy means of moving to related articles. The chapter describes the Hyperties user interface and the internal structures used. Guide is a system developed at the University of Kent and marketed by Office Workstations. The chapter by Peter Brown describes an application of Guide for helping to 'launder' fault reports. The application is designed to help a team of diagnosticians (launderers) who answer telephone calls about hardware faults. The goal of the system is to assist in locating the fault and to ensure that an engineer is sent to the customer's site with the correct spares if needed. Replacing paper documentation with a Guide hypertext resulted in a considerable improvement in diagnosis and a corresponding saving in engineers' time.

The second section focuses on human factors. This includes the physical interface with the hypertext system but concentrates rather more on the tasks a user performs and effective ways to present information. The chapter 'Expertext: Hyperizing Expert Systems and Expertizing Hypertext' by Dan Diaper and Roy Rada also tackles another interface area where hypertext and expert systems are coming together.

The third section looks in a little more detail at the internal models and structures used in hypertext systems, including references and links. The relationship between text and hypertext is considered in 'Converting Text to Hypertext and Vice Versa' by Roy Rada and Dan Diaper and in 'Hypermedia for Multi-User Technical Documentation' by Ian Williams. Some consideration is also given in this section to the use of existing standards (like SGML and ODA) for hypertexts.

Object-oriented databases do not appear explicitly in the titles of chapters until the fourth section, but this does not mean that databases have been entirely neglected in the earlier chapters. This section contains two chapters devoted entirely to the database side of the interface. The chapter on the 'Structure and Scope of Object-oriented Databases' by Stuart Roberts provides a clear introduction to the essential ingredients of object-oriented databases: objects, object classes, encapsulation, generalization and aggregation, and inheritance. It also evaluates some current products and prototypes. The chapter on 'Object-oriented Databases – Evolution or Revolution?' by John Spiers looks at the evolution of more flexible databases and takes a slightly cynical view of the current fashion for describing everything as object-oriented.

Finally, the chapter by Graham Kemp and David Melvin describes a graphical interface developed for an object-oriented database containing data on protein structures. The final section of this chapter discusses some of the differences in the browsing and searching capabilities of hypermedia system and object-oriented databases.

ABSTRACTS

1 Usability Considerations in Introducing Hypertext

J. Nielsen

After a brief look at the definition of the word 'hypertext', we survey the surprisingly extensive history of the field starting from the never implemented 'Memex' from 1945 over the pioneering systems from the 1960s and the research systems from the 1970s to the commercial systems of the 1980s. We briefly consider the future systems of the 1990s. We then discuss the reasons why hypertext has become so popular now and conclude with the consideration of usability problems in hypertext implementations.

2 An Overview of Hyperties, its User Interface and Data Model

C. Plaisant

Hyperties stands for the Interactive Encyclopedia System, based on Hypertext. It is composed of an author tool and a browser. It allows users to easily traverse databases of text, pictures and videodisc images. Our main goal in the past has been to design interfaces for novice users. Common applications of Hyperties include museum exhibits, kiosks etc. Hyperties features such as screen layout, link representation and multiple window strategies are discussed from a user interface standpoint. A PC version has been available since 1987 and the Human-Computer Interaction Laboratory has implemented a workstation version on Sun using NeWS.

3 Hypertext: Dreams and Reality

P. Brown

The aim of hypertext is simple and practical: to create a better world for readers of on-line documents. There is a danger, in any field of research and development, of the researchers moving into a dream world, far divorced from the real needs of users. This can happen throughout computing research – and doubtless in other disciplines – even when the topic is severely practical. It happens in relatively mature disciplines, such as software engineering, and is certainly not confined to new and fashionable disciplines like hypertext.

Often the dream world is encouraged by funding agencies, who push grandiose and ambitious projects. When these fail no-one wishes to acknowledge it, least of all the funding agency, and thus further even more grandiose projects are built upon the failure of the earlier projects.

We could all gain by following Ivan Sutherland's (Frenkel, 1989) wisdom: 'It seems to me the secret in research activities is to pick something easy enough to do, ... but a lot of people pick projects that are too hard. I've tried to pick easy ones to work on. And there are plenty of easy ones going begging'.

The purpose of this chapter is to act as a counter-weight to the dreams and hype surrounding hypertext. It takes a real project with down-to-earth aims, and examines how the lessons learned from that project throw light on the issues facing hypertext.

4 Exmar: Automating Marketing Planning

H. Wilson

The Exmar club of British companies aims to develop computerized assistance for strategic marketing planning, using AI Limited as technical contractor. Focused analysis emphasizing representation led to a logical model, including a generally applicable, sound data model, that unified the diverse formal techniques of market planning; a process model for marketing plan generation; and semi-structured assistance to the planner. These features were exploited in a demonstrator, an interactive system that supports a marketing planner by enabling one's markets and products to be represented and interpreted, leading to a better understanding of the business and an appropriate course of action. Having established the feasibility of building such a tool and obtained evidence for its utility, prototype development is under way. Conclusions are drawn on the analysis approach and the role of the computer in such systems, and on project management in clubs.

5 Hypertext and Added Value

P. Baird

Novel media for the presentation and dissemination of information are increasingly being devised. In a world where information and documentation is ever increasing, information services are continually exploiting ways in which the new technologies can ease their burden by consigning labour-intensive tasks to the machine; can manage and manipulate large stores of information; can assist information retrieval within their environment etc.

Often what they neglect is an exploration of how new technologies can benefit information management, can add value to the service they provide, can release professional staff from drudgery, can give them strategic advantage over their competitors: in other words which can enable them to offer a better information service to their users.

Hypertext as a concept is not new. It is a forty-year-old-plus idea which recently, with powerful computer support, can translate the idea into reality. This chapter will explore hypertext as an added-value information resource.

6 Human Factors Issues in the Design of Hypermedia Interfaces

A. Dillon

Designing a suitable interface for any hypermedia application requires an awareness of numerous factors to do with the intended users, the tasks they will perform and the information they will be dealing with. The present chapter presents a framework for viewing these issues that suggests which factors are important and where the research needs lie.

7 Teaching with Hypermedia: Problems and Prospects

N. Hammond

Hypertext provides the basis for a new generation of exploratory learning systems, but should be supplemented by more directed mechanisms for information access, for learner guidance and for a variety of simulation and creation tasks. Different learning situations can require quite different tutorial approaches and facilities, and we argue that hypertext systems potentially provide an organizing structure for supporting a broad range of learning tasks.

8 Expertext: Hyperizing Expert Systems and Expertizing Hypertext

D. Diaper and R. Rada

An expertext system is one that combines some of the properties of an expert system and hypertext system. These two base systems are described and can be formally represented using graph theory. These descriptions are used to describe expertext options both formally and informally. A particular expertext version – Headed Records Expertext (HRE) – is then described and a simulated, worked example of the production of an HRE document is described in the domain of document generation and reuse. The conclusions of this study lead to a specification of both HRE authoring tools and HRE reader/user tools. Extensions of HRE applications to training and help systems are discussed.

9 Converting Text to Hypertext and Vice Versa

R. Rada and D. Diaper

The writing process involves network, hierarchy, and linear representations of ideas and text. The hierarchial and linear forms are handled in new international standards. Algorithms have been implemented which translate hierarchically and linearly structured text into hypertext form. Automatic methods for discovering non-hierarchical links which are implicit in a document are the subject of research. Economic motives for converting text to hypertext are multiple but have been less apparent for converting hypertext to text. These authors, however, claim that converting hypertext to text has many important applications. Not the least of these applications is that of allowing authors to represent their ideas in a network form and then providing computer support in translating this hypertext into text. In particular, the linearization strategies of the MUCH system are presented.

10 Hypermedia for Multi-User Technical Documentation

I. Williams

With the advent of commercial hypermedia software products, designers are addressing the problems of adapting this new technology to complex documentation systems. The challenge is twofold: to extend the technology so that it meets user needs in a variety of contexts and to integrate the technology with conventional paper-based systems. Rather than address the related design issues from a theoretical viewpoint, this chapter reflects recent experience in developing several complex systems for the engineering industry.

11 Extending Software into the Future

L. Bottaci and A. Stewart

This chapter is concerned with exploiting hypertext in the development of software, particularly in the writing and documentation of large software systems. The software crisis gained widespread and official recognition at the first NATO conference on Software Engineering in 1968. The crisis is now 21 years old and we are faced with the question of what the future has in store for the development of software technology. Clearly, there is yet much scope for better working methods, programming languages, tools and environments and progress is slowly being made on all these fronts. This chapter argues that hypertext has an important role to play in extending the power of software as a technology.

12 The Office Document Architecture and Hypermedia

H. Brown and F. Cole

Interactive editors for complex documents have much in common with hypertext systems. Both allow users to create structured bodies of information and to read or browse through this information online in an interactive fashion. There are no accepted standards for representing interactive documents or hypertext of this nature.

The Office Document Architecture (ODA) is an international standard designed to aid the representation and interchange of paper-based documents such as memoranda, letters, and reports. ODA provides comprehensive facilities for describing the structure and content of complex multimedia documents. This chapter looks at the possibility of using ODA as a standard for interactive documents and hypertext.

13 Structure and Scope of Object-oriented Databases

S. Roberts

The main aim of this chapter is to examine the features expected from an object-oriented database to assess whether these features are useful in principle and available in practice. The features we shall discuss include the object as the unit of modelling; generalization and aggregation hierarchies; methods and encapsulation. Reference to a number of available packages will be made in order to illustrate object-oriented database features. A simple application will be used to show the benefits of object-oriented techniques and comparison will be made with traditional data models where appropriate.

14 Object-oriented Databases—Evolution or Revolution?

J. Spiers

The role of a Database Management System (DBMS) is to automatically enforce representation, structure and increasingly, meaning and behaviour of data.

This chapter reviews the area of object-oriented database requirements in the light of the existing standards and investments in today's relational systems. A number of evolutionary directions for relational systems are identified and illustrated.

15 A Graphical Interface for an Object-oriented Database

G. Kemp and D. Melvin

An object-oriented database system has been implemented in a combination of Prolog and C, and is being used to store data on protein structures. Queries against the database explore protein structures by navigating through the database, following relationship links from one object to others. The database can be queried using Prolog or the query language Daplex. A graphical interface to the database which enables simple queries to be expressed easily is described. Search and query in an object-oriented database is compared with that in hypermedia systems.

Part One

Hypertext and its Applications

1. USABILITY CONSIDERATIONS IN INTRODUCING HYPERTEXT

J. Nielsen

Technical University of Denmark

The simplest way to define hypertext is to contrast it with traditional text like this paper. All traditional text, whether in printed form or in computer files, is sequential. This means that there is a single linear sequence defining the order in which the text is to be read. First, you read page one. Then you read page two. Then you read page three. And you don't have to be much of a mathematician to generalize the formula to determine what page to read next.

Hypertext is non-sequential, however. This means that there is no single order which determines the sequence in which the text is to be read. Hypertext presents several different options, and the individual reader determines which of them to follow at the time of reading the text. This means that the author of the text has set up a number of alternatives for readers to explore rather than a single stream of information.

The same is true of footnotes in traditional printed texts since the readers have to determine upon reaching the footnote marker whether to continue reading the primary stream of text or to branch off to pursue the footnote. Therefore hypertext is sometimes called the "generalized footnote".

Many other computer techniques may match various aspects of the definition of hypertext at least partly, but true hypertext should also make users feel that they can move freely through the information according to their own needs. This feeling is hard to define precisely but certainly implies small overhead with respect to using the computer. This means short response times so that the text is on the screen as soon as the user asks for it. Small overhead also requires low cognitive load when navigating so that users do not have to spend their time wondering what the computer will do or how to get it to do what they want.

So when asked whether I would view a certain system as hypertext, I would personally not really rely so much on its specific features, command, or data structures, but more on its user interface "look and feel".

One of the most important advantages of hypertext is that it is a method for integrating three technologies and industries which have been separate until recently: publishing, computing, and broadcasting (in the form of television and film). Hypertext provides the opportunity to publish information structures to the general public in much the same way as books or newspapers are currently published. But these new information structures would be highly based on moving images in the tradition of the film and animation industries and would be under computer control to allow for user interaction.

As an example, consider the NewsPeek system developed at the MIT Media Lab under the direction of Walter Bender. NewsPeek watches the nightly television news for you and records those parts which it knows are of interest to you. You can then browse through the news structures generated by NewsPeek at your convenience.

Systems like NewsPeek can turn the tables of the power structure in journalism. Until now, the general public has been on the bottom of a pyramid populated by journalists and editors who decided what the individual readers and viewers should spend their time on. Computer-based news systems put the power in the hands of the individuals, however. If you watch one hour of television news every night then you will spend more than twenty thousand hours on this one activity over your lifetime. A computer technology which could save you half of this time would be equivalent to a medical breakthrough which would increase your expected life by two years.

NewsPeek-like systems can gather news from many sources such as broadcast and cable television and various newswire services. It can then integrate this news in a hypertext structure with links between related news stories downloaded from the *Times*, tables from the Dow Jones service, and film clips from the TV. If a newswire service mentions a topic which is not covered on the TV news, your computer might link to illustrations it could generate itself from a stock of illustrations on a CD-ROM which would include e.g. maps of the world.

All of this news would be presented in a format edited by your own computer to match exactly your own interests and preferences. For example, the computer might know that you were going on a business trip to Brussels because it had taken care of your airline reservations. It would then give news stories from Belgium higher priority than stories from other countries, and it would present a story about, say a forecast for a snowstorm in the Brussels area as "front page" material on your personal newspaper.

Scenarios like this are an example of another reason many computer scientists are excited about the potential inherent in hypertext. Even more modest applications of hypertext show that hypertext is fundamentally a computer phenomenon as observed by Gilbert Cockton from Glasgow University. Hypertext can only be done on a computer while most other current applications of computers might just as well be done by hand. You can only get so excited about designing yet another word processor or accounting program since you are fundamentally doing nothing except making slight improvements to activities which have been conducted almost as well without computers in the past. Hypertext applications, in contrast, only make sense if you have a computer. Except maybe for Presidents and Prime Ministers, nobody gets a personalized newspaper now, but everybody will when hypertext becomes more established.

As further discussed in (Nielsen, 1990) hypertext has a surprisingly extensive history considering how recently most people have heard about the concept. Table 1.1 gives a short survey of some of the main events in the history of hypertext.

In the short term of three to five years, I don't really expect significant changes in the way hypertext is produced compared to the currently known systems. Of course new things will be invented all the time, but just getting the things we already have out in the world will be more than enough. I expect to see two major changes: the emergence of a mass market for hypertext and the integration of hypertext with other computer facilities such as artificial intelligence and simulation systems.

Towards the end of the 1990s we should expect to see widespread publishing of hypertext material. It is also likely that the various forms of video which are currently quite expensive will be part of the regular personal computers people have in their homes and offices. So we should expect to see true hypermedia documents for widespread distribution.

What will happen in the really long term future more than twenty years from now? In the computer business, ten to twenty years count as long term future indeed, so any further projections are reserved for the science fiction authors. I recommend that you read for example Gibson (1984), Vinge (1984), or Bova (1989).

In any case, developments in user interface design for hypertext will determine whether hypertext ends up as a success or failure. Even in a small document which could be read in one hour, users experienced the "lost in hyperspace" phenomenon as exemplified by the following user comment from our field studies (Nielsen and Lyngbaek, 1989): "I soon realized that if I did not read something when I stumbled across it, then I would not be able to find it later". Of our respondents 56% agreed fully or partly with the statement: when reading the report, I was often confused about "where I was".

The hypertext used in our field study was implemented in Guide, and users had too many problems using the inverse operations of the Guide hypertext buttons to return to their previous system states as can be seen from the 44 % agreement with the statement: when reading the report, I was often confused about "how to get back to where I came from". One reason for the confusion felt by many users is probably that Guide uses different backtrack mechanisms depending on which type of "button" (link mechanism) was used originally. Several users complained that Guide does not re-establish a completely identical screen layout when returning to a previous state after a backtrack operation. This makes it more difficult to recognize the location one returns to and thus complicates the understanding of the navigational dimensions of the hyperspace.

For a fairly detailed example of a hypertext user interface, let us next consider The Manhole (Activision, 1988). This is an interactive fiction for "children of all ages" published on a CD-ROM for the Macintosh. It takes place in a fantasy world with talking animals and dragons where magic bean stalks grow into the sky. The fantasy world is displayed to the user in a first-person perspective (i.e. graphically showing what you would actually see if you were positioned at the current location in the world) and users move through the world by clicking onto the place they want to go.

It took me approximately two hours to get through all of The Manhole's navigation space. The fantasy world of the disc actually has some structure to it in a one-dimensional ordering of the locations from the bottom of the sea, via the sea surface and the street level with the manhole itself, to a tower in the sky. There is a

1945	Vannevar Bush proposes Memex
1965	Ted Nelson coins the word hypertext
1967	the Hypertext Editing System and FRESS
	Brown University, Andy van Dam *et al*
1968	Doug Engelbart demo of NLS system at FJCC
1975	ZOG (now KMS): CMU
1978	Aspen Movie-Map, first hypermedia videodisk
	Andy Lippman, MIT Architecture Machine Group
1984	Filevision from Telos; limited hypermedia database widely available for the Macintosh
1985	Symbolics Document Ecaminer, Janet Walker
	major system which went into practical use.
1985	Xerox NoteCards announced, Frank Halasz *et al*
1985	Intermedia, Brown University, Normal Meyrowitz
1985	Schneiderman Hyperties (University of Maryland)
1986	OWL introduces HyperCard, first widely available hypertext
1987	Apple introduces HyperCard, Bill Atkinson - stackware latest craze
1987	Hypertext'87 Workshop, North Carolina
	250 participants out of 500 applicants

Table 1.1 Overview of the history of hypertext

magic bean stalk which covers this distance, thus providing a kind of landmark. This navigation space is set up with little regard to normal conventions regarding landmarks and orderly user movement, however, and users are frequently magically transported to new locations and have to discover where they are in the navigation space. The very structure and connectivity of the navigation space did not even become apparent to me before I had spent about one hour in it.

Fig. 1.1 shows one example of navigational support provided by the bean stalk landmark while Fig. 1.2 shows an example of navigation violating traditional expectations. This latter kind of "magical" movement in the world of an interactive fiction adds spice to the experience of using the system and is probably good in a system having entertainment as its main purpose. It also seems to make it harder to acquire a conceptual model of the navigation space, however, so it would probably not be suited for more work-oriented situations.

The Manhole uses the English language to a large extent in the form of messages from various characters to the user. These messages are printed on the screen in cartoon-like speech-bubbles and are also read out loud by the system using good quality sound and some interesting voice characterizations. There are four main characters with which the user interacts: an elephant which paddles the user around in a small boat, a dragon, a walrus, and a rabbit. Each character has a tone of voice consistent with the way it behaves (e.g. the walrus is lazy and the dragon is a "hip dude"). Other sound effects, including both music and various naturalistic sounds are also used to good effect.

Because of its heavy use of the English language, I have not been able to experiment with the use of The Manhole by Danish children. The Inigo Gets Out hyperstory about the adventures of a cute cat, in contrast, is a totally non-verbal interactive fiction, and we found (Nielsen and Lyngbaek, 1989) that Danish children were indeed able to move through that story easily and had great fun doing so. But Inigo Gets Out has a much smaller navigation space than The Manhole (only 31 screens) so one probably cannot generalize about this result . In Inigo Gets Out, the user returns every few minutes to a single landmark location (a screen where the cat can either look in the bushes, follow a road, or climb a tree) which children easily recognized.

I did experiment with one test user of The Manhole in addition to myself. This person (an adult business professional) enjoyed using the system for about 30 minutes but frequently complained about the difficulty of knowing which parts of the screen were active hypertext anchors (clickable areas) and what the results of her actions would be. Also, she found it difficult to know when the system was in a state where it would respond to input from the user and when it was running through a pre-defined animation sequence. This was probably because The Manhole sometimes will display an animated screen (e.g. containing drifting seaweed) or play music in situations where it is really waiting for user input. In other situations, the user is prevented from performing any action until the system has finished displaying some animation. If the user clicks anyway, there is often a risk that the system will "remember" that click and use it to activate some choice on whatever screen is displayed at the end of the animated sequence. The test user frequently had problems with a click made on one screen becoming active on the next screen, but this is probably more of a problem with the underlying HyperCard system than with The Manhole.

To conclude, The Manhole is indeed enjoyable and your initial experience, the first hour or so you use it, will give you a good idea of the feeling of reading/participating in the open or truly large-scale interactive fictions we will probably see in the future. Children will probably take more time to discover the closed nature of the fantasy universe and may even continue to enjoy moving through then-familiar territory after they have been through the entire navigation space and have discovered its internal structure.

As discussed above, the magic dimension of The Manhole would probably not be appropriate for more work-oriented hypertexts. This is one indication of the need to carefully match hypertext features to specific user needs. Further evidence is derived from a meta-analysis of hypertext usability studies (Nielsen, 1989) which concludes that the three largest effects on hypertext usability are: first, individual user differences; second, differences between users' tasks, and third, the fact that hypertext is used differently than paper and other computer systems.

	Compared with paper	Compared with traditional computer systems
Advantages of Hypertext	Can show moving images, animations, film Easier to update - perhaps automatic downloading of changes May be shipped over networks Making single copies is easy Takes up less physical storage space Can be shared by several people Potentially: The whole world's literature a click away	Data structures have user-oriented semantics A single framework to handle unstructured data (free text), semi-structured data (semantic nets etc.), and structured data (tables etc.) Does not require "programming" skills to be able to construct complex structures
Disadvantages of Hypertext	30% slower reading speed on current displays Lower resolution graphics Not portable Overhead in having to learn system and setting up computer No user interface standard No standard for data transfer No regular publishing channels, bookshops, libraries, ISBN, etc. No "romance" - first editions, leather binding etc. Computer text "homogenized"	Possible spaghetti structure No central definition of the structure of the data, and therefore no easy way to specify general actions or computations on the data

Table 1. 2 Summary of the advantages and disadvantages of hypertext

Because of these results there is little hope for a single, universal hypertext user interface design which will be optimal to everybody. Table 1.2 gives an overview of the advantages and disadvantages of hypertext compared with paper and other, traditional computer systems. Obviously hypertext has enough advantages to ensure it has a bright future if we can design sufficiently usable interfaces to at least partly overcome those disadvantages which have the largest negative impact on our users. Current empirical research on hypertext usability has no clear evidence for whether hypertext is in fact superior to paper. For some applications hypertext was best and for other applications paper was better than the current generation of hypertext. It seems clear that hypertext is indeed better in some cases even now. For many potential hypertext applications, the disadvantages will be larger than the advantages as long as we are restricted to current technology and interface designs, so we have to strive for significant improvements in both.

Furthermore, we have almost no experience with really big hypertexts. Almost all the hypertexts which have been tested in formal usability experiments have been very small and have contained only about a hundred nodes or less. A few larger hypertexts have been constructed such as the Electronic Whole Earth Catalog with its approximately ten thousand nodes.

But a really large hypertext would contain at least a hundred thousand nodes and we should expect to see some hypertexts with millions of nodes in the future. It may well be that many of the major advantages of hypertext will not become apparent until we have such great hypertexts integrating major fields of human knowledge. But we are also guaranteed to discover new usability and implementation problems as we move to such huge information structures.

Acknowledgement

This paper is partly based on work performed within the SAFE project, partially funded by the Commission of the European Communities under contract number D1014 of the Exploratory Action of the DELTA program. The views expressed in this paper are those of the author, however, and do not necessarily reflect those of the SAFE consortium.

REFERENCES

Activision: *The Manhole*, Activision, P.O. Box 3048, Menlo Park, 94025-3047, USA (1988) Commercial product, $59.95 (floppy disc version with poor sound costs $49)

Bova, B. (1989) *Cyberbooks*, TOR Books.

Gibson, W. (1984) *Neuromancer*, Ace.

Nielsen, J. The matters that really matter for hypertext usability, *Proc. ACM Hypertext '89 Conf.* (Pittsburgh, PA, USA, 5-8 November 1989).

Nielsen, J. and Lyngbäck, U. Two field studies of hyprmedia usability, *Proc. Hypertext II Conf.* (York, UK, 29-30 June 1989).

Vinge, .V., (1984), *True Names*, Bluejay.

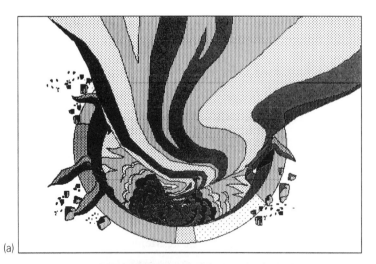

(a)

(b)

Fig.1.1(a) and (b).   Two screens from The Manhole showing support for literal navigational dimensions through the use of a landmark: The bean stalk is a linear object which connects the sea, ground, and sky levels. In fig. 1.1(a) the user's viewpoint is slightly above ground level since the figure is a snapshot from an animation of climbing down the bean stalk. The manhole (which gives the story its name) is seen at the ground level, and through it we can also see the sea level, where the bean stalk grows up from an island. In fig. 1.1(b) we are in the sky level kingdom and we can see the top of the bean stalk in the background (it grows up into the sky). If the user moves to the bean stalk in fig. 1.1(b) and then climbs down, fig. 1.1(a) will be displayed. The fact that the bean stalk is visible in the background of fig. 1.1(b) gives the user a sense of location when looking at this screen, since it would not otherwise be obvious that the tower was located at the sky level.

(a)

(b)

Fig. 1.2(a) and (b).   An example of a magical navigational dimension from The Manhole: When users move into the tower from fig.1.1(b), they will see fig.1.2(a) after having been through some screens showing a winding stairway leading to the top of the tower. Because of this movement and the presence of the flamingo on the top of the tower, users initially view the tower as a traditional building located in the forest seen in the background of fig. 1.1(b). When users move to the objects seen outside the tower in fig.1.2(a), they get to fig.1.2(b) where it is revealed that the tower has been magically transformed to a rook on a chess board (this visual pun is actually better in Danish where a chess rook is called a taarn (tower) so that the pun also becomes verbal). At the same time, the user's navigational location has been moved from the sky level to the sea level where the chess board floats in a labyrinth.

2. AN OVERVIEW OF HYPERTIES, ITS USER INTERFACE AND DATA MODEL

C. Plaisant

Human-Computer Interaction Laboratory, University of Maryland

2.1 INTRODUCTION

Hyperties has been under development at the University of Maryland since Autumn 1983. It was originally called TIES (The Interactive Encyclopedia System), but the new name was chosen to indicate the close relationship with hypertext concepts. Hyperties allows users to traverse textual, graphic or video information resources in an easy way. They merely touch (with their fingers or with a mouse or by pressing arrow keys to move a cursor onto) highlighted words or objects that interest them, and a brief definition appears at the bottom of the screen. The users may continue reading or ask for the full article about the selected topic. An article can be one or several pages long. As the users traverse articles Hyperties retains the path and allows easy reversal. Hyperties has been designed to be used by novice computer users, and to build confidence and a sense of control. Experimental studies are regularly conducted to test out design alternatives and observe user behaviour.

A PC version of Hyperties has been available since 1987, and the Human-Computer Interaction Laboratory has implemented a workstation version (on a Sun using NeWS window system) which provides a richer environment to explore advanced features.

Both versions are closely related and databases convertible. Some very practical features (like printing) are only implemented on the PC version, while some more advanced features (such as free shape selectable graphic or multiple windows) are only available now on the workstation. Because this Chapter's purpose is to describe desirable functionalities more than to present a specific product, both versions are unified.

Hyperties is written in C. The PC version accepts PC paintbrush graphic, the Sun version Sunraster images and Postscript display.

This Chapter presents a general overview of Hyperties and discusses user-interface issues, then describes the database structure of the new workstation version.

2.2   OVERVIEW OF HYPERTIES

The Hyperties browser was initially designed for novice users. The user's attention should be focused on the content of the database and not on the technical aspects. Hyperties makes a clear distinction between the authoring and browsing of a database. We believe that the quality of the authoring tools will play an important role in the design of the database and of its interconnection, and that the quality of the database is one of the main success factors for any hypertext application.

2.2.1 Hyperties encyclopedia metaphor

Using an encyclopedia metaphor, an Hyperties database consists of a set of articles, each covering a topic. Each article has a title, a short description (definition or abstract) and a content (the article itself). It can consist of one or several screens or pages, the size of each article is only a function of the topic covered (down to consisting only of one definition).

There is only one type of article, but some articles use a reserved title, for example the "table of content" article, the "introduction" article , the "index" article.

There is no underlying structure imposed on the database links. Even though a large number of existing documents have a hierarchical structure, we think it is important not to limit the research to a very specific structure, but to study old and new structures that make better use of the Hypertext concepts.

The database is assumed to be static, i.e. the contents of a database will not change during browsing (but this restriction could be relaxed in the future). There is no underlying limitation to the number of articles.

2.2.2 Links

Links are embedded in the content of the article. They can be included in text or in graphics.

In the text components of the article, the default type of link proposed to the author is an embedded link where the highlighted words in the text correspond to the title (or a synonym) of the article referred to. In fig. 2.1 the boldface string "Smithsonian museum" indicates the link to the article whose title is "Smithsonian museum" . The transparency of the link gives the user a good idea of the reference's nature and a sense of continuity. Much can be done to automate the author's job of establishing links between entries. When an author specifies a reference in an article (by simply putting tildes around the string), the author tool merely examines a list of entry names and synonyms to establish the link.

```
WASHINGTON, DC: THE NATION'S CAPITAL              PAGE 2 OF 3

     Located between Maryland and Virginia, Washington, DC
  embraces the White House and the Capitol, a host of
  government offices as well as the Smithsonian museums.
  Designed by Pierre L'Enfant, Washington, DC is a graceful
  city of broad boulevards, national monuments, the rustic
  Rock Creek Park, and the National Zoo.

     First-time visitors should begin at the mall by walking
  from the Capitol towards the Smithsonian museums and on
  ------------------------------------------------------------
  SMITHSONIAN MUSEUMS: In addition to the familiar castle and
  popular Air & Space Museum there are 14 other major sites.
  FULL ARTICLE ON "SMITHSONIAN MUSEUMS"

  NEXT PAGE  BACK PAGE    RETURN TO "NEW YORK CITY"      INDEX
```

Fig. 2.1   This Hyperties display on an IBM Personal Computer shows highlighted embedded menu items that can be selected by touchscreen, mouse or arrow keys. The reader can follow a topic of interest, turn pages, return to the previous article or view the index.

We strongly believe that the use of the article titles as navigation landmarks is an important factor to limit the disorientation of the user in the database. It is only with caution that we introduced what we call "opaque links" or "blind links" (a link where the highlighted word is not the title of the referred article), to satisfy what should remain as special cases.

In the graphic components: the commercial version on the PC only allows graphic pages to be displayed or used as background for a page of text.   Other PC versions allow rectangular shaped targets to be selected. The Sun version allows the use of selectable targets of any shape. A selectable graphic item is highlighted when the mouse cursor passes over it, and all the selectables are shown when the user clicks the mouse on a non -selectable part of the screen.

The default destination of a link is the beginning of an article. With some caution we are introducing located links to jump directly inside an article to a specified location, but believe that this type of link demands an important re-orientation effort from the user. These located links should only be used when the context of the jump is such that the user can expect to land in the middle of a document.

Links are unidirectional because bidirectional links can be very confusing. When reading about the play *Les Miserables* you may want to read about France, but when reading the article France you may not want to see the thousands of articles referring to it. The user can always consult a separate cross-reference table if necessary, and the author(s) of the database can create paired links when they make sense.

Links are made visible only if the content of the destination article has been created.

The links are part of the article (unlike some other systems that store links and nodes separately, e.g. Intermedia).

Before jumping to a new article, Hyperties first displays the short description of this article. The user then decides to follow the link to the full article or not. The description provides a smoother transition between articles and limits the possibility of irrelevant jumps. In some cases an article consists only of a definition. The author of a database can also decide to bypass the presentation of definitions in a given database.

2.2.3 Other Hyperties user interface aspects

(a) Screen layout

The original PC version of Hyperties displayed a single page of information. The title appears at the top left, the page number (Page x of y) in the top right corner. A four line area is reserved for the definition display in the low part of the screen. The bottom of the screen is used for the standard commands (e.g.: NEXT PAGE, BACK PAGE, INDEX, QUIT, etc.).

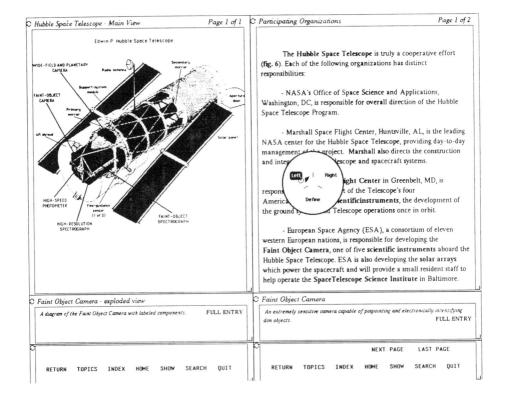

Fig. 2.2   Example on the Sun using two windows

In the Sun version, we are exploring several multiwindow strategies. For the novice users we are in favour of carefully designed tiled windows (as opposed to moveable overlapping windows) to limit the manipulation of the windows by the user. Simple but effective window switching mechanisms should still be studied, as well as a command language to allow "advanced" users to describe or modify those default strategies. Fig. 2.2 shows a pie menu used to specify which window should be used to display the links destination article. Pie menus allow click ahead (a quick click and slide right or left is sufficient). In fig. 2.3, an overlapping window shows the short description of the destination article, the user chooses the destination window among four.

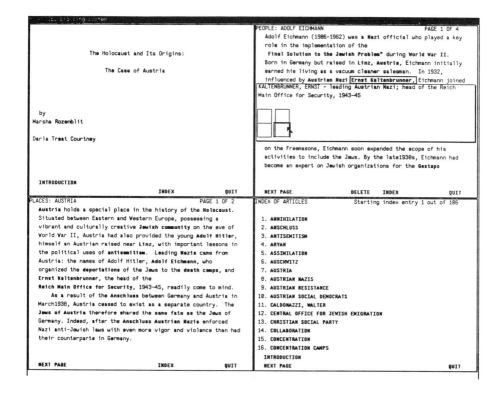

Fig. 2.3 A four windows example on the Sun

(b) Make clear what is selectable

The text domain allows relatively simple assumptions to be made about the nature of the selectable items and permits a simple approach to their representation (e.g. using boldface or colours). The text selectable items are references in the article and control commands available in the control panel at the bottom of the screen. By default the selectable strings are highlighted in light blue in the PC version and in bold on the Sun.

The incorporation of graphics into hypertext systems presents a challenge in interface design. In the graphic domain there is no simple technique for emphasizing the targets that is acceptable in all cases and the author must laboriously link all targets to their references (they are not self naming, as in the text case). Another problem to be addressed is that of indicating the selectable elements of a graphic. The user should not have to hunt for the targets on an image by trial and error. The chosen scheme should identify unambiguously the location and scope of the target, not interfere with the comprehension of the image and require little or no effort from the user. Possible solutions includes dynamic indicators, outlines, inverse video, fixed symbols, colour, shading, and image manipulation [Weiland and Schneiderman, 1989]. This last solution has been implemented in the Sun version of Hyperties. The pop-out technique causes the target to be redisplayed slightly shifted vertically and horizontally, with an apparent shadow underneath. This gives the appearance of having the object pop out of the screen. The slight movement of the object makes it readily detectable to the eye. This is especially effective where arbitrary-shaped objects are to be used (e.g. maps) and does not clutter the screen. All targets are revealed when the users try to select a non-selectable part of the image (e.g. click on the background).

(c) No commands to remember

At any point the user only has to select one item among the selectable items available, with the mouse, the arrow keys or a touch screen.

(d) No error messages
Only the valid links to existing articles are highlighted, and only the valid control commands are available on the control panel.

(e) Where are we?
Hyperties keeps track of the articles visited. A command "Return to (name of the previous article)" is always available in the control panel and allows users to reverse their traversal. A "history" command is also available to jump back directly to any article previously visited (PC-version).

(f) Retrieving information
Apart from following embedded links, several commands allow the user to identify articles of interest. The INDEX command displays the alphabetical list of articles. The TABLE OF CONTENTS command displays the table of content articles. The SEARCH command gives access to a full text string search which constructs a list of articles containing the searched string(s) (currently only on PC version). All lists are handled in a consistent way and mark the already visited articles with an asterisk.

(g) The commands available
NEXT-PAGE, BACK-PAGE, RETURN TO (previous article), INDEX, TABLE OF CONTENTS, SEARCH, HISTORY, QUIT. The commands are highlighted on the screen. Short cuts are also available via the keyboard (e.g. CTRL-Q for Quit).

2.2.4 The authoring tool

(a) For the PC
The authoring tools are used to enter (or import) the text of each article and mark the links. The authoring tools automatically tie the articles and provide an index to the entire database. Articles can be added, deleted, renamed. Cross-reference   tables are provided. The browser can be directly called by the author to check the formatting of an article and its links. Hyperties allows the author to mark special articles as the table of contents, the front-matter article used to include the preface, credits etc. Only

a simple text editor is provided in the authoring tool, but text and graphic files can be imported from other commercially available editors. Formatting comands are used to polish the presentation of information.

Databases can be easily converted from the PC to the Sun.

(b)   For the workstation
We are now exploring a new environment for the authoring tool as well as a new markup language to describe the information to be presented in each article. Unipress Emacs provides a multiple windows, menus and programming environment to author a database. Graphics tools are launched from Emacs to create or edit the graphic components and target tools are available to mark the shape of each target and set the attributes of the pop-out or other target identification method used. The authoring tool checks the links and verifies the syntax of the article markup. It also allows the author to preview the database by easily following links from Emacs buffer to buffer. Author and browser can also be run concurrently for final editing.

2.2.5   Current research directions

The current research directions are as follows:

- graphic searches;

- "advanced browser" (annotation, bookmarks, tours.);

- automatic importation strategies ;

- automatic exportation to linear print formats ;

- better authoring tools .

2.3   HYPERTIES DATASTRUCTURE

Hyperties has been in use for almost six years running under MS-DOS. The original
Hyperties was specialized to this environment and to a particular set of capabilities
and interface features.   There have been ongoing efforts to explore a variety of
extended capabilities: large, bitmapped displays and multiple windows (on the Sun
workstation); alternate input devices (touchscreen); graphics and other media; global
textual search; and numerous possible interface variations. From these efforts have
sprung a number of divergent Hyperties systems, each customized for a particular
investigative task, but based on the original Hyperties architecture. A more modular
and extensible Hyperties architecture has been developed which, it is hoped, will
facilitate future research by providing an open framework for experimentation and
revision.

2.3.1   General Considerations

The Hyperties database system is implemented in the standard file systems available
in most operating systems (though Unix and MS-DOS are of primary concern). In
general, a document (i.e. a node in the hypertext network) is represented by a collection
of files, one of which serves as the primary description of the document's format and
content: the "storyboard". Other "associated files" contain graphical images (or other
data, such as digitized sound, that will not normally be represented as human-readable
text) and eventually information used to allow rapid presentation of the document at
browsing time. One special file, the master index, exists to provide the association
between the document files and the database as a whole. The new Hyperties database
format permits great freedom in the organization of a database's component files. An
author can impose a hierarchical structure, using the features of the standard file
systems found in Unix and MS-DOS, to simplify access to components of the database
when a fully-integrated authoring environment is not available, and to "flatten" the
structure of a database to optimize use of storage when authoring is fully supported.

2.3.2 Database Components

In general, the files of a Hyperties database fall into two categories, portable (system-independent) files, and non-portable (system-specific) files. Of the portable files, the most basic file type is the storyboard, which contains a pure text description of an individual article in the system. Pictures and targets may also be portable, provided that the host browser supports the file format, and can compensate for differences in screen aspect ratio, etc. Non-portable files are the master index, which gives the correspondence between identifiers and system-specific file names, and graphic files . A convention adopted is that all database components are referred to by an identifier, which is a user-supplied name of arbitrary length, and that components contain their own names, so that they may be identified and collected automatically, without requiring user intervention.

(a) Storyboards

The storyboard files are pure text descriptions of the individual documents (nodes in the hypertext network) of a Hyperties database. These files are broken into fields. Today the five main fields are the title (the identifier of the document), synonyms (alternate identifiers by which the document may be referenced), description (a brief textual, graphical, etc. piece, usually used to summarize the document), content (a lengthy multi-media piece: the document proper), and notes (an optional collection of textual remarks maintained by the author). The content (and possibly the description) may contain references to other documents. Since the storyboard is a pure text document, it uses a special markup language to indicate page layout, font types, specify the inclusion of graphics etc.(see fig.2.4)

.title < Text and picture example >

.synonyms <

< Hubble Space Telescope >

~~< test and picture >~~

.description

An artist's conception of the space telescope in orbit.

(A text and picture example)

.contents <

Here is an example of article having text and a picture. The links are specified by placing ~ tildas ~. around the string.

An artist's conception of the space telescope in orbit. The picture is suppose to appear on the next line on the left part of the screen. The picture has one target (the telescope itself) which jump back to the ~ introduction article ~ ...

.nl

.picture < orbital view >

.target < orbital view - shape telescope > < introduction >

.nl

Figure 2.4   An example of storyboard. This file can be written directly by the author. Most of the marks can be added automatically with the assistance of the author-tool. It can also easily be created from pre-existing documents.

The author has to create an auxiliary file that gives the name of the target (here : "orbital view - shape telescope") and point to the actual data necessary to display the target (for example the line around the shape of the telescope itself, or a bitmap of the telescope alone). Ah... making real touchable graphic is not easy! But the author tool helps you create, assemble and verify the database

(b) Auxiliary files
A Hyperties database will also contain a number of auxiliary files, which allow images (and associated targets), generated by various graphics editors, to be included. These exist simply to provide an identifier, and description of the format, for such images, without having to modify the image files themselves (so they remain editable).

(c) Master index
The master index provides the mapping of identifiers to actual file names in a file system. It thus defines the collection of files that constitute a database. The master index is constructed automatically by the database compiler, but is a human-readable text file.

REFERENCES

Weiland, W. J., and Shneiderman, B. (1989), Interactive graphics interfaces in hypertext systems, Proc. ACM DC 28th Technical Symposium, Washington DC, USA, August, 1989.

FURTHER READING

Faloutsos, C. Lee, R. Plaisant, C. and Shneiderman, B. (June 1989), Incorporating string search in a hypertext system: User interface and signature file design issues, *Technical Report, CS-TR-2266, CAR-TR-448*

Furuta, R. Plaisant, C. and Shneiderman, B. (1989) A spectrum of automatic hypertext constructions, Technical Report. (to appear in *Hypermedia.*)

Marchionini, G. and Shneiderman, B. (January 1988), Finding facts vs. browsing knowledge in hypertext systems, *IEEE Computer*, 21, 70-80.

Seabrook, R. and Shneiderman, B. (April 1989), The user interface in a Hypertext, multi-window program browser, *Technical Report CS-TR-2237, CAR-TR-437*.

Shneiderman, B. (1989), Reflections on authoring, editing, and managing hypertext, In *The Society of Text,* (ed. E. Barrett), MIT Press, Cambridge, MA, USA.

Shneiderman, B. and Kearsley, G. (1989) *Hypertext Hands-On!*, Addison-Wesley, Reading, MA, USA.

3. HYPERTEXT: DREAMS AND REALITY

P.J. Brown

The University, Canterbury

The aim of hypertext is simple and practical: to create a better world for readers of online documents. There is a danger, in any field of research and development, of the researchers moving into a dream world, far divorced from the real needs of users. This can happen throughout computing research, and doubtless equally in other disciplines, - even when the topic is severely practical. It happens in relatively mature disciplines, such as software engineering, and is certainly not confined to new and fashionable disciplines like hypertext.

Often the dream world is encouraged by funding agencies, who push grandiose and ambitious projects. When these fail no-one wishes to acknowledge it, least of all the funding agency, and thus further even more grandiose projects are built upon the failure of the earlier projects.

We could gain by following Ivan Sutherland's (Frenkel, 1989) wisdom: "It seems to me the secret in research activities is to pick something easy enough to do, ... but a lot of people pick projects that are too hard. I've tried to pick easy ones to work on. And there are plenty of easy ones going begging."

The purpose of this paper is to act as a counter-weight to the dreams and hype surrounding hypertext. It takes a real project with down-to-earth aims, and examines how the lessons learned from that project throw light on the issues facing hypertext.

3.1 THE PROJECT

Just as you can prove anything with statistics, you can prove anything by choosing the right projects as examples. Too many "research advances" in computing are justified by toy examples which are so small and so over-simplified that all the real issues are avoided.

A more subtle effect comes from a project being the first in the field, as any project that exploits a new research technique will inevitably be. There is extra excitement and commitment from the people involved (including the so-called Hawthorne effect), and funding criteria may be different - the project may not need to justify itself economically, but instead may be regarded as a research exercise.

The project chosen for this exercise is the Locator project, undertaken by ICL at Stevenage in collaboration with the University of Kent at Canterbury. It is certainly not a toy project and had strictly economic funding criteria, and competition from other groups. It was, however, a pioneering project and, during development, was blessed with excellent and well-motivated staff. The overall results may therefore be better than a normal project, though, to counter this a little, the project faced, during its application stages the familiar problems of "We have done it this way for 20 years. Why should we change to your new approach?"

3.2 DETAILS OF THE LOCATOR PROJECT

The project involved many ICL staff, but four of the leading roles were taken by George Rouse (the overall manager), Brian Brough, Des Meehan (who deserves huge credit for technical and implementation matters) and Mike Thomas. Further details are given in Meehan (1987).

The project is concerned with what ICL calls **laundering:** dealing with hardware fault reports from customers. A team of diagnosticians sit at telephones (they were originally called "launderers" before the grander title of diagnostician was used) and receive calls from customers; their aim is to elicit enough information from the customer so that:

- an engineer can be sent to the customer's site only if needed. (Lots of "faults" turn out to be the customer's error);

- the engineer, if sent, has the right spare parts.

Prior to Locator, the laundering system was based on shelves of paper manuals with numerous cross-references ("If it is a printer problem go to Section...of Volume..."), plus the diagnosticians' experience and expertise. The aim of Locator was to provide a better way for the diagnosticians to find their way round the information. Locator did not therefore set out as a project to test hypertext techniques: instead it was a project to solve a problem, and hypertext techniques turned out to be (part) of the solution.

The hypertext system used was Guide, in its implementation that runs on Unix workstations (Brown, P.J, 1989a), in this case Suns. (There is also a widely-used implementation of Guide that runs on IBM PCs and Macintosh machines. This was developed by Office Workstations Ltd (OWL), based on the original ideas from the University of Kent. It differs in detail from the Unix implementation - every hypertext system must fit its environment - but is similar in principle).

The standard version of Unix Guide was specially tailored to meet ICL's needs. For example, the normal menu was cut down and made more specialized to the laundering environment.

3.3   A LOCATOR CALL

With the Locator system the diagnostician works exactly as before, except that the documentation, instead of being on paper, is now displayed by Guide on a workstation screen. When a customer phones to report a fault the diagnostician views the initial screen shown in fig. 3.1 The big window on the left-hand side is running Guide (We shall discuss the rest of the screen later.) The Guide window contains **replace-buttons** (shown in bold, e.g. Acoustic Hood) corresponding to the types of fault the customer may report. Replace-buttons are used in Guide to expand detail: a button is replaced in-line by more detailed material that relates to that button.

Assume the customer says the laser printer is the problem. The diagnostician then selects the LASER Printer replace-button by pointing at it and clicking the mouse. This then leads to the screen shown in fig. 3.2. In fact the whole of the document seen in fig.3.1 is a Guide **enquiry:** a collection of replace-buttons interspersed with text/graphics that is treated as a unit. If any button within the enquiry is selected, the whole enquiry is replaced by the **button-replacement** of the selected button.

The document that the user sees in Guide appears as a scroll. Selecting replace-buttons within the document causes the content of the scroll to change, and reveals information previously hidden (folded) behind the button. The user continually refines detail by selecting the appropriate replace-button until the scroll contains the desired information. This scroll model is different from the frame-based model exemplified by HyperCard, and we shall discuss the implications of this later. However, if, as in fig.3.1, a Guide enquiry occupies the whole screen, then Guide behaves like a frame-based system.

Replace-buttons are used to build a hierarchy into a document. Hierarchies are an important facet of many hypertext systems - indeed some only offer hierarchies - and we shall discuss the importance of hierarchies later.

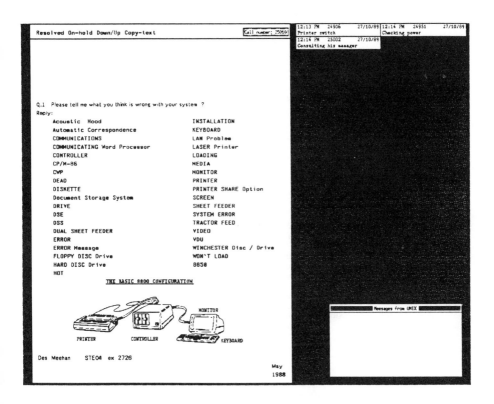

Fig. 3.1 The complete screen with the initial locator window

In fig. 3.2 the screen consists of one line of text ('A.1 LASER Printer') followed by a further enquiry. The diagnostician need not, of course, be aware of mechanisms such as enquiries, or, indeed that he/she - we shall here assume she - is using a hypertext system. To her, selecting buttons causes the appropriate text to appear magically.

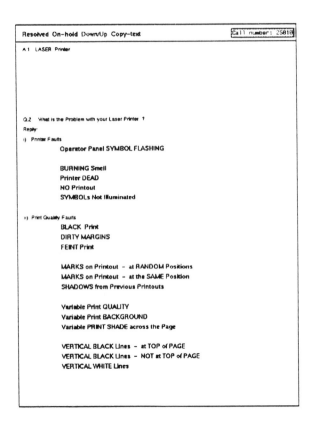

Fig. 3.2   The effect of selecting the LASER printer button.

Fig.3.3 shows the result of selecting the 'Operator panel SYMBOL FLASHING' button in fig. 3.2 This in turn leads to an extra line at the top of the screen to give the customer's second response, and a further enquiry. (The extra lines at the top of the screen are provided by Locator to tell the diagnostician how she reached the current position; it is a disciplined use of Guide's facilities; in general a button-replacement can take any form.)

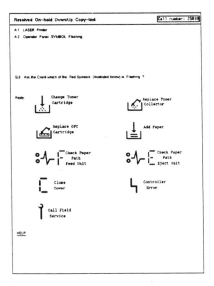

Fig. 3.3 .. after a further reply from the customer

A design aim of Guide is that it should contain a small number of facilities. Reading from a hypertext system will never be quite as simple as reading from paper, but you want to get as close as you can. To the diagnostician Guide contains just four facilities: the menu, two types of button - one of which we have just covered, and "undoing" (explained later).

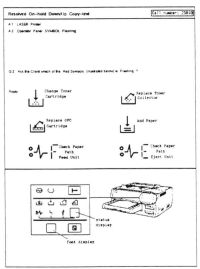

Fig. 3.4 .. after selecting the HELP glossary button

The other type of button is the **glossary-button.** Glossary buttons are underlined on the screen, and are used for such purposes as explaining jargon terms, footnotes, citations, etc. The button-replacement of a glossary-button does not appear in-line, in place of the button, but instead appears in a separate sub-window (in OWL'S Guide this is an ephemeral one). In fig.3.3 HELP is a glossary-button, and its button-replacement is a picture of the laser printer showing where the operator panel is. Fig.3.4 shows the effect of selecting it.

3.4 USABILITY FACTORS

When you move from the research laboratory to real use you always hit vagaries of human behaviour. In Locator, three such aspects of customer and diagnostician behaviour were of special importance.

Firstly, many of the Locator customers are naive in computer terms and often change their mind during a conversation ("Did I say I had a laser printer? My colleague now tells me it is a daisy-wheel printer"). Secondly, and more frustrating still, some of them do not know the answers to "simple" questions and have to go off and find out; they then might call back later, perhaps the next day, and expect the diagnostician to resume the conversation where she left off.

Thirdly, ICL maintains its service even if, for example, all the diagnosticians are struck down with food poisoning on the same day. In such cases a new partially trained stand-in diagnostician needs to be brought in.

The last problem is ameliorated by Guide's minimal set of features. A new diagnostician can be using Guide effectively after only a quarter of an hour. The same is true of almost every other hypertext system: the user can be presented with a minimal set of facilities so that training is no problem.

We shall now discuss the first problem: the customer changing his mind.

3.5 UNDOING

Unix Guide assumes a mouse with at least two buttons. One is used for "going forwards". i.e. selecting replace-buttons or glossary buttons, and the other is used for 'going backwards', i.e. undoing any previous selection. The exact rule is that if you point at any material on the screen and click the "undo" mouse-button, then Guide undoes the button selection that caused the material to appear. (This undoing does not have to be done in the same order as button-selection; it is easy to undo any previous selection.)

The design of the Locator button-replacements, where the first line gives the customer's decision, makes undoing particularly simple. The diagnostician just points at the wrong statement and clicks the "undo" mouse-button.

More generally, if the "undo" mouse-button is held down a moment before releasing it, a pop-up menu appears. This shows the diagnostician the current position in the hierarchy, i.e. all the button selections that caused the pointed-at material to be reached. Fig.3.5 contains an example of this. The pop-up menu can be used to undo any of these button selections. As the user moves up and down the pop-up menu. Guide highlights the corresponding button-replacement that might be undone; on a monochrome display, as in our Figs, highlighting is done by inverse-video.

The undoing facility caters well for the customer who changes his mind, and it does not even matter if he changes his original answer after giving several subsidiary answers. It represents the third of the four Guide Facilities the diagnostician needs to know about.

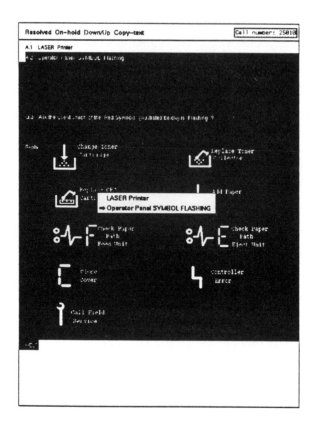

Fig. 3.5 The pop-up menu to allow "undoing" of previous decisions

3.6 RESOLVING A CALL

Eventually the goal of the customer and diagnostician will be reached and the cause of the fault will be resolved. This is shown in fig.3.6, a Guide screen with no further questions. If the customer is satisfied with this conclusion, the diagnostician then selects Resolved from the menu, and Locator is ready for the next call. The diagnosis of the previous call is automatically saved so that the next stage of curing the customer's problem can proceed, e.g. sending out an engineer with the appropriate parts.

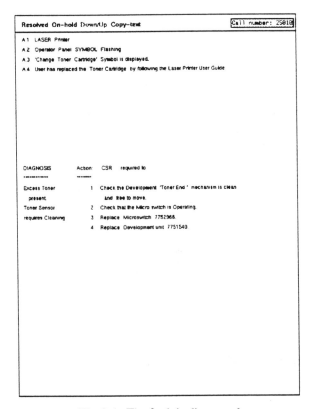

Fig. 3.6   The fault is diagnosed

3.7   HELD CALLS

We mentioned that calls may need to be 'held' while the customer finds out some information; when the customer phones back such calls are resumed where they left off.

The diagnostician places a call on hold by selecting On-hold from the menu. The call is then stored as a icon representing a Guide session that can be resurrected later. Fig.3.1, which shows the whole Locator screen, contains three such icons, labelled "Printer switch", "Checking power" and "Consulting his manager".

If the workstation is closed down overnight and then re-booted the next morning, Guide automatically saves the state of its 'on-hold' sessions, and restores them when it starts again the next morning.

3.8 TAILORING

As we have said, Locator uses a specially tailored version of Unix Guide. This contains extra mechanisms to cover the 'On-hold' and 'Resolved' facilities. There are other changes, mostly concerned with removing facilities that are not needed for this application so that they do not confuse the diagnostician.

All these changes are directed towards making the hypertext system sit naturally in its working environment. Certainly the message from the market-place has been that each application has different needs. As a result Unix Guide now contains much fuller facilities for tailoring of menus and other objects.

3.9 SUMMARY OF THE APPLICATION

The above is a somewhat oversimplified description of the hypertext technology used in Locator. Although we have given the impression of a tree structure the underlying data structure is, in fact, a more elaborate directed graph, since the same goal can be reached by many routes, as we shall discuss later. Nevertheless there is nothing special in the hypertext technology used. Instead the interest of the project is to throw light on some of the issues currently facing hypertext, and to gain from some of the excellent skills shown by those concerned with authorship and design.

In the rest of this paper we shall focus on seven issues facing hypertext. These issues are taken from Brown (1988), though no knowledge of that paper is assumed.

3.10 ISSUE 1: INTEGRATION

No user wants a hypertext system *per se.* The user wants a solution, and, at best, the hypertext system will only be part of that solution. It is vital therefore that the hypertext system be able to work in conjunction with other existing tools. Such tools may cover:

- Preparation of material. If hypertext documents are in some standard format this helps greatly. International standards such as ODA and SGML may offer long-term solutions (Brown,H.,1989a) but most of today's standards are generally more *ad hoc* ones.

- Checking version control and maintenance.

- Extraction from the hyperbase. A company may make a huge investment in creating a hyperbase (i.e. a collection of hypertext documents) covering, say, its personnel. Given this valuable resource, the company will want to get the maximum benefit from it; the company would not, for example, be pleased if one of their existing tools for producing some management information could not be run because of some incompatibility concerning the layout of the hyperbase.

- Capturing existing material and converting it to hypertext form.

Unix Guide uses **troff-style** mark-up to represent structure (e.g. a . **BU** request in a Guide document marks the start of a button). The reason that this, albeit imperfect, form was chosen is that it is a Unix standard. The Unix spelling checker, for example, works naturally with this format. The Locator project used a wide range of existing and newly-created Unix tools and this standard format has been invaluable.

A further facet of integration is that it can be *intimate* in the sense that the hypertext tool may run simultaneously with other tools in a single seamless package. In Locator, for example, Guide works intimately with some software that logs telephone calls. More ambitiously, hypertext systems would gain greatly from working seamlessly in tandem with drawing programs, editors, expert systems, etc (Meyrowitz, 1987).

3.11 ISSUE 2: AUTHORSHIP

The biggest opportunity arising from hypertext is for creative authors to present material in an entirely novel way, exploiting the new medium rather than using techniques taken from paper documents.

Sadly, however, large hypertext projects rarely start from scratch. Instead there is normally an investment in existing documentation, designed for paper but usually stored inside a computer in some word-processor format. This investment needs to be protected, and, indeed, the cost of re-gathering the material would often be prohibitive. Thus a largish project that really does start from scratch, such as Glasgow Online (Baird and Percival, 1989) is an unusual opportunity.

Capturing existing documentation consists of two stages:

- using an automatic tool to convert the existing material to hypertext form. This tool should capture text, pictures and, ideally, structure. Thus for example section headings might be turned into replace-buttons;

- tailoring the converted material by hand in order to reap the full advantages of the hypertext system.

The second stage is expensive, but, in the Locator experience, worth a good deal of investment. As Oren (1987) has remarked, if you just take an existing paper-based document and apply some automatic conversion procedure to it you add nothing.

3.12 ISSUE 3: TESTING

Quality assurance in Locator is multi-faceted. Comparatively easy matters are spelling checks (use an existing tool) and linkage checks (use Unix Guide's option which, on loading, checks that all glossary-buttons have corresponding definitions and that all cross-references lead somewhere).

More difficult is testing the quality of the material:

- Is it easy to read?

- Are the buttons natural to use?

- Is the granularity right?

Equally difficult is testing the mechanics of usability:

- Does the diagnostician sometimes 'miss' when trying to select a button?

- Can she simultaneously handle both Guide and a phone call?

There are, of course, no easy answers to these questions any more than there are easy answers to producing good paper documents. A pre-requisite to achieving anything, however, is to have a method of recording sessions so that the problem can be subsequently analysed.

In Locator, one of the problems that arose was wholly unexpected. When diagnosticians become adept at using Locator, they are often tempted to explore by selecting possible buttons before the customer has answered the question. This sometimes leads to conversations getting out-of-phase. Perhaps it has been made *too* easy to explore documents.

3.13   ISSUE 4: LARGE DOCUMENTS

In the field of programming it took a while to learn that large programs are inherently different from small programs. In a large program complexity dwarfs all other considerations, and unless one's methods successfully tame complexity all is lost. In hypertext we are still exploring the limits.

It is undoubtedly true that in hypertext, as in programming, discipline is vital in taming complexity. The haphazard author, even if blessed with flair and imagination, is a menace.

The Locator hyperbase is of medium-to-large size - a few megabytes of text, plus some pictures. A key to the success of the project is that authors have used a strict discipline throughout. As we have seen from the above figs, material follows a prescribed form. During the project a strong house-style evolved. Following Engelbart's (1987) suggested 'hypergrammars', this house-style was designed specifically for the Locator project rather than for every hypertext application within ICL. Discipline helps both readers and authors. It is boring, anti-creative, but necessary.

We have explained that the Guide user sees a document as a continuous scroll, which expands and contracts as buttons are selected/undone. This is unlike those hypertext systems that work in units such as cards, pages or frames. Guide's approach is not inherently better or worse than the card-based approach. If the underlying information is naturally divided up into separate card-sized units, then the card-based approach is best. If not, dividing the material into cards adds an extra and unnecessary level of complexity.

The underlying data for Locator is probably equally suitable for either approach. The Guide 'scroll' for Locator is in fact never bigger than the screen, so no scrolling takes place. (This is highly unusual in a Guide application, but was a Locator design aim.) On the other hand the Locator display presented by Guide is not based on fixed pages: recall that the top part of the display gives the customer's decisions that caused the current point to be reached: this exploits Guide's in-line replacement facility. The information is dynamic: several different paths can lead to the same point, so the path (i.e. the list of customer decisions) cannot be wired into the destination.

3.14 ISSUE 5: GETTING LOST

At hypertext conferences half the papers tend to be about navigation, specifically about avoiding getting lost. Yet on the Locator project, and probably on most other real-world hypertext projects, the getting-lost issue is a minor one compared with many of the others we are considering. In Locator getting lost is not a big problem for readers (in this case diagnosticians), and is only a moderate problem for authors.

The biggest reason why navigation problems have been kept in check was good authorship: in this case one of the added benefits of the discipline used by the authors has been that readers and authors are less likely to get lost.

A secondary reason was Guide's relative lack of gotos. This is a more technical point, and we shall spend a little time explaining it.

3.15 GETTING AWAY FROM GOTOS

Links in hypertext are like gotos in programming languages. They represent a low-level feature that causes problems in maintenance and, more specifically, in getting lost. Guide has made modest steps in getting away from gotos by means of its usage-buttons. Usage-buttons are employed in Locator when two or more paths join.

Paths that join are extremely common in Locator. More generally in any information system it should be possible for a user to reach the same piece of information in many different ways. In Locator, assume that the underlying problem is with the power - the customer may even have forgotten to switch it on. The problem may manifest itself in many different ways, e.g. 'Will not boot', ; 'Screen blank', 'Disk light not on', etc. Thus many paths through Locator will lead eventually to the section dealing with lack of power. In the old paper manuals on which Locator is based, this information was in one manual - in this case the manual concerned with disk booting - and all the other occurrences had cross-references to this: 'This is a power problem: see Section...in Volume...'.

If converting to hypertext is done without thought the same arrangement will be followed. Users who approach the lack-of-power material via 'Will notboot' will see a hierarchy, but for other users the hierarchy will be broken by a goto that leaps into the 'Will not boot' material. A hierarchy is a powerful aid to orienting the user - indeed it is the only higher-level abstraction he has. Breaking it in a case like the above is arbitrary and unnecessary, and Guide's usage-buttons avoid the break.

What a usage-button does is to make a cross-reference appear to the user to be an ordinary hierarchical replace-button. The abstraction is that the referenced material is copied to the position where it is used. Thus in our example, if the diagnostician approaches the lack-of-power fault through the 'Screen blank' route, then, when she comes to the cross-reference to the material on lack-of-power, this material is notionally copied into the 'Screen blank' hierarchy. To the user it appears to be naturally part of this hierarchy, just as it does to the user who approaches it through a 'Will not boot' hierarchy. In summary, usage-buttons enable a host of different hierarchies to be built on the same underlying material, and each user sees their hierarchy as the 'true' one.

In Locator, the underlying hyperbase is an acyclic directed graph. Perhaps surprisingly, usage-buttons are equally valuable with cyclic directed graphs, e.g. for instantiating grammars (Brown,P.J.,1989b).

3.16 ISSUE 6: ABSTRACTIONS

We have been discussing one abstraction, the hierarchy, but there is a need for much more.

Indeed, abstractions are another area where the needs of hypertext authors are similar to the needs of programmers. We have learned from programming languages that abstractions are a powerful way of understanding programs: instead of talking about bit-patterns one creates abstractions that relate to the current problem. Thus one might have a data structure called 'wheel' and a procedure called 'reduce size'. For authors to represent and to understand the structure of hypertext we need similar abstractions that are at a higher level than the goto link. The previous section described how a higher level abstraction, the hierarchy, could encompass gotos.

As Engelbert observed when explaining his hypergrammars, many of the most useful abstractions are one tied to the problem in hand, rather than general ones that a hypertext system might provide for all users. In Locator one abstraction is the particular style of question that pervades the Locator system - we call this a Locator-question. A Locator-question is made up of a variable number of lower-level Guide constructs such as enquiries, replace-buttons, usage-buttons, etc., following rules dictated by the house-style adopted for Locator.

To provide these abstractions, ICL have developed a tool that creates Guide source files. This tool is specifically designed for creating Locator-questions and other abstractions, together with the links between them. It has a pleasant visual interface, and does checking on-the-fly, so that the author can easily correct mistakes. The tool has led to a dramatic increase in the productivity of authors, and has enabled ICL to extend the Locator hyperbase to cover six machine ranges. It merits a paper in itself but is unfortunately subject to commercial secrecy.

3.17   ISSUE 7: COSTED PROJECTS

Poor information has a huge cost. The potential benefits of hypertext are that information will be better - the readers will more frequently reach the information they need - and will be obtained more quickly. The hypertext literature is full of descriptions of "immensely successful" applications, but quantifiable measures of real projects are sadly lacking.

The Locator project was in an environment where budgets were strict, and competing projects were all too keen to show that they could get better results. Thus measurements of effectiveness needed to be made, and the results of these were very pleasing.

In the paper-based system that preceded Locator, 68% of faults were correctly diagnosed as a result of the phone conversation with the customer. The effectiveness of Locator was tested first after two weeks of operation, and again after six weeks, when the diagnosticians were more practised. After two weeks 88% of faults were correctly diagnosed, and after six weeks this had risen to 92%. The overall result was a huge saving in engineers' time.

Although the benefits of Locator have been quantified I cannot, unfortunately, reveal details of costs, other than that ICL management thought the project was cost-effective and, indeed, awarded it a prize. Originally, the biggest concern was authorship costs, but ICL tamed this problem by using the authorship tool we have mentioned earlier.

Locator runs on expensive hardware: graphics workstations. The verdict, albeit a subjective one, is that the extra cost of such hardware is justified.

3.18 CONCLUSIONS

There are still a large number of problems and research issues facing hypertext. Indeed experience of areas such as software engineering shows that, as the state-of-the-art advances and bigger applications become tractable, the number of current problems increases rather than decreases. The problems facing hypertext are not by their nature problems that will ever be 'solved' - no-one will solve the authorship problem. The scale of the problems will, we hope, be reduced over time, and there is scope for spectacular advances in some areas.

Experience of Locator has shown that these problems can be surmounted, and that there are numerous opportunities to make effective use of hypertext in real applications.

As for researchers, the 'easy problems', which will eventually lead to the most glory and the fewest tears, probably lie in the more mundane areas such as testing and abstractions rather than in glorious navigation aids or multi-media extravaganzas.

REFERENCES

Baird, P., and Percival, M. (1989) Glasgow Online: database development using Apple's HyperCard, in *Hypertext: theory into practice*, (ed. R. McAleese) Blackwell, Oxford, pp.75-92.

Brown, H. (1989) Standards for structured documents, *Computer J.* 32, 6.

Brown, P.J. (1988) Hypertext: the way forward, in *Document Manipulation and Typography*, (ed. van Vliet), Cambridge University Press.

Brown, P.J. (1989a) A hypertext system for UNIX, *Computing systems*, 2 (1), 37-53.

Brown, P.J. (1989b) Do we need maps to navigate round hypertext systems? EP-odd, 2(2),pp.91-100.

Engelbart, D.C. (1987) Keynote address, *Hypertext'87*, University of North Carolina, USA.

Frenkel, K.A. (1989) An interview with Ivan Sutherland, *Comm. ACM*, 32, 6, 723-728.

Meehan, D.P. (1987) *Locator: a system for service-desk 8801 fault diagnosis*, MSc thesis, Kingston Polytechnic, Kingston, UK.

Meyrowitz, N. (1987) The missing link: why we're all doing hypertext wrong, position paper, *Hypertext'87*, University of North Carolina, USA.

Oren, T. (1987) The architecture of static hypertexts, in *Hypertext'87*, University of North Carolina, USA, pp. 291-306.

FURTHER READING

Conklin, J. (1987) Hypertext: introduction and survey, *IEEE Computer*, 20, 9, 17-41.

4. EXMAR: AUTOMATING MARKETING PLANNING

H. Wilson

Artificial Intelligence Limited

4.1 INTRODUCTION

4.1.1 The Exmar club

The Exmar club (Expert Systems in Marketing) is a club of ten major British companies. Formed in 1987, its objectives are to investigate the possibility of computerized assistance for strategic marketing planning by the development of a prototype, and to spread awareness of expert systems in club member organizations. It is funded by contributions from the member companies, and by the Department of Trade and Industry.

The club's primary source of marketing expertise is Professor Malcolm McDonald of Cranfield School of Management. Marketing experience within club member companies is also being tapped.

The involvement of AI Ltd with the club as technical contractor began in the second half of 1988, when AI Ltd conducted an analysis phase, followed by production of a demonstrator and an appraisal of the way forward. The demonstrator was built in the Interlisp programming environment and the Loops object system on Xerox 1186 workstations.

The Requirements Specification for a prototype, to be used for experimentation and evaluation by club members in their own organizations, was completed in March 1989, and work is now in progress on the functional and design specifications. The prototype will run on IBM-compatible 386 machines, using Smalltalk-80 and Analyst, and is scheduled for delivery by the end of 1989.

4.1.2 Strategic Marketing Planning

Marketing is about matching an organisation's products or services with the needs or wants of the markets in which the organization operates, subject to constraints imposed by the organization's environment, in order to achieve the organization's objectives (McDonald,1987)

A strategic marketing plan is a plan outlining the marketing strategy of an organization over a period of time. It is strategic in various respects. Firstly, the period of time covered is longer than for a tactical or operational plan (typically three years as opposed to one year). Secondly, for the sake of simplicity and clarity only the most important products and markets of the organization will be included, and with a coarse level of detail. Thirdly, the plan will ignore detailed tactical decisions on pricing, promotion and so on, in order to concentrate on the broad strategy for a product which would then bound these decisions - that is, an understanding of the nature of the market in which the organization operates, and decisions in broad terms about how the product will meet these needs.

4.1.3 Structure of Paper

Section 4.2, Previous Work and Early Observations, outlines the approach taken to the analysis process at the start of the project, discusses the nature of the logical model that emerged, and gives the system objectives that were then derived .

Section 4.3 discusses the nature of the logical model that emerged, and briefly describes the demonstrator system based on it, emphasizing the nature and style of the support to the user provided by the system, how this reflects the logical model, and how this meets the system objectives.

Section 4.4, Demonstrator Feedback, discusses the feedback received to date on the demonstrator, and its influence on the prototype now being developed.

Section 4.5 draws conclusions on the appropriate approach to systems development in such "soft" areas as marketing planning.

4.2 PREVIOUS WORK AND EARLY OBSERVATIONS

AI Ltd's first involvement with the club was to conduct an assessment of the work previously carried out for the club. This assessment drew various conclusions about the appropriate technical approach in this area.

- need for focus

The previous work had been on a broad front, involving analysis into all aspects of strategic marketing planning. This is a vast topic, tackling many of the most fundamental problems inherent in business activity, and progress was therefore slow. There was a need to focus on a subset of the overall problem.

- feasibility and utility to be established

The very title of the club, "Expert Systems in Marketing", suggested that the use of expert systems techniques in this area was possible and appropriate. This assumption of feasibility was based on the observation that there existed demonstrable expertise, but why this might imply a classic rule-based expert system had not been addressed. This was a doubly large assumption as no previous systems (or work towards systems) were known in this application area. There was a need to address this early, and the related issue of how any system would be of use to the marketing planner.

- modelling and representation

It was decided that the appropriate first step was to carry out analysis in a closely defined subset of the problem, with the emphasis on modelling the area using whatever formal techniques were appropriate. An example of the choices deliberately not made at the start was whether any modelling of expertise adopted the " low road" of embedding the expertise in data structures and procedures, the "high road" of an explicit, "deep" representation, or the "middle road" of an explicit but heuristic representation (Brown,1984). In this modelling work, the emphasis would be on representation rather than computation, as the essential first step towards any computer system.

- the marketing swamp

Marketing has been described by Professor McDonald as a swamp of intuitive, experience-based practice with the occasional rocky peak of formal techniques. In our experience, the best place to start when modelling such "soft" domains was often on the boundary between the soft area and neighbouring more readily formalizable areas. In this case, that meant starting with the established formal techniques and working out from there.

4.3   RESULTS OF ANALYSIS WORK, AND DEMONSTRATOR

Several analysis sessions were held with Professor McDonald, and with marketing practitioners in club member organizations. This resulted in an overall Exmar system objective, an outline model that was used as the basis for a demonstrator system, and a list of areas where further work was required.

The overall Exmar system objective was defined to be: to provide assistance for the marketing planning process in such a way as to spread knowledge and further understanding of how and why the multifarious factors of the market interact and serve to define the parameters of the business activity.

The remainder of this section describes features of the model, and how these were exploited in the demonstrator. The structure is an interleaved description of the two: each subsection describes a model feature, and the relevant aspects of the demonstrator.

4.3.1   Assistance to aid in interpretation and understanding

The model covers the data manipulated by a marketing planner when developing a strategic marketing plan, and structures the marketing planner's task. Many of the individual subtasks or processes of this task involve modelling by the user of the business context, or interpretation by the user of the information entered. There is much that a computer system based on the model cannot do for the user, and where its most appropriate aim is to assist.

The objective of the demonstrator was therefore to provide an interactive system that supports a marketing planner by providing tools that help the user to represent the state of the markets and products under consideration; to interpret this information so as to gain an understanding of the markets and one's place within them; and to determine a course of action based on this understanding.

4.3.2 Model of process of Generation of Marketing Plan

A hierarchical breakdown of the process the marketing planner should adopt to generate a marketing plan was defined. Encouraging the user to adopt this process is of value in itself, as the process incorporates much experience that helps avoid common pitfalls: for example, the need to arrive at an appropriate understanding of the current situation before setting objectives for the future.

The demonstrator uses this hierarchy as a basis for the user's navigation round the system. The initial screen display is shown in fig.4.1. Also shown is a window for more detailed navigation round a particular stage.

Each box in the graphical browsers represents a stage of the process. The user carries out a stage by selecting a box with the mouse: the system then takes the appropriate action, which may for example be to present the user with a form to fill in, or to open a more detailed browser of the process for that stage.

To give an overview of the process: Select/Define Business Unit identifies which area of the business the marketing plan is for, and records the purpose of the business area. Focus identifies which of the unit's markets and products are of interest. Conduct Audit assesses the current position of the products and markets. Forecast predicts the future position of the products and markets, assuming we do not intervene, as a base-line for objective setting. Finally, Set Objectives and Strategies sets objectives for the business unit based on the information collected, analysed and summarized; and defines strategies by which the objectives are to be met.

Detailed browsers contain icons showing the nature of the support offered for a particular stage: for example, there are icons for graphical displays of information, for tables of numbers, and for free text. The Predict relationship with markets browser is illustrated as an example. The user will largely go through the process depth first and top to bottom; but he or she is free to do otherwise, as there are many cases where he or she may legitimately wish to do so.

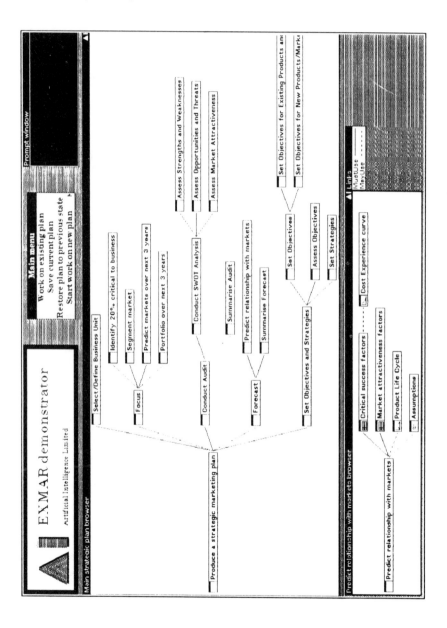

Fig. 4.1 Initial screen display, with an example of a detailed browser.

4.3.3 Generally applicable, Sound Data Model

A data model was developed that captured and related the information considered during production of a strategic marketing plan. It has proved essentially sound, and of general applicability to the wide range of marketing situations represented by the diverse club member companies. A simplified entity-relationship diagram of the model is given in fig.4.2, and briefly described.

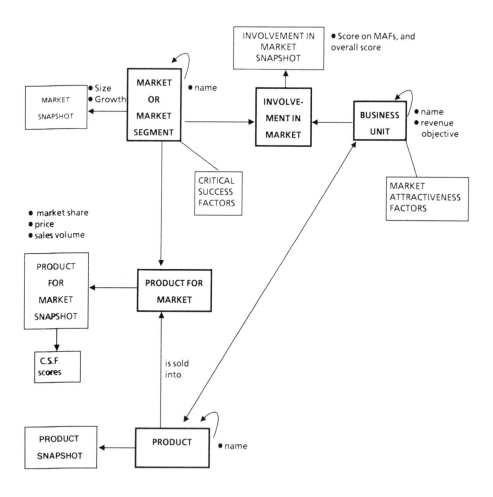

Fig. 4.2 Simplified data model in entity-relationship notation.

The model has three cornerstone entities: Business Unit, the part of the organization for which the plan is being developed; Product, the products or services offered by the unit; Market, the markets in which it operates.

Critical Success Factors model the workings of a market by documenting the factors critical to the success of any product in the market, from the consumers' viewpoint. They are an objective assessment of how the market works, independently of the Business Unit's presence in it. The matching of products to markets is represented by the important Product For Market entity: a product's score on the Critical Success Factors relates to this entity.

Market Attractiveness Factors model the priorities of the business unit by documenting the factors determining how attractive a market is to the unit. Being a subjective assessment of the business unit's priorities, the criterion for their correctness is the agreement of key executives. The matching of markets to business units is represented by the important Involvement In Market entity: a market's score on the Market Attractiveness Factors relates to this entity.

4.3.4 Time-dependent information is held in Snapshot entities.

For each plan, the demonstrator system holds data structures closely based on the data model. The user's primary means of manipulating the data is by using forms which are illustrated below.

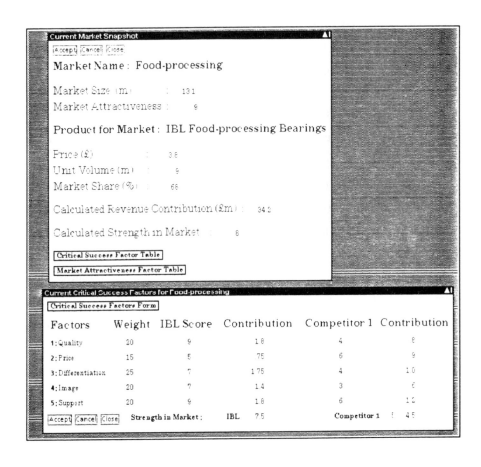

Fig. 4.3 Typical forms for data manipulation

The top form shows current information about the Food Processing market for the fictional International Bearings Limited (IBL) company, which sells bearings into a variety of markets. The bottom form shows the Critical Success Factors defined for this market, with weights to illustrate their relative importance. For example, while price is important in this market, it is less so than several other factors, such as product differentiation and quality, the product's image, and the engineering support provided. It also shows a score for IBL and its main competitor against these factors, and a weighted average computed by the system, to represent IBL's overall strength in the market. This is copied to the top form by the system. The Market Attractiveness score on the top form results from a similar weighted average form for the attractiveness of the market against such criteria as the market's size, growth and profitability.

4.3.5 The use of the data model by techniques

The "rocky peaks" with which the analysis work started are "textbook" techniques for analysing an organisation's markets and products, such as Directional Policy Matrix which is illustrated below, the Boston and Porter matrices, and so on. These view different aspects of the data model using differing graphical representations, to aid in the data's interpretation. To extend our analogy, the data model thus forms the bridges between the rocky peaks to enable us to navigate the intervening swamp.

The screen snapshot (fig. 4.4) gives an example of how the demonstrator exploits these features by showing the underlying data presented in the standard formats. The Directional Policy Matrix plots, for each of IBL's markets, the market attractiveness against IBL's strength in the market. The size of the circles is proportional to the market's contribution to IBL's revenue (though it could have been set to any useful metric). Different circle shadings illustrate the current, forecast and objective situations for the product/market. (In terms of the data model discussed earlier, each circle strictly represents a Product For Market.)

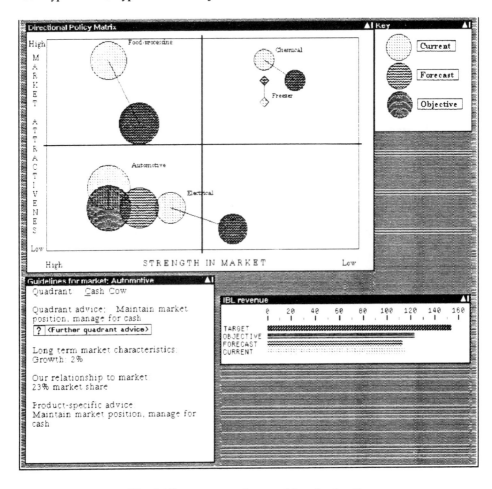

Fig. 4.4 Data presentation to aid understanding

The matrix aids in understanding both the situation of an individual product/market, and the balance of the portfolio of products. An example of the matrix's interpretation is that in all its markets, IBL is moving downwards and rightwards from the current to the forecast situation. This indicates a general weakening of IBL's position: the matrix illustrates what IBL intends to do about this for the automotive market by maintaining its competitive position while cutting costs where possible.

The demonstrator also provides on request standard, "textbook" advice for a product-for-market in a given position on the matrix, as a guide to the planner in setting objectives. For example, for the automotive market, the system advises that the market position (strength in market, and market share) be maintained, but that subject to this the market be managed for cash to fund development of more attractive markets. This is the only case in the demonstrator where it was felt appropriate that the system should take an active role of giving advice, rather than the passive role of presenting information in differing forms to aid the user in interpretation.

The diagram also shows a "gap gauge", a bar chart showing the financial gap between the business unit's target revenue and the sum of the individual objectives so far set for the various markets.

4.3.6 Less structured information: checklists, free text

Some parts of the marketing plan were best expressed in text: for example, the business unit's mission statement, and lists of opportunities and threats. Also, in several areas, marketing expertise was identified that was not formalized beyond free text in the model. Examples are checklists of common critical success factors; assistance with definition of a business unit's mission statement; and checklists of possible opportunities and threats to consider. This unstructured information was related, however, to specific points in the planning process, or to specific items in the data model. The demonstrator exploited this by making available text windows at appropriate points with icons on the browsers and elsewhere. This was implemented using the NoteCards hypertext system.

4.4   DEMONSTRATOR FEEDBACK AND PROTOTYPE

4.4.1 Initiative is with the user

The demonstrator leaves the user to decide what to do next. This was liked by the club members, who felt it to be appropriate for this application.

4.4.2 Evidence of utility

Club members felt an operational system based on the demonstrator's ideas could be of significant use in the vital process of strategic marketing planning. This is an example of utility being addressed by the clients rather than by the developers.

4.4.3 Communication of nature of proposed prototype

The demonstrator served to communicate the nature of the support that would be offered to a marketing planner by a fuller computer system, to club members and to the primary expert, Professor McDonald. We found that with this innovative system, this was difficult to achieve on paper.

4.4.4 Use in specification of prototype

The demonstrator has been used effectively in discussions with club members to aid with specification of the prototype now being developed.

4.5 CONCLUSIONS

The approach to the work adopted at its inception (see section 4.2) proved a productive and efficient one. The analysis and demonstrator gave a sound basis for system development to deliver genuine benefits, and took about 20 person-weeks. All deliverables have been produced on time, and within a maximum of 10% over budget. There are some general conclusions that can be drawn.

4.5.1 Analysis approach

The analysis approach was undogmatic and modest: to model the available expertise with whatever modelling techniques proved most appropriate, starting with the most well-established and documented, and verified, expertise. "Don't run before you can walk" should not need emphasizing: but the early experience of the club shows that perhaps it still does. The very term "expert systems" has led to some unjustified assumptions not just of the feasibility of building computer systems based on expertise, but also of their utility, and of the most appropriate modelling and system-building tools (Bobrow, Mittal and Stefik, 1986). The alternative is classic software engineering, with an expanded toolkit of analysis and implementation techniques to draw upon as appropriate.

This may lead to the question how and to what extent the model and demonstrator may be said to incorporate expertise. All aspects of the model and demonstrator can reasonably be said to be based on expertise: the process, the data model, the means of presentation of information, the checklists provided, and the one case where data-dependent advice is given. The system thus takes the "low road" according to Brown's categorization discussed earlier. There is certainly much available (but not necessarily formalizable) expertise that has not been captured: the critical design task has been the effective definition of the boundary between the system and the user such that the user is encouraged to think about the issues that the system cannot of itself address. This conforms to the stated Exmar system objective quoted in section 4.3, of providing assistance for the marketing planning process in such a way as to spread knowledge and further understanding of the business and its markets.

4.5.2 Role of the computer

The potential benefits shown by the Exmar demonstrator are due mainly to its assistance with the understanding and interpretation of the information entered. The end result may include a marketing plan, but it also includes an enhanced and readily communicable understanding of the business gained by the marketing planner. These benefits are largely due to appropriate and varied display of the information. Systems do not necessarily have to do much to be justified, if the combination of system and user is more effective than the user alone.

4.5.3 Project management in clubs

The club members have been closely involved in the software development process, in particular through a very active Working Party. This close involvement has been important in ensuring that the project is kept on the most effective track. An example is the quality assurance criteria for each stage of the work, that have been agreed with the Working Party at the start of the stage. The use of a demonstrator has assisted in this communication.

REFERENCES

Brown, J.S. (1984) in *The AI Business* , (eds. P.H. Winston and K. Prendergast), The low road, the middle road, and the high road, MIT Press, Cambridge, Mass., USA.

Bobrow, D. G., Mittal, S. and Stefik, M. (September 1986) Expert systems: perils and promise. *Comms. ACM* 29,9, 880-894.

McDonald, M.B.H. (1987) Marketing Plans: How to Prepare Them, How to Use Them, Heinemann.

5. HYPERTEXT AND ADDED VALUE

P. Baird, B. Cronin and L. Davenport

University of Strathclyde

5.1 HYPERTEXT AND INFORMATION MANAGEMENT

The position of hypertext in the world of business information no longer needs a defence; it now has a secure niche as the tool for handling unstructured text (in any medium). The advantages it offers in terms of links and cross references are summarized in the label "associative information management system (AIMS)" which neatly points the contrast with traditional structured processing technologies, "database management systems (DBMS)". These two features, freedom of scope and freedom of movement, allow hypertext to extend or add value to three main areas:

- storage

- auditing

- access

These areas, which are specifically intended to add value to information in the business context, will be discussed, and then some of the current projects at the Department of Information Science at the University of Strathclyde will be described.

5.2 STORAGE

Hypertext adds value to information storage in two ways:

- its loose structure allows managers to trap information which has hitherto escaped the organizational net,

- its loose structure allows hypertextured information to be exploited across the organization - the information cake can be sliced as often as required.

5.2.1 Survival strategies

The first point relates to what may be called business strategy. Strategy may be seen from two perspectives: biological, and military. In evolutionary terms, strategy is what allows you to survive: you must know the terrain, you must know your own niche, you must know your friends and your enemies (or when to cooperate and when to compete), you must have foresight to recognize turbulence ahead, and you must have flexible responses; to survive is to be informed. An extension of survival strategy is gaming strategy, which is a common source of analogy in the literature of business. This involves guessing the intentions of other players, and preventing them from guessing yours. Hypertext can enhance such activities by offering a maximized information store for pattern matching and scenario spinning.

5.2.2 Secrets and subgroups

Much of this information will be intimate, volatile, informal, and you will not want to share all of it. Competitive advantage will lie in having information that no one else has: monopoly; or having information before the others in the field: priority. Information will be shared only where there is some advantage in cooperation, and it will be the binding force in such a cooperative group: confraternity.

Monopoly, priority, and confraternity are, of course, recognized as levers of advantage in business strategy. Fraternities lubricate many sectors of business; they are the commercial equivalent of the secret service, and the information they embody must be regarded as intelligence. If, however, you look at the literature on business intelligence, no attempt is made to address the problem of exploiting such stuff. It is labelled "informal", and is regarded as fixed that way.

What is recommended, as a source of strategic advantage, is a blend of information from inside and outside the company. The information inside the company will have been heavily structured to fit some kind of DSS or MIS system; *de facto*, it will have been heavily edited to conform with the protocols of field and file formats. The sources of external information will be accessed through large and sophisticated online hosts offering company information, market analyses, press digests, which are updated daily (or more frequently) in most cases, and can be downloaded and manipulated as required. Such systems offer rapid access, and customization; we describe below a project at Strathclyde which uses HyperCard as an interface to such a resource.

Commercial intelligence of the fraternal kind, is rarely trapped and tapped. Such information remains in people's heads, and is transmitted in cabals, coteries, closet meetings (Cronin and Davenport, 1990). Bureaucracy, as Weber has pointed out, thrives on secrecy and secret unions; this, especially in the case of large, established corporations, can be counterproductive. Hypertext offers a countervailing technology, which can capture commercial intelligence, and allows it to be exploited for the strategic benefit of a larger group, the organization as a whole. Levels of protection will safeguard genuinely critical items. IDEX, a product from Office Workstations Ltd in Edinburgh, is available for the PC. IDEX has evolved, from the flagship product Guide, as a file server-based system designed for corporate users who need online access to large volumes of documentation, but with different access levels for the critical items.

5.2.3   Export intelligence

Let's look at a specific environment: a firm who wishes to export to Europe by 1992, a large manufacturer for example. The objective of such a firm is to secure as many outlets as possible at the lowest cost to the company. The strategic information required will not lie in the public domain (accessible through commercial vendors) as one's competitors can also access such information, but with the ground contacts acquired through a network of Chambers of Commerce, dealers, industry insiders, "deep throats" and so on.

Such information may be used by senior managers for long-term planning, by picking out patterns and matching them with current and projected overviews, and middle management can use it to locate overseas offices. But these benefits can only be realised if the information remains relatively unstructured: if it has to be formatted to conform with the rigid protocols of dBase III, or Lotus, it will loose much of its latent value. Hypertext is an essential medium in this context, in that it lends itself to continual metamorphosis. The structure is always fluid, but always valid, in that it reflects current intelligence.

5.2.4   Feeding the five thousand

The second area where hypertext adds value to storage is the extension of flexibility. Because information is unstructured, the cake can be cut in as many ways as required: the feeding of the five thousand phenomenon. Input from one department or one division can be exploited across other units; a hyperbase is the clay which is moulded into whatever shape users require. Think of our exporting scenario: we stressed how integrated information might be exploited at different levels. It might also be exploited by different divisions of the company: the production facility for example might wish to differentiate output to meet foreign demand; the demand would be gauged by the marketing department on the basis of intelligence from the export unit. Such cross-departmental referencing has been labelled "value linking" by Parker and Benson (1988), and is seen as an important factor in gaining competitive edge.

5.3 AUDITING

By auditing we mean the capacity offered by hypertext to back track through a database and examine the roots of decisions. In many organiza.tions, versions are discarded as they are superseded, and electronic systems often store a later version at the expense of the first. This may be done by accessing the many versions which have developed into current documents, projects, policies in any organizations (as would be allowed in systems like Xanadu, which proposes to construct versions out of fragments of existing and amended text). Or it may be achieved by tracing the links which individual decision-makers have made between cards, or comparable storage units. Perhaps we can backtrack from "auditing" in the metaphorical sense described above, to its literal sense of the process by which an opinion is formed on the financial statements of a company. In California, the Price Waterhouse Technology Centre are developing an electronic system for this complex task with the inclusion of hypertext features. Their model of the audit process can provide the basis for reasoning about relationships among contents of working papers and can also, through hypertext, explore and better understand the collaborative nature of the task (De Young, 1989).

Such a capability may have far-reaching effects. In traditional print-based environments, decision-making is supported by sheaves of documents. To prevent overload, a format for the information contained in such documents has developed over the years, which is tied to due procedure in reporting. Meetings are embodied in minutes, which are extracted and combined into summary reports. There are innumerable manuals and guides to house style and due procedure, and they can offer guidelines for the future by recording the consensus of the past: they are an essential instrument to ensure fair play. But due procedure can preclude the apportioning of

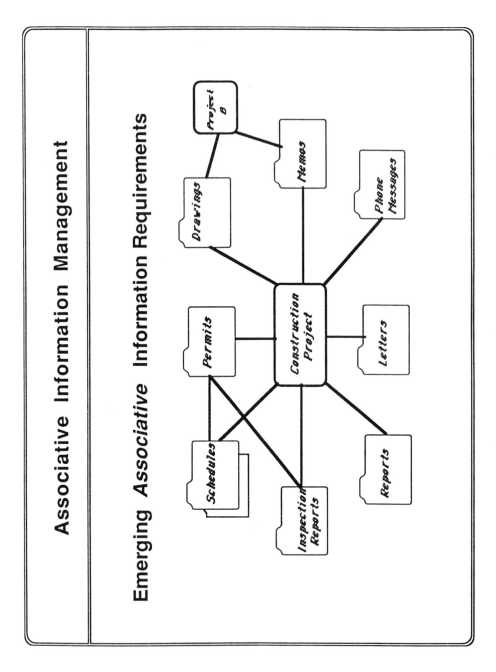

Fig. 5.1 Associative information management.

praise or blame, or blur the balance of consent and dissent by stifling the individual voice.

Hypertext, as we have suggested, can add value to the decision-making process by allowing the substrata to be explored, by trapping, much more completely, the input which lies behind decisions, and by allowing critical decisions to be explored, either backwards (starting from the present) or forwards (starting from some historical point). Decisions, designs, reports (and other products of meetings) can be scrutinized; key or controversial points can be traced back, and accountability improved (fig5.1).. In other words, hypertext can help track how the organization actually functions by monitoring the information flow. Large corporations are discovering the value of history, the value of archiving the process by which the organization grows - that it can be the key to the future. However, successful systems depend on open structures (with the caveat for critical information mentioned earlier), total flexibility and the absence of protocols - both access to and input of information.

5.4 ACCESS

Information is a commodity which derives its value from meaning and use. If a useful information system or service within an organization is to be provided, the system structure must act as the intermediary between the user and the information. It must adapt to, or augment, the user's skill in exploiting the system, presenting an interface to overcome, rather than impose, barriers to the information. System and user must work in unison to determine the outcome of the enquiry. In traditional information retrieval environments, access procedures tend to be explicitly adapted to the system's structure. Some systems have structures which impose esoteric entry and access mechanisms. These systems may be very successful for information retrieval purposes, but in the main, they suit those users who have achieved a certain level of knowledge and expertise. Novice users, by definition, do not have this expertise and so are disadvantaged. Nelson has said that traditional databases will not satisfy the data needs of the non-computing public (Nelson,1988), and this latter group often includes business managers who have the domain knowledge and expertise, but who are repelled by the protocols and complexities of existing technologies.

5.4.1 The medium and the message

New media for the presentation and dissemination of information are increasingly being spawned and nurtured. How do we evaluate the efficacy of the new arrivals? Evaluation of systems for the effective transmission of information centres on two criteria: the interface between machine and user; and the degree to which the technology adds value to existing information.

5.4.2 Transparency

Successful systems imply easy access. Easy access is synonymous with transparency; the technology is the window on the information. It must not interfere with information seeking; must not impose structures which veil the information. If access is impeded or dictated by the technology or the complex data structures, then the interface is not successful. In the corporate context, the interface should not only satisfy data needs, but should also offer added value to existing data by allowing clean and rapid access; by allowing user, as opposed to machine, the choice of how to navigate; where to go; the ability to backtrack; access to networks of expertise within the environment which traditional information resources do not reach or allow; elimination of drudgery and time-consuming duplication of transactions which paper-based resources spawn. Think of the mountains of paper required to pass a new set of procedures or regulations in any organization!

To summarize, successful information systems depend on open structures in which data can be massaged, squeezed and moulded, allowing new perspectives and new insights into the same information by a variety of personnel. It may be useful at this point to examine some information-seeking scenarios and possible solutions which are being developed at the Department of Information Science, University of Strathclyde.

5.5   ADDING VALUE AND HYPERACTIVITY AT STRATHCLYDE

There are at present four hypertext developments being undertaken at the University. They are not being developed within specific business environments, but are indicative of the ways in which large established corporations could handle and milk large information spaces. All but one decant already existing sources of information into a hypertext structure, which in itself adds storage value by integrating information and allowing access through one interface.

The movement towards integration of information packets is something which has been taxing the minds of many organizations. The validity of motion video, sound, graphics, animation and so on, as information sources within a domain, along with text-based sources, is increasingly being recognized. What is achieved beyond integration, and what is more relevant to the concept of adding value to the information itself, is the hypertextualiaztion of the data. This offers users access to a vast, non-linear, cross-referenced, resource-rich information environment which would not be possible through the medium of print. Access, in its fullest sense, does not only mean the ability to read; it also implies writing. The capability is there within the system for users to write to the database, creating their own links, leaving their footprints which subsequent users can benefit from without disturbing the integrity of the original text - the history of decision-making.

5.5.1 Community information

Glasgow Online is a database of information on the city of Glasgow which combines text, graphics, images and animation. It was developed using Apple's HyperCard software and exploits the associative power of HyperCard by enabling the author to link disparate nodes within the database allowing users to navigate at will. The database is approximately 16Mbyte in size and covers areas such as the history of the city, what to see and do in Glasgow, business and commercial information, local government services, education, leisure activities and shopping, restaurant and pub guides (fig.5.2). The end product is a public domain utility to meet the information needs of tourists, inward investors and the resident population of the city.

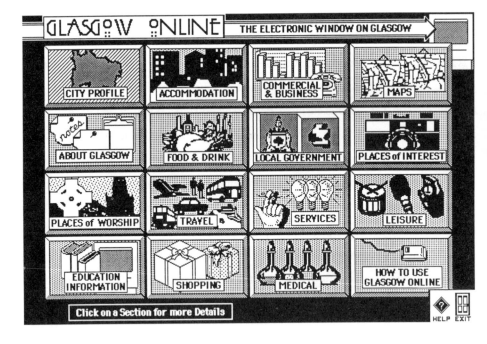

Fig. 5.2 Click on a section for more detail.

Glasgow Online does not present new information, but adds value by repackaging and restructuring existing information within a hypertext context. Pamphlets, guide books, maps, timetables, listings of hotels, restaurants, services information are combined and presented in an integrated environment which, through the hypertext links, provides a whole knowledge backdrop of information on the city. Patterns of association can be supported as the user moves from one information enquiry to another. Full accounts of the system and its development have been documented elsewhere (Baird,1988. Baird and Percival,1989).

5.5.2 HyperCard And CD-ROM

The Department is also currently working on a project called Europe in the Round, which hypertextures information available from the Euopean Community on ""Education, training and work opportunities in post-1992 Europe". It is intended to act as a handbook for those seeking work or commercial opportunities abroad, like students, trainees, young workers, employers, trade unions, advisors and teachers and lecturers. (Figs 5.3,5.4 and 5.5 indicate the breadth of the system.)

The project will combine the user-friendliness of Apple's HyperCard software with the ability to search mass data on CD-ROM. It is being funded by the Training Agency which has awarded £227 000 to a consortium consisting of the Department of Information Science, Vocational Technologies (Guildford) and Open Technologies (Glasgow). Priorities will be given to five areas:

- details of official programmes such as ERASMUS and COMETT;
- information on courses, qualifications, educational establishments;
- background information on all EC countries;
- survival information (e.g. travel, currency, cost of living);
- a glossary/encyclopaedia with definitions and illustrations.

Textual, numeric and graphic information will be supported by sound and animation. The possibility of various language versions will also be examined, which would allow access across Europe.

Fig. 5.3   Click anywhere for information.

Fig. 5.4 Click on a topic.

Fig. 5.5 Click any box for information.

Just how does such a system add value? It pulls together disparate information, which users might have to access across a range of sites (public libraries, specialist EC documentation centres, government agencies). It will offer guided tours through a dense information set which might otherwise be impenetrable by the layman. (Those who have attempted to penetrate "Eurospeak" documents will recognize the picture). It can suggest activities which might enhance the user's engagement with the material ("Do you know that...?"), and it offers basic help in the form of dictionaries (for synonyms, or translated terms) and bookmark facilities.

We can see extensions of the project into other areas. The background and survival information might remain intact, and the educational component be replaced by an appropriate set of specialist data, export information, for example (mentioned earlier in the context of sales and marketing). The implementation team have gained considerable experience reformatting European databases and providing uniform access to mixed media on CD-ROM.

An export hyperbase of the sort described above would obviously benefit from a mixture of Euro and informal information and local input. HyperCard, like most of the other commercially available hypertext packages, is a read/write instrument, and input by experienced users, or comments on the quality of the information can technically be accommodated. The designers of Europe in the Round have deliberately chosen for the moment not to include such glossing; a public domain system is open to abuse, and glossing may degenerate into graffiti. But subsets or adaptations of the database could provide such export intelligence.

5.5.3   Hypertext and legal information

This research will develop a prototype hypertext system covering the legal aspects of copyright with special emphasis on its application to new information products and services. The research team will examine the background to copyright law in the UK and its importance to the information industries, particularly in the areas of intellectual property and piracy. Related issues subsumed under GATT etc., will also be assessed. The prototype will be beta tested with law students, legal professionals and information specialists during development. The potential for extension of the system into a hypermedia environment will also be investigated.

Decanting and assimilating legal information into a hypertext vessel will offer the ability to capture new ideas within specific contexts, articulate the structure of complex entities such as patents, trade marks, copyright etc., and structure and support links and cross-references between any of these nodes and prior art, since so much in the legal environment depends on precedent. Simultaneous access to a shared database within a law firm offers a platform for information layering and collaboration with other lawyers and support staff who are involved.

5.5.4   Access to online systems

A last area of research, and the one that this paper will concentrate on because of its business potential, concerns the use of hypertext software as a front-end to electronic information services such as electronic mail and online databases. The availability of highly reliable national and international data communications networks has stimulated the development of value-added network services. Two of the best known types are online information retrieval services and electronic mail, both of which provide new opportunities for business, commerce and the public sector to acquire, process and disseminate time-critical information. However, although the market for such services has been growing, it has been inhibited by the difficulties experienced by users in retrieving information. The problems of storage and retrieval (for the expert user at least) have to a great extent been solved. New and less experienced users of online systems want simplicity and results and they also want that additional element from systems which traditional database management systems will not allow. They want systems which offer not only structured but also free text retrieval access to information. They are not interested in the mysteries and complexities of systems; what language is being used; how the data is processed. They are only interested in getting data as simply and as intuitively as possible. Problems abound.

Difficulties can be experienced in establishing communication links with external systems. Users may experience additional problems because the host system requires the search terms to be specified in synthetic command languages, which often vary greatly from system to system and which do not correspond to natural language. Moreover the languages often have extremely strict syntactical structures which are highly sensitive to error and little adequate help is given.

The problems do not end there. Other factors which deter the inexperienced user from using online information resources include:

- insufficient knowledge of the range and appropriateness of databases (globally in excess of 4200 in 1989);

- how to formulate a search strategy - selecting terms to match information needs;

- the need to make allowances for variations in terms, using all possible synonyms;

- the need to be aware of collateral relationships between terms.

These difficulties and others associated with online systems lead to under-utilization and ineffective exploitation of valuable information resources. In turn, potential revenues and opportunities are lost for network operators and information providers. Within the past eighteen months, however, SQL (Structured Query Language) has become increasingly important as a way, according to Personal

Computing, (Personal Computing, 1988), of giving users "a standard means of accessing data in any database" and so bring databases to the computing masses.

For non-professional users, however, SQL is not an intuitively understandable interface, but another esoteric programming language. Moreover, it is thought that intelligent gateway services, like EasyNet for example, are not encouraging additional take up of online services (Information World Review, November 1988), although Tome Associates, who are in the business of developing user-friendly front-ends to online databases, say that demand for Tome Searcher and other Tome products has been growing (Information World Review, December 1988). Tome also launched (early 1989) their Tome Selector, a database selector covering 1000 databases. There is a need, however, to continue with the quest to develop tools which would ease the problems of novice users: hypertext may prove to be such a tool.

The greatest asset of hypertext lies in its malleability. It can be moulded to facilitate semi or unformalized access to systems and information retrieval. Hypertext can help end users overcome the "slings and arrows of outrageous" systems. In its simplest versions, hypertext offers diverse paths through a contained set of materials, or hyperbase, perhaps the documentation attached to an organisation, or a research project. More ambitious proposals will permit collaborative work across disciplinary and geographical boundaries. The elements of these systems are basically similar. The fragments of text, links, a non-linear storage structure, and a user interface, though terminology differs across systems.

An evaluation of the potential of hypertext to provide user-friendly interfaces to electronic services (which would appeal to non-specialist - in the sense of non-systems specialists :users) formed the basis of this research. An extension of the programme will concentrate on

- developing and refining the functionality of the interface to electronic mail services enabling access entirely through a pointing device e.g. mouse or touch screen;

- analysing the problems of retrieving information from online hosts e.g. technical specifications, data structures, viewing versus downloading information;

- evaluating hypertext as an intelligent tool for database searching;

- examining the potential of exploiting hypertext capabilities to generate personalized information at local level.

An analysis of user requirements, within business enterprises will be undertaken along with user testing throughout project development. The final objective is twofold:

- to simplify the problems of online access for business managers as end users;

- to offer the end user a transparent, seamless information environment capable of supporting local processing and manipulation.

End users who are still resistant to online services require to be convinced that not only can an intelligent, user-friendly interface make it easier for them to get access to information they know exists, but to be guided to information which they do not know about, and are therefore unable to ask for.

Research so far at Strathclyde suggests that the theory of using hypertext in this field is sound, but that probably a much more powerful hypermedia engine than HyperCard will have to be developed. Whether this is possible or not remains to be seen. Research at Rutgers University [Kesselman and Trapasso, 1988) in the USA suggests that, even with a very user-friendly front-end like HyperCard, the main problems for the inexperienced end user lie in the inability to construct definitive search statements and effectively use Boolean logic.

However, when these problems are overcome, searching from a full-text database, for example, could result in a locally-generated database of downloaded items using HyperCard as a front-end.

HyperCard's linking capabilities at that stage could be used to massage the local database into a customised, desktop hypertext integrating relevant existing data with the downloaded information. Simultaneous access is envisaged to the expanded and enriched desktop facility, through its incorporation in a shared or a distributed system within the corporate setting. The added value potential is at once apparent.:

- the storage and integration of all necessary information packets

- the elimination or reduction of due procedure in reporting

- the ability to capture interrelationships

- the exploitation of business intelligence

- ease of access to time-critical information, often vital to decision-making

- the extension of fraternal, and often informal, commercial intelligence

- AIMS rather than DBMS.

REFERENCES

Baird, P. HyperCard opens an electronic window on Glasgow. *The Electronic Library.* (October 1988) 6, 5, 344-353.

Baird, P. and Percival, M. (1989) *Hypertext: Theory into Practice.* Glasgow Online: database development using Apple's HyperCard. Blackwell Oxford Scientific Publications, pp.75-92.

Business data move for Tome. *Information World Review.* (December 1988) p36.

Cronin, B. and Davenport, E. (1990) *Elements of Information Management,* New York Scarecrow Press.

DeYoung, L. (1989) Hypertext challenges in the auditing domain. *Hypertext '89* proceedings. ACM, New York pp 169-180.

Kesselman, M. And Trapasso, L. (1988) Hypertext and the end-user. *Online information '88,* Proc. of the 12th int. Online Information Meeting . Learned Information, Oxford, pp. 219-225.

Leading the questions. *Personal Computing.* (April 1988)

Nelson, T.H. (January 1988) Managing immense storage. *Byte.* 13,1, 225-238.

Parker, M. and Benson, R. (1988) *Information Economics.* Prentice Hall, Englewood Cliffs.

The online market column. *Information World Review.* (November 1988), p9.

Part Two

Human Factors

6. HUMAN FACTORS ISSUES IN THE DESIGN OF HYPERMEDIA INTERFACES

A. Dillon

HUSAT Research Centre, Loughborough University of Technology.

6.1 INTRODUCTION

The human-computer interface has gained such importance over the last decade in the domain of system design that an application or system is often judged more on the strength of its user interface than its functionality. However, the euphoria surrounding hypermedia systems and their potential for re-structuring large amounts of information in previously impossible ways has led some developers to forget or overlook the fact that even with such systems, a user still ultimately interacts with a machine. This fact alone necessitates careful consideration of the user interface issues.

Human-computer interaction can be conceptualized as a communicative dialogue whose purpose is to complete a task. The interface is therefore the communication channel afforded by the computer, allowing transfer of modality independent information between machine and user. As a communication channel the interface is both physical (keyboard, mouse, display) and representational (iconic, metaphoric) i.e., it offers the means of control as well as providing a model of its operations, whether this model is made explicit (e.g. the Macintosh desktop) or not (e.g. the MS-DOS operating system). The physical aspects are becoming reasonably standard across systems, the representational ones can vary even at the application level.

6.2   USERS, TASKS AND INFORMATION SPACES

From the traditional human factors perspective, the users and their tasks are the important factors to understand in designing any computer. In the hypermedia context it is worth adding the notion of information space in which the task is being performed. By information space is meant the document, database, texts, graphics and sounds etc. that the user works on. This information space varies tremendously and can be shown to interact with both users and tasks i.e., people utilize information differently depending on its type, their experience and what they want from it (Dillon, Richardson and McKnight, NYP).

As the range of users, information spaces and tasks that are computerized increases, our lack of knowledge about how people effectively satisfy their information needs becomes more obvious. Even now, with comparatively few real-world hypertext or hypermedia applications in service, it is difficult (if not impossible) to provide useful guidelines that extend beyond the specifics of any given situation. While this will not stop the inevitable flood of guidelines in the literature (Hardman and Sharratt, 1989) sensible design decisions are best made in the light of informed awareness of these three aspects of the hypermedia application under consideration rather than any slavish adherence to published recommendations.

Ultimately, the perspective outlined in the present paper encourages a view of the hypermedia system in total as an interface between a user and an information space. The advantage of this approach (which might be termed the "system is the interface " or "the interface is everything" approach) is that it emphasizes focusing very early on in the design process on the most important aspects of the application: the user, the information and the task. Such a view of the interface is necessarily broader than many computer scientists' perspective which tends to limit discussion of the interface to aspects of the display layout or message wording but is vital for those who wish to understand the nature of human interaction with complex devices.

From this perspective we conceive of the user interacting with a system to gain some information i.e. they are task-driven. Their behaviour may appear chaotic and error-prone, or smooth and efficient, depending on numerous factors such as skill, experience and so forth, but it is nonetheless purposeful.. The information they seek may vary from the general (e.g.,"What is in this folder?") to the specific (e.g., "What is X's telephone number?") but the interface is the medium or communication channel through which they obtain it.

A schematic representation of the human factors issues involved in using hypermedia is proposed here (see fig.6.1). This is a three-tier framework based loosely around the impact of size of information space. It is suggested that the major issues to be addressed alter as this space becomes larger. At the simplest level, reading a single screen or page of text (such as a note or letter), the major limiting factors are the visual ergonomics. Once the information space becomes larger than can be put on a single screen the user must manipulate the information in order to view it all. This necessitates the use of whatever facilities are available in the interface and focuses attention on aspects such as button selection, scrolling, searching mechanisms etc. As the information space becomes even larger it seems that the reader's model of its structure starts to play an increasingly important part, aiding navigation, suggesting where information might be found and so forth.

This is a generic representation of the factors involved. It is also a gross over simplification for example to lump issues under a heading such as "access structures" and attempt to rigidly separate them from other factors on the basis of information space size, but it suffices to give an indication of what human factors issues need addressing when designing a hypermedia application. Furthermore, such a framework can provide, I believe, a useful handle on the rapidly expanding experimental and discursive literature on human factors in hypermedia applications that is now appearing. In a paper of this length it is impossible to cover these issues in any detail but they are briefly discussed in the following sections.

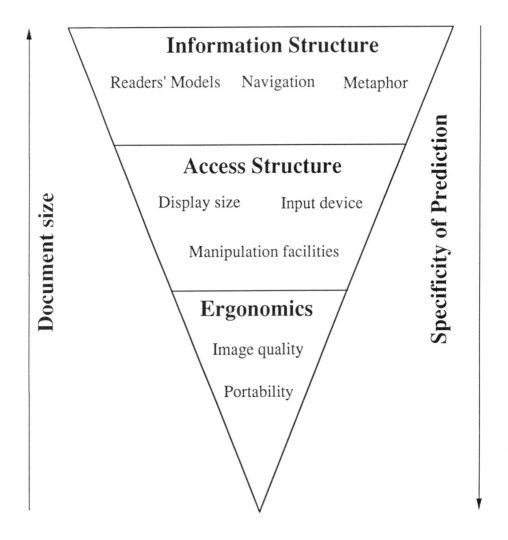

Fig. 6.1 Issues involved in Hypermedia design as a function of document size.

6.3 EMPIRICAL FINDINGS

6.3.1 Basic ergonomic issues

Even though the hypermedia user will inevitably find himself or herself sitting in front of a VDU (at least for the foreseeable future!) it is interesting to note how little attention is actually paid to the associated issues of screen reading. Much of the work in this area in the last ten years has addressed the issue of likely differences between reading from screens as opposed to paper (for a review see Dillon, McKnight and Richardson, 1988). Empirical investigations of the area have suggested five possible differences between them:

- speed (Wright and Likorish 1983)

- accuracy (Creed, Dennis and Newstead, 1987)

- comprehension (Kak, 1981)

- fatigue (Wilkinson and Robinshaw, 1987)

- preference (Cakir, Hart and Stewart, 1980)

It seems certain that reading speeds are reduced on typical VDUs and accuracy may be lessened for cognitively demanding tasks. Fears of increased visual fatigue and reduced levels of comprehension as a result of reading from VDUs remain unsettled, the latter issue in particular is unlikely to yield a simple answer. With respect to reader preference, top quality hardcopy seems to be preferred to screen displays, which is not altogether surprising.

No one variable is likely to be responsible for the observed differences. Gould et al. (1987) have shown that the speed and accuracy deficits could be overcome by using a high quality screen that combined positive presentation, high screen resolution to avoid flicker and anti-aliased characters. This equates more typically with the type of screen on which many hypermedia applications are presented though as an issue of empirical comparison between paper and hypermedia it tends to have been surprisingly overlooked.

Interestingly, any empirical attempt to tie the differences to factors such as the orientation of the display (paper is usually read in a horizontal position while screens are vertical), aspect ratio (paper tends to be portrait rather than landscape, the reverse holds for screens), visual viewing angle, or user characteristics (such as age, sex and experience in reading from screens) which are popularly supposed to affect screen reading, has failed to provide reliable effects (Gould, 1986).

As hypermedia, not just hypertext, become more commonplace ergonomic issues pertaining to sound quality and the interaction of sound and visual images are likely to emerge.

6.3.2   Access Structures

As information spaces increase in size other issues than those covered above come into play and need to be considered. With paper, users have acquired a range of physical and cognitive skills for manipulating text and the relatively standard format of texts allows for easy transfer of these skills across the spectrum of paper documents. The term access structure was coined by Waller (1977) in his work on text genres to refer to the facilities provided by the author to aid the reader. In paper this can take the form of headings, indices, spacing etc. while with electronically presented information it can be taken to include the range of interactive facilities available. It is less clear how hypermedia should be designed to facilitate equally easy use. Several relevant human factors issues which have been investigated are:

- display size, for which many people claim "bigger is better" although the literature shows few performance effects when reading short amounts of text (Duchnicky and Kolers, 1987; Elkerton and Williges, 1984) but significant preference effects for large display sizes over small ones (40-60 lines compared to 20 lines) when reading lengthy electronic texts have been reported (Richardson, Dillon and McKnight, 1989),

- scrolling versus paging, for which it is hard to make firm recommendations though novices seem to prefer paging (Schwarz, Beldie and Pastoor, 1983), and psychological evidence on readers' spatial recall of items in text suggests advantages for it (Rothkopf, 1971),

- colour coding, for which effects have been very difficult to assess though it seems to be universally popular with readers (Wright and Liickorish, 1988),

- text splitting across screens which seems to be a nuisance factor and causes users to return significantly more often to the previous screen (Dillon, Richardson and McKnight, NYP),

- input devices, though the mouse has been described as supporting a rate of movement nearly maximal with respect to the information processing capacities of co-ordinated eye-hand movement (Card, English and Burr, 1978), Milner (Milner, 1988) concludes that there is little evidence in the literature supporting its supremacy and Ewing et al. (1986) report a performance benefit for function keys over the mouse for a HyperTIES application.

The advent of hypertext applications with selectable buttons and linked nodes of information has brought a new sophistication to text manipulation facilities and it seems plausible that the ability to "point-and-go" has distinct advantages over paging or specifying goto jumps on a menu. However not all information is so easily manipulated and where information nodes are large or depend heavily on context, other factors such as display size, scrolling etc., come back into play. Specific work on these issues would be useful.

6.3.3   Organizing and Structuring the Information Space

While the preceding sections are often not considered directly relevant to hypermedia applications by many researchers and developers, the issues relating to re-structuring of information together with the nature and amount of linking involved have become central. It is almost taken on faith by many that traditional documents consist of a linear format which demands serial reading while hypermedia allows non-linear formats which offer more flexible and "natural" methods of use. Hypermedia is often proposed as the liberator, freeing the user from the confines of traditional linear documentation. Such a distinction is dubious. It assumes for example that paper text can only be read in one way and that readers will prefer to have texts re-structured into linked nodes. There is little evidence to support either assumption.

Navigation through hypermedia is the most commonly cited difficulty (Edwards and Hardman, 1989) and major research effort is now expended on developing browsing facilities and maps for users. Wright and Lickorish (1989) provide evidence that the suitability of the navigation facilities varies with the task and information space again highlighting the need to consider the relevant attributes of users, tasks and information in designing usable hypermedia interfaces.

It is clear that readers form mental representations of a paper document's structure in terms of spatial location [Rothkopf, 1971] and overall organization (Dillon, 1989). Such representations or models are derived from years of exposure to the information type (e.g. academic journal articles) or can be formed in the case of spatial recall from a quick scan of the material. Such models are useful in terms of predicting where information will be found or even what type of information is available. Consideration of existing models is vital in the design of new versions so as to avoid designing against the intended users' views of how the information should be organized.

To date most work on hypertext has been discursive rather than experimental but of the studies that have been carried out it is obvious that hypermedia will not be a universal panacea to problems of information presentation. It comes as a surprise to many that most comparative experimental work in the area has shown that users perform better or at least as well with paper [McKnight, Dillon and Richardson, 1989; Monk, Walsh and Dix, 1988). This is not always so (Egan et al. (1989) provide evidence for improved performance by students using the SuperBook over a paper text on statistics) but is typical. However such findings must be interpreted in terms of the users, tasks, and information spaces being investigated as there will be many instances of the hypermedia concept available in many different task domains to many different users. To assume that all hypermedia are better (or worse) than paper on the basis of several limited empirical examinations is clearly short-sighted.

6.4   CONCLUSION

The extent to which there is a weighting on any of these factors is interesting. Getting the image quality right is, as mentioned earlier, a necessary but insufficient condition. However, adopting the other approach, and getting the model correct without addressing access structure or low level ergonomic issues is equally insufficient, though whether it is as damning as good image quality and poor structuring is an empirical question.

Trade-offs can only be reliably made when the target users are understood. Though not well disposed to formal guidelines for design I realise that to many people such advice is considered useful. To this end I will summarize some steps that should be taken when seeking to design hypermedia for usability:

• Know the users, their tasks and the information space involved in terms of how the application is to be used, why it is to be used and what perceptions users have of the information's organizing principles.

- Plan the structure of the information space (rather than attempting to incorporate everything and then linking it all together).

- Design suitable access structures.

- Optimize image quality.

- Test the design and test it early! Adjust accordingly.

The first step is important and will provide information of direct relevance to the next three steps. The last step is probably the most important although is often seen as a luxury that cannot be afforded. Failure to test the design is bound to lead to problems as no theoretical models or formal guidelines exist that can even approximate the quality of information obtained from observing real users interacting with a system. These steps will not guarantee success but they offer better prospects of achieving it than any others.

REFERENCES

Cakir, A., Hart, D. J. and Stewart, T. F. M. (1980) *Visual Display Terminals* John Wiley and Sons, Chichester.

Card, S., English, W. and Burr, B (1978) Evaluation of mouse, rate- controlled isometric joystick, step keys and text keys for text selection on a CRT. *Ergonomics*, 21, 601-613.

Creed, A., Dennis, I. and Newstead, S. (1987) Proof-reading on VDUs. *Behaviour and Information Technology*, 6, 1, 3-13.

Dillon, A. (1989) Readers' models of text structures. *HUSAT Technical Report,* PQ/LUT/AD06.

Dillon, A., McKnight, C. and Richardson, J. (1988) Reading from paper versus reading from screens. *The Computer Journal* 31, 5, 457-464.

Dillon, A., Richardson, J. and McKnight, C. (1989) The human factors of journal usage and the design of electronic text. *Interacting with Computers*, 1,2, 183-189.

Dillon, A., Richardson, J. and McKnight,C. (in press) The effect of display size and text splitting on reading lengthy text from screen. *Behaviour and Information Technology.*

Duchnicky, R.L. and Kolers P.A. (1983) Readability of text scrolled on a visual display terminal as a function of window size. *Human Factors*, 25, 6, 683-692.

Edwards, D. and Hardman. L. (1989) Lost in Hyperspace: cognitive mapping and navigation in a hypertext environment, in *Hypertext: Theory into Practice.* (ed R. McAleese) Intellect, London, UK.

Egan, D., Remde, J., Landauer, T., Lochbaum,C. and Gomez, L. (1989) Behavioural evaluation and analysis of a hypertext browser, *In Proc. of CHI'89,* ACM, New York, USA.

Elkerton, J. and Williges, R. (1984) Information retrieval strategies in a file search environment. *Human Factors,* 26, 2, 171-184.

Ewing, J. Mehrabanzad, S., Sheck, S., Ostroff, D. and Shneiderman, B. (1986) An experimental comparison of a mouse and arrow-jump keys for an interactive encyclopedia. *International Journal of Man Machine Studies,* 24, 29-45.

Gould, J. D. (1986) Reading is slower from CRT displays than from paper: some experiments that fail to explain why. *IBM Report RC 11709 (#52588)*, IBM Research Centre, Yorktown Heights, New York 10598, USA.

Gould, J.D., Alfaro, L., Finn, R., Haupt, B. and Minuto, A. (1987) Reading from CRT displays can be as fast as reading from paper. *Human Factors,* 26 5 , 497-517.

Hardman, L. and Sharratt, B. (1989) User-centred hypertext design: the application of HCI design principles and guidelines. Paper presented at *Hypertext II, the 2nd Annual UK Conference on Hypertext,* University of York, UK.

Kak, A. V. (1981) Relationships between readability of printed and CRT- displayed text. *Proc. of Human Factors Society - 25th Annual Meeting,* 137 - 140.

McKnight, C., Dillon, A., and Richardson,J. (1989) A comparison of linear and hypertext formats in information retrieval, in the proceedings of *Hypertext II, the Second Annual UK conference on Hypertext,* University of York, UK.

Milner,N. (1988) A review of human performance and preference with different input devices to computer systems, in *People and Computers IV* (eds. D.Jones and R.Winder)   , Cambridge University Press, Cambridge.

Monk,A., Walsh, P. and Dix,A. (1988) A comparison of hypertext, scrolling, and folding as mechanisms for program browsing, in *People and Computers IV*, (eds. D.Jones and R.Winder), Cambridge University Press, Cambridge.

Richardson,J., Dillon, A., and McKnight, C. (1989) The effect of window size on reading and manipulating electronic text. in *Contemporary Ergonomics*, (ed. E. Megaw), Taylor and Francis, London.

Rothkopf, E. Z. (1971) Incidental memory for location of information in text. *Journal of Verbal Learning and Verbal Behaviour*, 10, 608-613.

Schwartz, E., Beldie, I. and Pastoor, S. (1983) A comparison of paging and scrolling for changing screen contents by inexperienced users. *Human Factors,* 25, 279-282.

Waller, P. (1977) Typographic access structures for educational texts, in (eds. P.Kolers, M. Wrolstad and H. Bouma), *Processing of Visible Language,* Vol 1., Plenum, New York, USA.

Wilkinson , R.T. and Robinshaw, H.M. (1987) Proof-reading: VDU and paper text compared for speed, accuracy and fatigue. *Behaviour and Information Technology,* 6(2), 125-133.

Wright, P. and Lickorish, A. (1983) Proof-reading texts on screen and paper. *Behaviour and Information Technology,* 2, (3), 227-235.

Wright, P. and Lickorish, A. (1988) Colour cues as location aids in lengthy texts on screen and paper. *Behaviour and Information Technology,* 7, 1, 11-30.

Wright, P. and Lickorish, A. (1989) An empirical comparison of two navigation systems for two hypertexts, in the proceedings of *Hypertext II, the 2nd Annual UK conference on Hypertext,* University of York, UK.

7. TEACHING WITH HYPERMEDIA: PROBLEMS AND PROSPECTS

N. Hammond

CTI Centre for Psychology, University of York

> *Men must be taught as if you taught them not,*
> *And things unknown proposed as things forgot.*
>
> *Alexander Pope*

7.1 INTRODUCTION

Traditionally, computer-based learning (CBL) has divided into systems based on tutoring and systems providing exploratory environments. The former direct the course of learning by controlling instructional dialogue and strategy, while the latter encourage the learner to explore concepts using a constrained set of tools, often within a programming environment.

The philosophies underlying this dichotomy still flourish, although the clash is now leading to productive compromises. Hard-line proponents of the AI technologies which underlie intelligent tutoring systems claim that the course of training must be driven by explicit models of the learners' and experts' states of knowledge and of the underlying acquisition processes. Proponents of hypertext-based learning systems, on the other hand, argue that there is no need to model the student, and that more effective learning is achieved by allowing learners maximum freedom to explore information bases, to discover relationships for themselves and to form integrated structures as their learning goals demand. Thus strict intelligent tutoring has been criticized on the grounds that "to treat the learner as a dumb patient and the computer system as an omniscient doctor is both perverse and arrogant" (Megarry, 1988), while strict hypertext-based systems can be ineffective if users merely ramble through the knowledge base in an unmotivated and haphazard fashion.

However, many recent approaches to CBL have steered away from these two extremes. The iron grip of model-driven control in intelligent tutoring is loosening, through the development of advice-giving systems, guided discovery techniques, intelligent agents and the like. Tutoring systems are moving away from the prescriptive towards the advisory. Likewise, recent exploratory systems (such as the Alternate Reality Kit, (Smith, 1987)) provide the means for some degree of tutorial control. Advocates of hypertext-based learning acknowledge that letting the learner sink or swim in a sea of links and nodes has its problems, and talk increasingly of tools for navigation and guidance, of more directed support for learning activities, of intelligent or adaptive links and even of AI-based advising tools.

This characterization is of course simplistic. Learning is not unitary; there is room for a spectrum of approaches to CBL. Knowledge domains differ hugely both in their natural structures and in the requirements they pose for the learner. Learners differ, not only in terms of ability, strategy and temperament, but in their goals and contexts. To use current parlance, learning is situated: mobilization of the learners' cognitive resources and deployment of their strategies depend heavily on the nature of the learning situation. Thus a great range of activities is typically called upon in learning: some active, some passive; some creative, some reactive; some directed, some exploratory. The nature of learning, and of the tools and situations that support it, is task dependent. This message is by no means a new one, and is sometimes taken as grounds for a cognitively-based approach to the design of instruction and instructional systems (Di Vesta and Rieber, 1987).

In this paper I argue that hypertext provides a framework for a range of tools supporting the plurality of learning activities necessary for truly effective CBL. First, I outline some of the problems with learning from hypertext alone. I then discuss some ways in which hypertext may be extended to address the learner's and the teacher's needs. I shall use the term hypertext to refer to both textual and non-textual systems, whether video, computer graphics or indeed any technologically feasible form of presentation: no distinction is made between hypertext and hypermedia. For a general review of hypertext systems and their use the reader is referred to Conklin (1987) and Halasz (1988).

7.2   PROBLEMS WITH HYPERTEXT

The use of hypertext tools in education and training is growing (e.g., Barden et al. (1989); Dufresne, Jolin and Senteni (1989)). In some cases, hypertext serves as the sole mechanism for delivering of information to the student (basic hypertext). Basic hypertext systems allow learners to explore materials by browsing through a knowledge structure, guided in part by their goals and in part by the imposed structure of the knowledge base. In other cases, additional facilities may be added to the basic hypertext mechanism, for example to guide the learner through the material, to provide tutoring information, or to allow learners to generate or inter-link materials for themselves. A number of authors point to the potential of hypertext for blurring the distinction between author, editor and reader (Conklin, 1987).

Experience with using hypertext systems for learning has revealed a number of problems (e.g., Hammond and Allinson (1989) and Jones (1987)). These problems do not of course occur in all cases, but they give some insight into issues which may prove important. Principal amongst the problems are the following.

First, users get lost. The knowledge base may be large and unfamiliar; the links provided will not be suitable for all individuals and for all tasks, and the user may be confused by the embarrassment of choice. Once in an unknown or unexpected part of the knowledge base, the user may have difficulty in reaching familiar territory; like a stranger in a foreign city without a map, he may miss the correct turning. Providing a backtrack facility is unlikely in itself to solve the problem.

Second, users may find it difficult to gain an overview of the material. They may fail to see how parts of the knowledge base are related and even miss large relevant sections entirely. In one study from our own laboratory (Hammond and Allinson, 1989) we asked individuals to explore a small knowledge base for a fixed time using a variety of hypertext tools. All users had available the basic hypertext mechanism for traversing links from one frame of information to another, but some users also had access to additional facilities such as maps (providing an overview), an index of keywords or a number of guided tours through the material. Compared with users of systems with these additional facilities, users of the basic hypertext version thought they had seen the most material when in fact they had seen the least. Basic hypertext systems do not make it easy for users to know what's there or where they've been.

Third, even if users know specific information is present, they may have difficulty finding it. The knowledge base may not be structured in the way that they expect, or their lack of knowledge might mislead them. Jones (1987) has pointed out that the number of alternative choices often makes appropriate selection difficult. A related problem is that of uncertain commitment, where the user is unsure where a link will lead or what type or amount of information will be shown. Raskin (1987) gives an example of a user pointing to the leg of a butterfly on the screen: will the system take this to indicate the whole butterfly, the leg, the tarsus, legs in general or even the concept of symmetry? In other cases, the user might expect a short explanation, perhaps in a pop-up window, only to find that she has moved on to a new area in the knowledge base.

Fourth, users may ramble through the knowledge base in an instructionally inefficient fashion, with choices motivated by moment-to-moment aspects of the display which attract attention. This will be a crucial issue in instructional situations. When a person is uncertain of their immediate goals or of how to attain them, they will search their environment for clues. A system which gives a multiplicity of choice but the minimum of guidance may not be the ideal way for learners to ask themselves the right questions or to help them to formulate and attain their goals. This will be particularly so for non-experts (Gay, 1986).

Finally, coming to grips with the interface for controlling the various facilities may interfere with the primary task of exploring and learning about the materials. Raskin (1987) claims that the central lacuna of hypertext systems is the omission of any specification of the user interface, and even enthusiasts admit that the generic nature of hypertext systems is both a blessing and a curse (Halasz, 1988). It is a curse because users are faced with a tool that may well be useful but is not well adapted to the specific task in hand. Getting the interface right is crucial in learning situations so as to prevent needless squandering of the student's resources on fighting the system.

These problems do not mean that hypertext is inappropriate for exploratory browsing or for learning, but rather that systems for specific activities should be supplemented by more directed access and guidance mechanisms, by appropriately tailored interfaces, and perhaps by learning activities outside the normal purview of hypertext. Hypertext methods should be seen as one tool within the educational technologist's toolbox, to be used judiciously alongside others.

7.3 LEARNING SUPPORT ENVIRONMENTS

The philosophy which underpins the exploratory learning environments is based on the observation that we know a good deal more about providing appropriate environments for learning than we do about the details of learning processes themselves. This is the case both at the level of cognitive theory and at a more applied level.

Cognitive theory furnishes us with a number of potentially useful distinctions in identifying conditions which will optimize learning. These include, for example, modes of learning (such as implicit and explicit), kinds of knowledge (such as declarative and procedural), forms of processing of materials (selecting, organizing, integrating), phases in learning (accretion, restructuring, tuning) and not least the consequences of learning activity for memorization and understanding (such as depth of processing, encoding specificity, schema integration). These issues will not be expanded upon here: see (Banner, 1988), (Di Vesta and Rieber 1987), (Hammond and Allinson, 1988) and (Russell, Moran and Jordan, 1988) for a more detailed discussion of their application to instructional design.

At a more practical level, many informal approaches to learning aim to optimize the general conditions without worrying too much about the moment-to-moment course of learning. For instance in "teaching" a child to talk the parent merely needs to give appropriate stimulation at appropriate times; details of intermediate states of knowledge and the processes of acquisition can safely be left to the child and to the research psychologist. Much learning is implicit and occurs without intention. An artificially imposed strategy may even impair learning (Berry and Broadbent, 1988), a long-recognized fact which perhaps underlies the quote at the start of this paper.

The distinction between implicit and explicit forms of learning is of particular interest since hypermedia provides a rich environment for implicit learning during exploratory tasks. It has been claimed that much routine childhood learning and some adult learning occurs implicitly, and psychologists are increasingly arguing for a distinction between explicit and implicit modes of learning (e.g. (Hayes and Broadbent, 1988)) and of memory performance (Graf and Schachter, 1985). For instance the latter authors demonstrated a dissociation between the two modes in amnesic patients. Models of learning based on connectionist principles (Pike, 1984) or on multiple-trace memories (Hintzman, 1986) have also given a spur to the idea that rules and structures can be abstracted from experiences without the need for them to be represented or taught explicitly. It may be important, therefore, to identify when implicit rather than explicit learning is appropriate and what the optimal instructional approach for each type of learning might be.

The proposition, then, is that such issues can take their place in a framework designed to support learning not by providing an explicit representation of the student's knowledge and the required activity to alter it but by suggesting how best to provide the right tools at the right time so that the student's learning processes - perhaps poorly understood - can flourish. The aims are theoretically more modest than those of model-driven intelligent tutoring: no attempt is made to develop a "complete" model of the student which can predict detailed learning behaviour, rather the aim is to ensure that the likely informational, task and cognitive requirements of the student can be helpfully met.

Hammond and Allinson (1988) propose the notion of a learning support environment or LSE as a system which provides the learner with a set of tools to support exploration of, or instruction in, some field of knowledge. The tools will include both a set of learning activities and range of aids for accessing information and making best use of the available activities. The set of tools, the extent of learner control and characteristics of the interface can be tailored by the author or teacher to match the requirements of the student. They should not only allow the user to access the knowledge base without getting lost or bogged down in a morass of information but the nature of the tools should encourage optimal learning strategies. In the rest of this paper, I briefly outline some possible extensions to basic hypertext which might fulfil this function.

7.4   EXTENDING HYPERTEXT

7.4.1   Helping the learner to choose

Fig. 7.1 summarizes some of the dimensions along which CBL can vary. Traditional tutorial methods, such as programmed instruction and drill-and-practice, allow the learner little control, and can be located near the top end of the vertical dimension. Although intelligent tutoring techniques may attempt to escape from this straightjacket by providing more directed remediation or conjectural forms of instruction, these have proved successful only in highly restricted and formal knowledge domains (Stevens, 1986). The requirement that the instructional dialogue should be driven by an explicit model of the student's state of knowledge places extreme constraints on the freedom that the learner can enjoy. Hypertext, on the other hand, allows the user complete freedom to explore the information available, and in some cases (such as in the Intermedia project, (Garrett, Smith and Meyrowitz, 1986)), to create and link materials.

However, such freedom can cause problems, as we have indicated above. Giving the learner appropriate access and control is not just a matter of providing a hypermedia interface to the knowledge domain; learners may need to inform their choices with signposts and access mechanisms to help them through the materials or with instructional strategies to optimize the route taken.

A number of studies have investigated tools for supporting learner choices. One technique is to provide additional signposts and access mechanisms. Both Edwards and Hardman (1989) and Jones (1989) have investigated the provision of an index to hypertext screens over and above normal hypertext navigation. Edwards and Hardman argued that provision of both techniques, as compared with either facility alone, can make it more difficult for users to form a cognitive map of the hypertext. Their novice subjects performed directed search tasks, and the effectiveness of the facilities varied widely depending on the specific content of the question. This content-dependency was also a feature of Jones' study (1989), in which use of an index was again compared with use of hypertext links in terms of directed search and incidental learning. The facility better supporting directed search depended on question content, whilst use of the index resulted in more incidental learning than did use of hypertext links. This last finding may have been an artifact of the route taken or a consequence of the task demands imposed by the different access facilities.

Hammond and Allinson (1988 and 1989) investigated a hypertext learning system providing a range of access mechanisms, incuding an index, a map (overview frames which give a bird's eye view of, and access to, the available material), and "tours" (optional linear sequences of frames to lead learners through particular topics). They found that these various mechanisms were used effectively by learners in a task-dependent fashion, the efficacy of a particular tool depending on the situation of its use. For example, the index was more likely to be used in specific directed tasks, while tours were more likely to be a feature of general exploratory tasks.

Well-designed maps or browsers can be highly effective in providing learners with navigational information. Not only can they embody (and make explicit to the learner) the structural relationships in the knowledge base, they can also act as an access mechanism (pointing to a map location takes the learner there directly) and provide "footprint" information (where I have been so far). Users find it hard to judge the nature and amount of information available in a basic hypertext if it has none of these additional access facilities (Hammond and Allinson, 1989).

A second way to help learner choice is to give the learner the option of relinquishing control for some activities. The use of tours, described above, is one such example. Hammond and Allinson (1988) found that tours were more likely to be used when students have little prior knowledge of a topic. Other forms of "soft" tutoring (in contrast to strict model-driven tutoring) of this type have also been advocated. For example Mayes, Kibby and Anderson (1989) describes the StrathTutor system in which one aspect of tutoring is to require the learner to make sense of dynamic hypertext links computed by the system on the basis of knowledge attributes of each display frame.

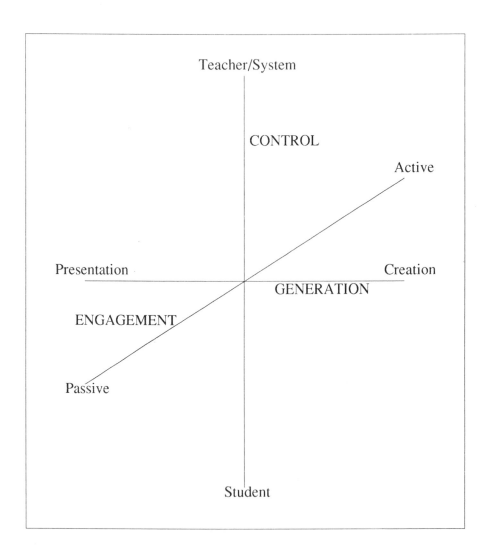

Fig. 7.1 Some dimensions of computer-based learning.

In general, there are two types of control which tend to feature in hypertext-based learning systems: control over the sequencing of the materials which the learner sees and control over the types and sequencing of learning activities (such as reading information, taking tests, solving problems or trying interactive demonstrations). The optimal level of control depends on the nature of the learners, on their familiarity with the materials, on their learning goals and not least on the nature of the knowledge domain. Handing complete control to the beginner may be as ineffective as forcing the expert through a drill-and-practice tutorial. The question of appropriate level of instructional control has been the topic of a certain amount of research, and there seems to be a consensus that more knowledgeable learners can capitalise on self-directed learning. Some of this work is reviewed in (Hammond and Allinson, NYP) and (Hammond, 1989).

7.4.2   Helping learners to structure knowledge

A second dimension of CBL shown in Fig. 7.1 is the degree with which learners engage with the materials. The task of understanding a domain is normally achieved more effectively if learners can be persuaded to think actively about the structures and relationships within the domain. All too often, designers of CBL conveniently forget that their goal is learner understanding rather than merely information provision. Meyrowitz (1986) notes that some users of the Intermedia system showed no learning benefits and suggests that this may have been because they used the system passively rather than actively. Basic hypertext systems, let alone ones as sophisticated as Intermedia, may not encourage active engagement. Additional activities, such as quizzes, problem-solving activities, interactive demonstrations or mini-experiments may all help, depending on the nature of the domain. We have incorporated some of these into our own learning system (Hammond and Allinson, 1988). It may also be helpful to provide external motivation for engagement, such as by requiring learners to perform tasks or assessments which demand thoughtful use of the system. The

StrathTutor approach, described above, is a more direct attempt to achieve active engagement.

The third dimension in fig. 7.1 also relates to the goal of helping learners to structure the knowledge. The act of creating information, whether from scratch or re-structuring existing material, provides a further range of important learning situation and activities. Although there are situations when it is appropriate to let the learner loose with the full power of hypertext authoring systems, more often than not this would be counter-productive. Bland talk of blurring the boundary between reader and writer is unhelpful on its own, even counter-productive: specific tools, tailorable to specific learning situations, are required. These may be tools to help the learner perform specific tasks, or might, for instance, require the student to "teach" the system using some form of instruction language or notation. Hewett (1986) discusses some of the issues in treating the computer as pupil.

An approach we are currently investigating is to help learners manipulate partly familiar material which they have difficulty organizing into a coherent structure. This is a characteristic difficulty with a good deal of conceptual knowledge. One of the techniques we are using is a knowledge jigsaw task; an example is shown in fig. 7.2. The top panel of the figure shows a mock-up of the screen at the start of the task. The learner has to assemble the boxes (nodes, in hypertext terminology) and arrows (semantically-typed links) into the correct structure (shown in the bottom panel of the figure). The boxes can be moved around using the mouse, and links of different types can be selected from the "arrow quivers". The learner can request further details of any box, which appear as a pop-up, as illustrated in the middle panel (the learner has displayed the pop-up for the Phonemic similarity effect box).

In this particular example, the knowledge is structured as a scientific argument, with nodes defining model components, hypotheses and empirical evidence, and links defining the relations of prediction, support and refutation. Other examples

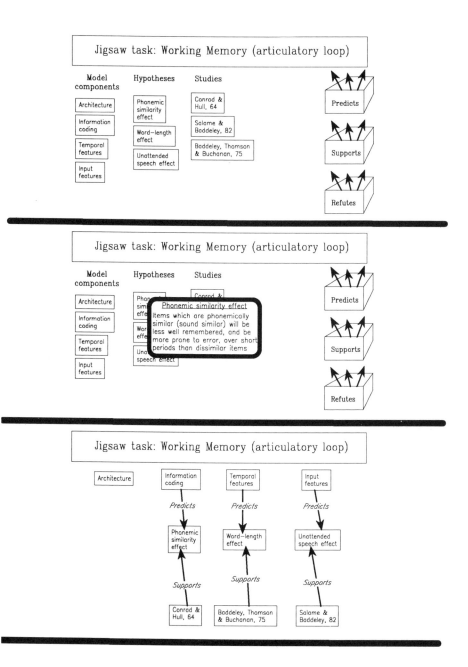

Fig. 7.2 Example knowledge jigsaw task (see text for details)

would require quite different node and link entities, but it would be quite feasible to develop generic authoring and presentation tools to support the creation of this kind of specific hypertext "tutorial". Just as with knowledge presentation we have to do better than dropping the learner in front of a basic hypertext system, so too with knowledge creation we have to provide a range of specific tools to meet the requirements of the specific learning situation and activities.

7.5 HYPERTEXT AS A FRAMEWORK FOR CBL

In the preceding sections I have argued that hypertext provides a basis for exploratory CBL systems, but of itself is a poor vehicle for many learning situations. Basic hypertext needs to be supplemented by a variety of tools, tailorable to specific learning situations by the course developer, by the instructor or even by the learner. Some of these tools (for instance browsers and indexes) are accepted as "hypertext" tools; others are not. This distinction is quite arbitrary in the context of CBL. Fortunately, recent hypertext systems are no longer flat: they provide "hooks" to the outside (computational) world, and at least some tools of use in developing courseware for learning. This makes hypertext an ideal framework for CBL. A "node" needn't just be a static display frame; it can contain any processing activity or set of interactions. In addition, there is no reason why strategic control (whether of a directive or of an advisory nature) should not be incorporated within the same hypertext framework.

It is worth finishing with a word of warning. In many ways the most important topic of all has been barely mentioned in this paper. Any learning system is only as good as its user interface; learning is hard enough even when nothing impedes the learners view and control of the knowledge domain.

ACKNOWLEDGEMENTS

Thanks are due to my colleagues Lesley Allinson and Anne Trapp for many valuable discussions on the topic of this paper. Some of the work described was supported by a grant from the Computers in Teaching Initiative of the UGC Computer Board for Universities and Research Councils

REFERENCES

Allinson, L.J., and Hammond, N.V. (in press)   Learning support environments: Rationale and evaluation. *Computers and Education.*

Barden, R., Storrs, G., Tang, H., Windsor, P. and Clifton, C. (1989) Extending your home with an ITS: Building a hypertext-based intelligent tutoring system, in *Proceedings of Hypertext II Conference,* University of York, UK.

Berry, D.C. and Broadbent, D.E. (1988) Interactive tasks and the implicit-explicit distinction. *British Journal of Psychology,* 79, 251-272.

Bonner, J. (1988) Implications of cognitive theory for instructional design: revisited. *Educational Communication and Technology Journal,* 36, 3-14.

Conklin, J. (1987) Hypertext: an introduction and summary. *Computer,* September, 17-41

Di Vesta, F.J. and Rieber, L.P. (1987) Characteristics of cognitive engineering: the next generation of instructional systems. *Educational Communication and Technology Journal,* 35, 213-230.

Dufresne, A., Jolin, N. Senteni, A. (1989)   Hypertext documentation for the learning of procedures, in *Proceedings of Hypertext II Conference,* University of York, UK.

Edwards, D.M. and Hardman, L. (1989). "Lost in Hyperspace": Cognitive mapping and navigation in a hypertext environment, in *Hypertext: Theory into Practice.* (ed. R.McAleese), Intellect Books, Oxford, pp 105-125.

Garrett, L.N., Smith, K.E. and Meyrowitz, N. (1986) Intermedia: issues, strategies, and tactics in the design of a hypermedia document system, in *Proceedings of the Conference on Computer-Supported Cooperative Work,* (Austin, Texas, USA, December), pp 163-174.

Gay, G. (1986) Interaction of learner control and prior understanding in computer-assisted video instruction. *Journal of Educational Psychology,* 78, 225-227.

Graf, P. and Schachter, D.L. (1985) Implicit and explicit memory for new associations in normal and amnesic patients. *Journal of Experimental Psychology: Learning, Memory, and Cognition,* 11, 501-518.

Halasz, F. (1988) Reflections on NoteCards: seven issues for the next generation of hypermedia systems. *Comm. of the ACM,* 31, 836-852.

Hammond, N.V. (1989) Hypermedia and learning: Who guides whom? in Computer Assisted Learning. (ed. H.Maurer), Springer-Verlag: Berlin, Germany, 167-181.

Hammond, N.V. and Allinson, L.J. (1988) Development and evaluation of a CAL system for non-formal domains: The Hitch-hiker's guide to cognition. *Computers and Education,* 12, 215-220.

Hammond, N.V. and Allinson, L.J. (1988) Travels around a learning support environment: Rambling, orienteering or touring? In *CHI '88 Conference Proceedings*: Human Factors in Computing Systems. (eds. E. Soloway, D. Frye and S.B. Sheppard), ACM Press: New York, USA, (Washington, May), pp 269-273.

Hammond, N.C. and Allinson, L.J. (1989) Extending hypertext for learning: an investigation of access and guidance tools, in , *People and Computers V,* (eds. A. Sutcliffe and L. Macaulay), Cambridge University Press: Cambridge, UK, pp 293-304.

Hayes, N.A. and Broadbent, D.E. (1988) Two modes of learning for interactive tasks. *Cognition.*

Hewett, T.T. (1986) When every student has a computer. A new perspective on courseware and its development. *Behavior Research Methods, Instruments, and Computers,* 18, 188-195.

Hintzman, D.L. (1986) "Schema abstraction" in a multiple-trace memory model. *Psychological Review,* 93, 411-428.

Jones, P. (1989) Incidental learning during information retrieval: A hypertext experiment, in *Computer Assisted Learning.* (ed. H.Maurer)., Springer-Verlag: Berlin, Germany, pp 23, 5-252.

Jones, W.P. (1987) How do we distinguish the hyper from the hype in non-linear text? in *Human-computer interaction - Interact '87,* (eds. H.J. Bullinger and B. Shackel), North- Holland, Amsterdam, 1-4 September, pp 1107-1113.

Mayes, J.T., Kibby, M. and Anderson, T. (1989) Signposts for conceptual orientation: Some requirements for learning from hypertext, in *Proceedings of Hypertext II Conference,* University of York, UK.

Megarry, J. (1988) Hypertext and compact discs - the challenge of multi-media learning. *British Journal of Educational Technology,* 19, 172-183.

Meyrowitz, N. (1986) Intermedia: The architecture and construction of an object-oriented hypertext/hypermedia system and applications framework, in *OOPSLA '86 Proceedings.* Portland, Oregon, USA.

Pike, R. (1984) Comparison of convolution and matrix distributed memory systems for associative recall and recognition. *Psychological Review,* 91, 281-294.

Raskin, J. (1987) The hype in hypertext: a critique, *in Hypertext '87*. North Carolina, USA, pp 325-329.

Russell, D.M., Moran, T.P. and Jordan D.S. (1988)   The instructional design environment, in *Intelligent Tutoring Systems: Lessons Learned.* (eds. J. Psotka, L.D. Massey and S.A. Mutter), Lawrence Erlbaum: Hillsdale, NJ, USA.

Smith, R.B. (1987) The alternative reality kit: An animated environment for creating interactive simulations, in *CHI '87*, ACM: Boston, USA.

Stevens, A.L. (1986) The next generation of AI-based teaching systems. *Machine-mediated Learning,* 1, 313-326.

FURTHER READING

Geisler-Brenstein, E. and Brenstein, R.J. (1989) The potential of HyperCard for psychological research and instruction: A general discussion and description of two research applications. *Behavior Research Methods, Instruments and Computers,* 21, 307-311.

8. EXPERTEXT: HYPERIZING EXPERT SYSTEMS AND EXPERTIZING HYPERTEXT

D. Diaper and R. Rada

University of Liverpool

8.1 INTRODUCTION TO EXPERT SYSTEMS AND HYPERTEXT

This section introduces some of the problems associated with expert systems and hypertext. The two technologies are discussed from a user orientated perspective which focuses on the distribution of intelligence between users and these computer systems during task performance.

8.1.1 Expert systems and explanation

At least one view of expert systems is that they are devices that attempt to offer advice, help or guidance consistent with that which would be provided by a human expert. One of the claimed findings following the implementation of the early expert systems was, that in addition to the system providing advice, that it was also necessary for the system to explain itself. Indeed, many workers have gone so far as to claim that expert system explanation facilities are a necessary requirement for such systems. While there may be expert system applications where explanation facilities are not necessary, for example, where the operator is an expert and frequent system user and is fully aware of the expert system's domain limitations, such cases are probably comparatively rare.

Clearly the ability to provide explanation requires that an expert system has some self referential or introspective ability and this is not a normal requirement of computer systems. The most common form of expert system explanation has used the same inference mechanism for both generating advice and explanation. Thus an expert system that uses forward and backward chaining has traditionally generated explanations of the type: Question X was asked because rules 2374 and 3186 are positive. The temptation has then been to attach short pieces of canned natural language text to various parts of such an explanation. While this characterization of expert system explanation facilities is unfair, it is sufficient to make the point that explanation facilities are generally inadequate and remain a major research area in the expert system field (e.g. Schank, 1986; Chandrasekaran *et al.*, 1988).

The central problem to expert system explanation facilities is one of context sensitivity in that users require explanations for many different purposes and in many different styles and that this diversity can only be accommodated if the expert system has an adequate model of the operator. It has turned out to be very difficult to implement such user models in computers: the classic example of this failure is in the area of intelligent tutoring systems where perhaps the major current bottleneck to development is the difficulty in providing the system with an adequate model of each particular student user (e.g. Cawsey, 1989).

8.1.2   Hypertext and browsing

The difference between a traditional linear document and a hyperdocument lies in the nature of the links between different sections of text. Linear documents, such as this paper, are intended by the author to be read from beginning to end, although there are references within it to forward sections of the text (cataphoresis) and to previous sections (anaphoresis) and to other documents not included, for example, references (exaphoresis). Some of these references are explicit, for example, when authors use phrases such as: "this will be discussed below"; and "as discussed previously".

However, the majority of the referential links are implicit and need to be made by the reader and held in memory. Perhaps one sign of a good author is that the reader does not find this referential activity too burdensome.

In contrast to linear documents, hyperdocuments attempt to make such referential links explicit and the user of a hypertext system (the computer system that allows a hyperdocument to be used) is actively encouraged to follow such links. In consequence, different hyperdocument readers will be presented with different sections of text, or other material, in different orders, depending on how they browse through the net of links.

One of the chief technical problems with hypertext has been in understanding and specifying the types of link that associate the textual nodes in the hyperdocument. Experience suggests that there are potentially many types of link and that while these may be used by the skilled linear document author, they are generally not explicit or easily verbalized. Furthermore, hypertext users are often not informed in sufficient detail as to the type of link (i.e. the link's semantics) that they are about to traverse.

A widespread finding from current hypertext implementations is that the user very easily becomes lost (e.g. Barlow et al., 1989). At least part of this navigation problem may be caused by the lack of link semantic specification as opposed to the sheer number of links. Considerable effort is currently being expended in providing additional facilities to aid hyperdocument navigation. While there is a wide range of styles to these facilities, the most common consists of a map of labeled nodes and links (e.g. Duncan, 1989). Indeed, (Monk et al., 1988) showed that a hypertext program editor only achieved levels of performance similar to those of a more traditional scrolling editor for relatively naive (i.e. undergraduate) programmers when such a map was provided.

However, there is a fundamental design issue involved with attempting to solve the problems of a poorly designed system by providing additional, external support, rather than changing the basic design. Hypertext navigation tools might, from one perspective at least, be considered to be analogous to providing buttresses to a building because the building contained design flaws. The alternative, of course, is to redesign and rebuild; something that is often no easier with large software systems than with physical buildings.

8.1.3   System intelligence

The systems of concern in computing virtually all include a computer system, one or more operators, and an environment in which tasks are carried out. Diaper (1989a) and Barlow *et al.* (1989) have argued that one useful perspective to adopt when considering an operator-computer sub-system is to identify where the intelligence lies within this part of the system. They argue that with traditional database technology, the intelligence lies with the user, who must specify the logical conditions necessary for extracting relevant information from the database. Hypertext is in this sense similar to databases in that a hypertext system requires the operator to specify the order of link traversal. In contrast, with expert systems it is the computer system that possesses the main intelligence and the operator is usually relegated to the position of answering questions generated by the expert system. In fact, the expert system's explanation facilities are often the only area where the user can take control of the dialogue.

8.1.4   Formalizing Expert Systems and Hypertext

Both expert systems and hypertext can be described using graph theory. Barlow *et al.* (1989) suggest that:

> "The differences between the use of semantic nets to support knowledge representation in expert systems and as a model of documents in hypertext lie

in the nature of what constitutes the node content and in the mathematical properties of the labelling relations." (i.e. the links.)

In fact, there is a certain degree of complementarity between the two types of system which is made obvious when both are formally represented as graph-theoretic models. The nodes are semantically rich in hypertext, as they are basically natural language text and relatively impoverished in expert systems because the nodes contain a formal knowledge specification, for example, as rules. In contrast, the links are well specified for expert systems whereas they are virtually unspecified semantically in hypertext. In fact, the very problem of hypertext links is that, in general, they are potentially so rich in meaning that they are not understood by either the hyperdocument author or reader. This, of course, accords with the "intelligence in the system" characterization presented above in that expert systems use a computable representation at the expense of a richness of their knowledge (i.e. all expert systems are severely knowledge domain restricted) whereas hypertext is so rich in meaning that it defeats even human intelligence and hence people become lost.

8.2   EXPERTEXT

Expertext is the neologism first suggested by Rada and Barlow (1989a; 1989b) to represent systems that combine both EXPERt systems and hyperTEXT. The obvious combination is to have the semantically rich nodes of hypertext with the well specified, computable links of expert systems. The opposite combination of a weak knowledge representation within nodes and a rich but uncomputable set of links is almost certainly disastrous as the users of such a hypothetical system would have problems understanding both the nodes and the links.

A potentially useful expertext system, in contrast, would have nodes that are readily understandable by users and rich because they would constitute natural language text, perhaps the richest of the representational forms available, and, of course, diagrams, figures, tables, photographs etc., are not precluded. Similarly, by having well specified computable links that can be operated on by an inference engine, the expertext user can be advised or guided as to the order of node presentation and thus the human navigation problems associated with hypertext may be considerably reduced or eliminated.

From the "intelligence in the system" perspective such an expertext system would distribute intelligence between the operator and the expertext computer system. Human intelligence would be involved with the understanding of node content and the machine intelligence with the traversal of the net's links. This is clearly a sensible division of labour between the two types of intelligence, human and machine. People are generally good at understanding complex problems where many facts or events are presented simultaneously (i.e. in understanding declarative type knowledge) but generally poor at coping with lengthy chains of relationships (i.e. in understanding procedural knowledge). In contrast, the history of AI has, with its emphasis on solving games such as chess, missionaries and cannibals, etc., and the GPS (General Problem Solver see Newell and Simon, 1972) approach, been principally concerned with lengthy causal chains of reasoning which generally defeat human cognition. Such a view is well supported by the work of Johnson-Laird (e.g. 1983) where it has been shown that people's ability to solve syllogisms is improved by increasing the richness of the syllogisms' form without changing the logical content, whereas machines are good at stripped logic problems using As and Bs but poor at real world problems involving, for example, travelling by cars or trains to cities.

8.2.1 Expertext Applications

Expertext systems have the potential to replace or extend both current expert systems and hypertext systems. In the case of expert systems, an expertext system would provide an additional style of interaction between the expertext system and its operator. Instead of the operator merely being able to ask for an explanation, in expertext, the operator would be offered a textual description of the rules being activated by the expert system part of the expertext system and the operator would have the ability to influence the traversal of the underlying semantic net during run time. Thus the operator could guide the expert system because she or he would be able to understand what the expertext system was attempting. Such an expertext system would potentially be less domain restricted than a traditional expert system as the operator would detect inappropriate rule activation at run time and could suggest more efficient strategies of traversing the net, without having to be concerned with the low level complexities of such traversals. However, these applications of expertext, it must be confessed, have not yet been properly explored and at present this application of expertext remains only a suggestion.

At the University of Liverpool, current efforts have centred on developing expertext as an extension or improvement to hypertext systems. In general, an expertext system will allow an expertext operator or reader to be presented with text and to be guided through task relevant parts of the whole expertext document. Guidance might take several forms. The system may sometimes automatically offer the next section of text, or it might offer a prioritized list of suggestions for what the reader should see next. Returning to a previously visited node and taking a different path from it will be particularly easy in expertext as the computable links will allow backward chaining by simple recursion so that this type of major navigation problem will also be solved. Obviously such an expertext system will prevent the inefficient redisplaying of text associated with a node unless this is demanded by the reader.

There are potentially many uses to such hypertext type expertext systems. Some innovative work by Narula (1989) produced a prototype hypertext system as a training tool for the diagnosis and treatment of anaemia by third world doctors. Normally this sort of application would have used an expert system, but the strength of the approach was that by allowing structured browsing of the hyperdocument, Narula's system did not require the computer to have an active model of the reader.

The problem with the system was that while the computer did not automatically present inappropriate information, the readers could still be presented with inappropriate or redundant information when they became lost in the system. An expertext implementation would have reduced such navigation problems while still leaving the user in general control of what information was presented.

Rada (in prep.) has identified a number of existing systems that may be considered to be expertext systems. Thus the RUle-Based Retrieval of Information by Computer (RUBRIC - Tong *et al.,* 1983; 1984) and the Intelligent Interface for Information Retrieval (I3R - Thompson, 1985; Daniels, 1985) both provide a more intelligent and sophisticated means of categorizing and retrieving documents and the COmposite Document Expert Retrieval system (CODER - France, 1986; Fox, 1987) is able to both automatically parse documents into the canonical form of the information retrieval system and to then handle user queries. Quite differently, the system JANUS (Fischer, 1989) combines the expert system CRACK, which is an advisory kitchen design system, with the PHI hypertext system for hierarchical issue-based information systems to overcome the main criticism of CRACK that it failed to sufficiently identify to users with its brief explanations when "to make the intelligent exceptions characteristic of good design" (Rada, in prep.). Within the field of Computer-Aided Software Engineering (CASE), the Knowledge-Based Software Assistant (KBRA - Czuchry, 1988) allows many types of information to be entered in any order and is able, following dialogues with its operators, to automatically generate requirements documents. Similarly, the Application Software Prototype Implementation System (ASPIS - Puncello *et al.,* 1988) attempts to automatically convert requirements into computer design specifications. All of these systems might be characterized as prototype expertext systems, although they are not, generally, so characterized by their designers. With the exception of JANUS, which is principally an expert system type application, as characterized above, that benefits from additional textual material, all the other systems applications are involved with either the processing of linear text documents (RUBRIC, I3R and CODER) or with the production of such documents (KBRA and ASPIS).

The application area addressed in the example expertext system described in this paper is also concerned with the production of linear documents from an expertext document. There is considerable potential for document reuse applications, particularly in commerce and industry (e.g. Hahn *et al.,* 1989). For example, nearly all manufactured end products, and particularly computer system products, require the generation of numerous different linear documents. Thus even a simple product such as a lawn-mower will require an owner's manual, a service manual, and a repair manual as well as numerous manuals and documentation associated with the actual manufacture and marketing of the product. The idea behind document reuse is that these many different linear documents can all be created from a single expertext document. The advantages of this approach are that these different documents will take less time to produce and will be consistent with each other. Some may be subsets of a larger linear document, while some will only share some portions of text. Thus, a service manual may be wholly a subset of the larger and more detailed repair manual whereas an owner's manual may contain some of the text from the service manual plus additional text sections that are not required for servicing. In addition, and discussed later in this paper, there may be considerable advantages to such expertext systems being able to support multiple authoring. As a CASE tool, expertext may allow the production by many programmers, system designers, managers quality assurance evaluators, marketing personnel and so forth, of a single expertext document during the whole development lifecycle so that at delivery the whole suite of necessary documentation can be automatically produced along with the software itself. Such a possible CASE application is described in more detail in Barlow *et al* (1989).

8.3   HEADED RECORDS EXPERTEXT

Headed Records Expertext (HRExpertext) is one proposed architecture for an expertext system. The nature of this system was first described by Barlow *et al.* (1989) and is there described formally using graph theory. The basic notion behind HRExpertext was borrowed from the human memory framework of Morton and Bekerian (1986). An HRExpertext system can, hardly surprisingly, be characterized as a semantic net. The links between nodes are fully specified, as they would be in an expert system, and thus may be automatically traversed. What is distinctive about HRExpertext is the nature of the nodes. Each node consists of a headed record. A headed record has two sections to it. First, it has a record that contains user readable natural language text (or indeed potentially, any other type of user understandable material such as graphics, mathematics, or even video sequences). Second, it has attached to the record a header which contains a semantic specification of the record. The contents of the header is, of course, an impoverished representation of the record but has the property that it is computable. The form of the header representation is currently an open issue. One avenue for future research may be to investigate rule type representations, similar perhaps to PROLOG rules, so that the headers and between header links form a fully executable expert system. The mapping between a record and a header can be considered to be a set of hypertext links in that these links need not be sufficiently well specified in their semantics to be machine executable. Thus HRExpertext allows the semantic richness of hypertext between each record and its header combined with the well specified, machine traversable linking between headers.

8.3.1   HRExpertext and document reuse

In the hypertext field, considerable effort has be placed on the problems of converting linear documents into hyperdocuments (hyperization) and of generating linear documents from hyperdocuments (linearization) - (e.g. Rada and Diaper, 1989). The problems associated with both hyperization and linearization have not been generally solved and it may be necessary to write documents in a special format when there is an explicit intention of subsequently carrying out either of these processes. With respect to document reuse and HRExpertext the problem is how to write an HRExpertext document so that it may then be linearized into an number of different, meaningful documents.

It is suggested that two different HRExpertext tools are required. One for authors and a second for either online readers or for the generation of a paper based linear document. The HRExpertext authoring tool will basically be a combined tool with the features of both a document authoring system and a knowledge engineering environment. At its simplest it would appear to be a combination word processor and outliner. The word processor component will be used for the generation of the contents of the records and the outliner the generation of the headers. Ideally the HRExpertext author should also be provided with a hypertext system that links these header and record generating systems. Other desirable components of the authoring tool might be graphical editors used in knowledge engineering environments such as KEATS (Motta *et al.* 1986) to allow the author to inspect the relationships between headed records via the headers and the other typical tools used for building expert systems such as provided by Intellicorp's KEE and SimKit systems (e.g. Stelzner and Williams, 1988).

Considering only the document reuse application of HRExpertext, the second tool that is necessary is the document generation tool. This tool must be able to take an input from the tool's user and then traverse the HRExpertext net of header to header links and select the appropriate records that will be combined to form the generated document. It is almost certainly the case that the tool will need to be able to support a dialogue with the user as she or he specifies the semantic and other requirements of the final document. A well developed implementation of this tool will probably support both user and tool directed browsing of records online as the user refines the specification of the final document. It is anticipated that modifications to such a sophisticated version of the document generation tool will support quite different applications such as training/education, problem solving, and so forth.

8.3.2 The current state of HРExpertext

With respect to document reuse, the most obvious limitation to HРExpertext is that it will clearly only be suitable for large applications because the use of the HРExpertext authoring tool will be more time consuming than the use of a simple word processor. Thus only when the HРExpertext document is large and many different linear documents will have to be produced from it will it be cost effective to use HРExpertext. Thus HРExpertext should be a good document generation CASE tool but will not be appropriate for more modest projects.

The worked example that is described below in section 8.4 is basically a manual simulation of an HРExpertext system. The purpose of the simulation was first to demonstrate that multiple document generation is feasible using a simple version of HРExpertext. Second, by not implementing an authoring tool the simulation exercise focused Diaper on the requirements of such a tool independently of any particular computer implementation.

8.4 AN HРEXPERTEXT SIMULATION

In the summer of 1989, Diaper was scheduled to write the opening address to a one day, commercial conference on "Knowledge Acquisition for Expert Systems" organized by IBC Technical Services Ltd. As the opening address the paper was to be an overview of knowledge acquisition and would review:

1. the status of knowledge engineering with respect to general software engineering;

2. the stages involved in the knowledge acquisition parts of knowledge engineering;

3. the technologies and tools available to knowledge engineers;

4.   the desirable personal and organisational characteristics of those involved in knowledge engineering.

He decided that such a paper could provide an opportunity to test the HRExpertext document reuse application as it was conceivable that one might wish to produce a number of differently biased introductions to knowledge acquisition. Thus, while the complete paper was called "Knowledge Acquisition in Perspective" (Diaper, 1989b), it would have been possible, perhaps for different conferences or for different audiences to have produced papers which concentrated more on the stages of knowledge acquisition and their associated technologies (i.e. a paper perhaps called "Knowledge Acquisition Tools in Perspective"), or alternatively, on the process of knowledge engineering and its personnel (i.e. a paper perhaps called "Knowledge Engineering Personnel in Perspective"). Thus the former would emphasize those parts of the full paper characterized under 2 and 3 whereas the latter would emphasise 1 and 4. In addition, it was thought that an executive summary of any of the possible versions of the paper might also be producible using the simulated version of HRExpertext. (Note that Diaper has never had any intention to publish these other possible paper versions). The complete paper was to be quite brief (eventually only 14 pages of A4 in single line space, including references), and thus was thought to be a manageable document on which to test the ideas behind HRExpertext and document reuse, whereas a real software engineering example would be too large to be able to cope with without real HRExpertext software tools.

8.4.1   Authoring an HRExpertext Document

With many years of experience, Diaper's usual style of writing involves sitting at a word processor and typing without notes. Such first drafts are usually near to a standard suitable for publication and the subsequent three or four drafts generally only involve very minor changes. As can be seen from this paper, even after redrafting, one aspect of his style is the tendency to write relatively long paragraphs. This tendency is in part due to Diaper eschewing any prior written structure or outline prior to typing. The first difference that simulating an HRExpertext authoring environment caused was that Diaper was compelled to produce an outline of the paper's contents. Fig. 8.1 is the actual final version that was used, although there were three other, even more scrappy ones produced first. Before producing these outlines, Diaper had tried to start the experiment by merely numbering a paragraph (a record) and writing a header which had two types of information in it: first, the contents of the paragraph; and second the relationship of the current paragraph being written to others that had already been written or were intended. In some cases Diaper wrote out several headers first and then wrote the paragraphs that corresponded to the headers and sometimes the paragraphs were written first and then had headers placed on them. This scheme quickly became unmanageable and all his time was being spent attempting to work out the appropriate links between header. The first successful outline resembled fig. 8.1, but with far fewer links and even the final version in fig. 8.1 is not complete as the "133 Technology" and "128 personnel" headed records (top right of fig. 8.1) were never unpacked in the outline. Thus one of the first lessons to be learnt from this HRExpertext simulation was that it was essential for there to be an outline that is produced early in the authoring process. The reasons why it was not completed are described below.

The second early lesson was that the act of attempting to specify a record's content in the header forced Diaper to examine more carefully than usual the actual contents of the written text in the notional records. Repeatedly the paragraphs were divided into shorter pieces to generate more headed records as the specifications in the headers grew larger. The header specifications at this time were written as notes either of the form: 1. TO/FROM headed record X; or 2. record HAS content Y. The former could not be done without the outline and the latter quickly became very cumbersome. Thus this first attempt was very unsuccessful.

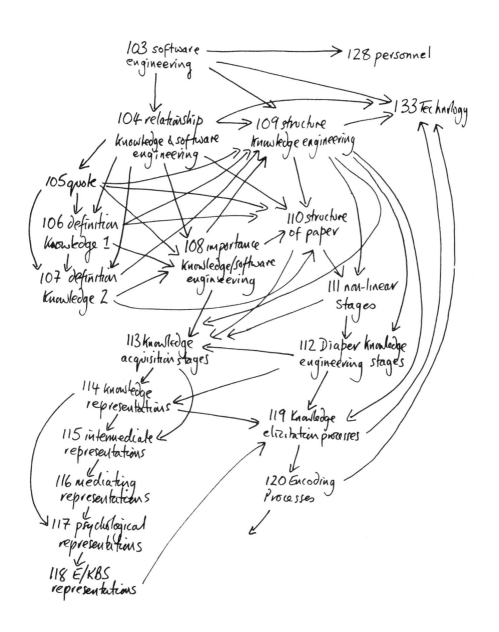

Fig. 8.1   Outline used in producing the paper "Knowledge Acquisition in Perspective"

Given the problem of specifying the header contents, a much simpler scheme was designed. As mentioned above in section 8.4, there were four main sections to the paper. These correspond to the nodes in fig. 8.1 near the top numbered 104, 109, 133 and 128. All headers were redesigned so that they simply contained six numbers. This design was only possible after the design of the document generation tool. The last four of these numbers could take only the values 1 or 0 and correspond to the four main topics of the paper (i.e. Software/Knowledge Engineering; Knowledge Acquisition Stages; Knowledge Acquisition Technologies; and Knowledge Acquisition Personnel). A 1 indicated that the record contained some reference to the main topic and a 0 no reference. A typical example is presented in fig. 8.2 and the hypertext like links between the record and its header have been drawn in by hand.

To explain the other two numbers in the headers it is first necessary to describe a number of decisions and discoveries that were made in the attempts to design the document generation tool. An early decision was that the semantic net that describes the header to header relationships would take the form of a Directed Acyclic Graph (DAG). This decision was made on the basis that DAGs possess a number of desirable properties which have been expressed by Koo (1989) and employed by Bench-Capon and Dunne (1989) as a means of ensuring that sections of documents can be coherently modified by representing their contents by graph modification rules (see also Barlow et al., 1989). The HRExpertext header to header semantic net is forced to be a DAG by the application of the simple rule that the order of records generated in any output document is invariant. Thus the first number in the header is the record number and records included in an output document are always printed in rank order starting with the lowest selected record number and, advantageously, this means that records can only be generated once within an output document.

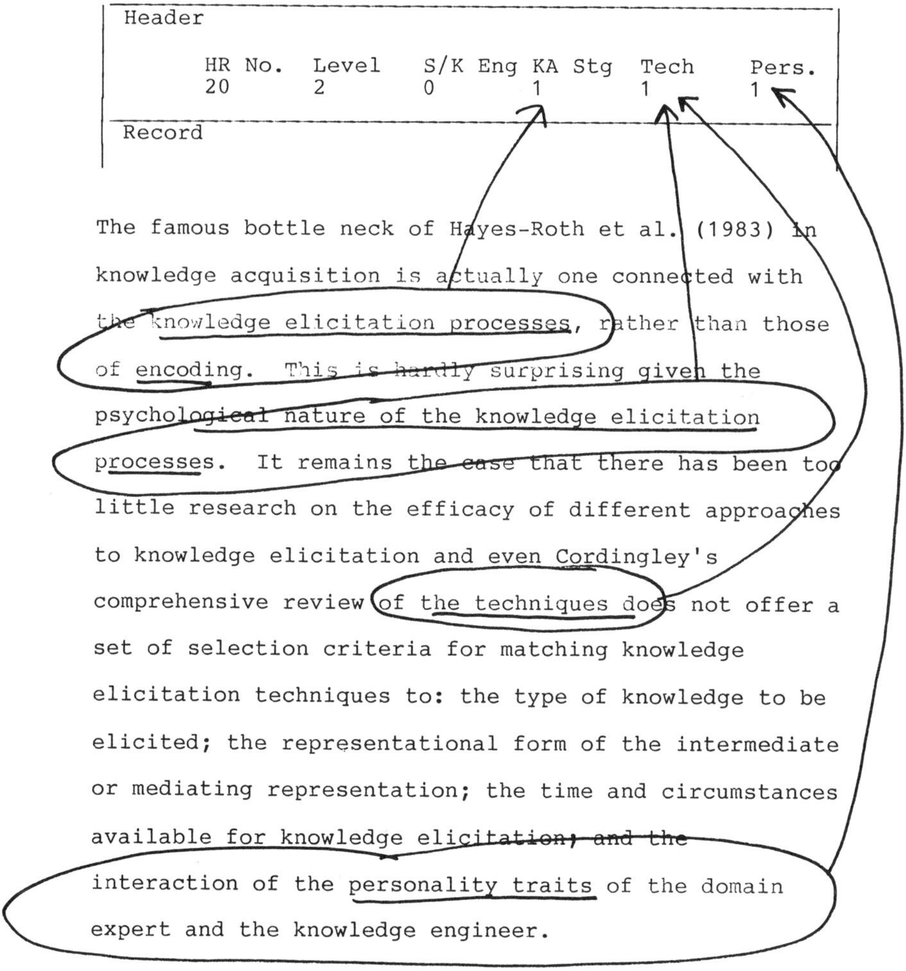

```
Header
    HR No.   Level    S/K Eng KA Stg   Tech     Pers.
    20       2        0       1        1        1
Record
```

The famous bottle neck of Hayes-Roth et al. (1983) in
knowledge acquisition is actually one connected with
the knowledge elicitation processes, rather than those
of encoding. This is hardly surprising given the
psychological nature of the knowledge elicitation
processes. It remains the case that there has been too
little research on the efficacy of different approaches
to knowledge elicitation and even Cordingley's
comprehensive review of the techniques does not offer a
set of selection criteria for matching knowledge
elicitation techniques to: the type of knowledge to be
elicited; the representational form of the intermediate
or mediating representation; the time and circumstances
available for knowledge elicitation; and the
interaction of the personality traits of the domain
expert and the knowledge engineer.

Fig. 8.2 Example record header.

This rule led to an interesting discovery which is represented by the links shown in fig. 8.1. Diaper started to go through the existing headed records that were associated with the first two of the four main sections of the paper. He asked the simple question: "Given a particular record is chosen to be printed in an output document, what records with higher headed record numbers can or cannot follow it?" The numerous arrows on fig. 8.1 represent the discovery that any subsequent record could follow. The ultimate test was to randomly select records and read them in the predetermined headed record order. To Diaper's surprise this generated reasonably coherent and meaningful documents, provided he was prepared to put some effort in to guessing what sort of reader would want each document generated in this manner. While of course not very satisfactory, there was a major difference between the results of this exercise and when the same exercise was carried out ignoring the headed record order.

The reason for this result is almost certainly caused by writing the records as if there actually existed an HRExpertext document reuse system. The author using such a system does not know when constructing records what, if anything, will be generated in an output document prior to, or after, the record currently being written. Thus the author cannot rely on either anaphoresis or cataphoresis and each record must be self contained. This turned out not to be too difficult a constraint, once appreciated, although it does lead to considerable repetition, particularly of references, across different records. Thus fig. 8.1 was never completed because Diaper could now revert to his more normal style of writing in that paragraphs as records could simply be written and numbered, although it was still necessary to write rather shorter paragraphs than he was usually accustomed if all the final four header numbers were not to be assigned the value 1. In general, paragraphs were split to form separate records if this occurred.

The final activity in authoring the document while simulating the HRExpertext system was to assign a "level of generality" to each record. These levels are represented as the second number in each header. Levels were simply produced by reading through the complete document and for each record asking two questions. First, "What is the degree of detail in the record?" (i.e. is this a major heading or sub-heading, or is it part of a sub-sub-sub-heading or an expansion or explication of a previous record); and second, "How important should its inclusion be in any final output document?". It can be seen in fig. 8.3, which lists the contents of each headed record's header, that 5 records were first judged to be the most general (records 7, 11, 18, 32, and 37). The second level of generality was determined by asking what were the next most general/important records after those judged to be at level 1. This was repeated until all the levels had been assigned a level.

HR No.	Level	S/K	Eng KA Stg	Tech	Pers.
1	4	1	1	0	1
2	2	1	0	0	0
3	5	1	0	0	0
4	2	1	0	0	0
5	4	1	0	0	0
6	4	1	0	0	0
7	1	1	1	1	1
8	2	1	1	0	0
9	5	1	1	0	0
10	3	1	1	1	0
11	1	1	1	0	0
12	2	0	1	1	1
13	3	0	1	1	1
14	3	0	1	1	0
15	5	1	1	1	1
16	4	1	1	1	0
17	3	0	0	1	0
18	1	0	1	1	0
19	5	1	1	1	0
20	2	0	1	1	1
21	3	0	0	1	1
22	4	0	0	1	1
23	4	0	0	1	0
24	3	0	0	1	0
25	4	0	0	1	0
26	3	1	0	1	1
27	4	1	0	1	1
28	3	0	1	1	0
29	2	0	1	1	1
30	3	0	0	1	0
31	4	0	1	1	0
32	1	1	0	0	1
33	2	1	0	0	1
34	5	0	0	0	1
35	2	1	1	1	1
36	3	0	0	0	1
37	1	1	0	0	1

Fig. 8.3   Table of Header Contents

That there were five levels of generality is an empirical fact carried out from performing this exercise. Clearly while this exercise was possible on a document as brief as Diaper's, which only contained 37 headed records, it would not be feasible with an HRExpertext document containing hundreds or thousands of headed records. Thus while this aspect of the simulation was unsatisfactory, a more appropriate method could involve using a hierarchically organized outline. The use of such an author's outlining tool is further discussed in section 8.5.1. While it must be recognized that there is a difficulty with aligning levels in different parts of a document in that the level of detail or importance in one third level sub-heading (e.g. 2.3.1.3) may not quite match that of another (e.g. 3.1.1.1), it is unlikely that even very large documents will have more than ten levels in them. This estimate is made on the grounds that even large, hierarchically structured thesauri such as that available in medicine, which contains tens of thousands of keywords, have no more than ten levels in them (Rada and Martin, 1987). Furthermore, provided the assignment of levels is approximately correct then the consequences are probably not too serious to the performance of the document generation tool.

8.4.2   Generating the HRExpertext Document

To demonstrate that documents with a different semantic bias and of a differing degree of detail could be produced in the HRExpertext simulation a simple BASIC program was written. The output of this program is a list of the headed records that would be printed in a particular version of the output document.

The program first requests that the user inputs a weight for each of the semantic categories (i.e. four weights, one for each category of: software/knowledge engineering; knowledge acquisition stages; technology and tools; and knowledge engineering personnel). These weights may be any integer. The program converts the weights to a real number between 0 and 1 by simply summing the weights and dividing each weight by this total. The program then calculates a critical value for each headed record which can take a value between 0 and 1. This critical value is calculated by taking each of the four semantic category values (0 or 1) and multiplying it by its weight (0 to 1) and by its level (linearly converted to between 0 and 1 such that 1 is the highest level and 0.2 the lowest with 5 levels). The critical value is the sum of this calculation for each of the four semantic categories. The user is then asked to input a threshold value between 0 and 1. This threshold value is used by the program to select the headed records that have a critical value that is greater than or equal to it. The program informs the user how many records have been selected, if the number is satisfactory then the headed record numbers are printed, otherwise a new threshold is entered and a different selection of headed records made (N.B. the higher the threshold the fewer records will be selected).

```
Semantic weight for:
          Software/Knowledge Engineering           1
          Knowledge Acquisition Stages             1
          Technology and Tools                     1
          Personnel                                1

              Threshold       No. of records
               value             selected

                0.8                 2
                0.7                 3
                0.6                 6
                0.5                10
                0.4                15
                0.3                21

Headed Records selected at a theshold of 0.6 are:
  7, 12, 19, 20, 29, 35

Headed Records selected at a theshold of 0.3 are:
  1,  7,  8, 10, 11, 12, 13, 14, 16, 18, 19, 20, 21, 26,
 27, 28, 29, 32, 33, 35, 37
```

Fig. 8.4 Threshold and Record Selection

Fig. 8.4 demonstrates that when the four semantic weights are equal varying the threshold value satisfactorily varies the number of headed records selected from the total set of 37. A threshold of 0.6 selects 6 blocks which might be appropriate for an executive summary and this document is reproduced in Appendix A. Fig.8.5 shows the consequence of semantic bias for a paper that might be titled "Knowledge Acquisition Technologies in Perspective" and fig. 8.6 for a paper with the title "Knowledge Acquisition Personnel in Perspective". The executive summary for this latter paper is reproduced in Appendix B. Comparison of the selected headed records in figs. 8.4, 8.5 and 8.6. demonstrate that different documents are being selected and a comparison of Appendices A and B shows that quite different executive summaries can be produced. Of course, where about 20 records are being selected from a set of only 37   then it is hardly surprising that quite a few records are repeated in the documents. While the difference between either of the semantically biased documents and the unbiased one in terms of blocks selected is only about 20%, the difference between the two biased documents is 43% (i.e. of the 42 records selected across these two documents, 18 occur only in one of the documents).

```
Semantic weight for:
        Software/Knowledge Engineering          5
        Knowledge Acquisition Stages           14
        Technology and Tools                   30
        Personnel                               0

        Threshold        No. of records
          value             selected

         0.7                   7
         0.3                  20

Headed Records selected at a theshold of 0.7 are:
 7, 12, 18, 19, 20, 29, 35

Headed Records selected at a theshold of 0.3 are:
 1,  7,  8, 10, 11, 12, 13, 14, 16, 18, 19, 20, 21, 26, 27,
28, 29, 32, 33, 35, 37
```

Fig 8.5 Semantic bias and record selection (a).

```
Semantic weight for:
        Software/Knowledge Engineering          8
        Knowledge Acquisition Stages            3
        Technology and Tools                    0
        Personnel                              17

            Threshold        No. of records
             value              selected

             0.7                  5
             0.2                 22

Headed Records selected at a theshold of 0.7 are:
 7, 32, 33, 35, 37

Headed Records selected at a theshold of 0.2 are:
 1,  2,  4,  7,  8, 10, 11, 12, 13, 15, 19, 20, 21, 22, 26,
27, 29, 32, 33, 35, 36, 37
```

Fig. 8.6 Semantic bias and record selection (b).

Thus the very simple, numerically based document generation program is surprisingly successful at being able to produce differently biased documents of different detail. It is particularly satisfactory that the very simple nature of the headers' semantics is apparently sufficient to achieve such results. The consequences of this simulation exercise for building real HRExpertext systems are discussed in the next section.

8.5 BUILDING A REAL HREXPERTEXT CASE TOOL

In software engineering the documentation associated with a product is generally vast, written by many people, in many independent documents. Not only is work often repeated in different documents but there is a major problem with consistency across documents. Furthermore, the problem of consistency errors between documents is exacerbated by there often being a series of different versions of each document. An HRExpertext CASE tool could potentially solve many of these problems.

First, such a tool would require only a single document to be written so that consistency would be less of a problem and less writing will be done as a piece of text which may appear in many output documents need only be written once.

Second, an HRExpertext system requires authors to explicitly structure their writing and this structuring is actually encouraged during the creation of headers. Such structuring should at least partially solve the coordination problems associated with multiple authoring of documents.

Third, if an HRExpertext CASE tool is used throughout the system lifecycle, from requirements specification to ultimate system decommissioning, then there is the possibility of improving software engineering project management as there would be only a single source document to be consulted, and it is one that can be accessed for many different purposes. Furthermore, during software development, headers can be created initially without records and thus HRExpertext could also function as a project planning tool.

Fourth, an online version of the HRExpertext document could not only form the basis for a context sensitive help system by the user providing a semantic specification, as was done in the document generation tool described in the previous section, but by tying it to the software such context sensitivity might be automatically generated.

Thus there is considerable potential utility to HRExpertext in software engineering and almost certainly in other areas where very large quantities of text in many forms needs to be produced. So far this paper has demonstrated that an HRExpertext system could be built using currently available computer technology. The final sections of this paper offer a discussion of a set of requirements specifications for an HRExpertext authoring tool and a document generation tool.

8.5.1   Requirements of an HRExpertext Authoring Tool

First, an HRExpertext authoring tool will require all of the standard facilities required for document generation (i.e. word processing, graphics, tables, etc.). In addition it will require a means of writing headers. A simple solution would be to present the author with a double window. One window would be for the document creation and the other for the header. The header window would contain a skeleton header. Where the record is constructed first, then a simple hypertext link system should be provided so that key concepts in the record can be explicitly linked to the relevant header specification. When the header is constructed before the record then activated elements in the header skeleton should force relevant text in the record to be linked to it by flagging any headed record that has unlinked skeleton elements. It will be desirable if a record can be easily split and new headers automatically generated for each new record.

Clearly one of the major difficulties will be in constructing a header skeleton. The six element skeleton used in the simulation will obviously be inadequate for much larger HRExpertext documents. In addition to the headed record number, which of course would need to be automatically changed as new headed records are added, and the level value, it is likely that at least two types of header element are required. First, and as used in the simulation, some header elements will need to represent the content of the record (i.e. its semantics). Second, and not used in the simulation, it will probably be desirable to have header elements that indicate the status of the record's contents with respect to its potential readers or its possible purpose for inclusion in output documents. At least one such element will need to be included for security purposes and another for version control. Constructing the initial header skeleton is likely to be a system critical task as even if a facility is provided to automatically change the header skeleton during the HRExpertext document's creation, this is likely to be a difficult and tedious task similar to changing the fields in traditional database software

While it may be the case, if the experience of constructing the simulation is borne out, that far fewer header elements are needed than might at first be thought, it is still likely that a real HRExpertext CASE tool will require at least tens of header elements. Obviously there will be problems for authors if they are presented with a header skeleton that simply lists, say, thirty such elements. A solution to this problem might be to arrange header elements hierarchically such that child elements inherit properties from parent elements. Such a technique could enormously reduce the author's effort in constructing headers as an author could either change a parent or, for a low level record, only a child element. The ability to copy a previously constructed header and edit it appropriately when two records are to have similar, or closely related contents is obviously a desirable feature

Ideally authors would also be provided with a specialized outlining tool. This tool might be presented in yet another window and show graphically the relationship of the headed record currently being constructed to other headed records. The display would, of course, need to be automatically updated when a new headed record is created. It might even provide the mechanism used to specify the construction of a new headed record and could perhaps even automatically generate a relevant, partially completed header skeleton, rather than the default one, where the new headed record is to have similar or related contents to an existing one. One function of the outliner would be to ensure that new headed records are assigned an appropriate level with respect to other headed records.

HRExpertext authors would also, of course, require online document generation and browsing facilities. The latter might be provided by selecting a node on the outlining tool display. It will obviously be necessary for authors to be able to generate partial documents so that they can check what they have written, perhaps in the context of several possible output documents.

8.5.2   Requirements of an HRExpertext Document Generation Tool

Obviously a real HRExpertext CASE document generation tool will have to be rather more sophisticated than the simple BASIC program used in the simulation described in this paper. It should be tied to the authoring tool in that it will be able to actually generate documents and, ideally, parts of documents. Users of the tool will still need to input specifications to the headers (i.e. by assigning weights to the header skeleton), but they should be supported in this in a manner similar to the support offered to authors. Thus, if a hierarchically organized header skeleton is used in the HRExpertext document then the document generation tool's users should also be able to input parameters to parent elements so that child elements, perhaps proportionally, inherit parameter values.

A browsing facility is also likely to be desirable and may be the same one provided to HRExpertext authors via the outlining tool. The same tool might also indicate, perhaps by highlighting, which headed records were selected for output when particular parameters and thresholds were selected. Obviously, if this tool is to be easy to use then the labelling and form of this representation of the output document will be crucial and there should probably be a text field included within each header.

8.5.3   Other HRExpertext Application Tools

A considerable number of other applications in addition to document generation have been suggested in this paper. If HRExpertext is to be used, for example, for project management, or to provide a context sensitive online help facility, or as an intelligent tutoring system, then specialized tools will have to be constructed, or at least additional facilities added to the basic document generation tool. It is likely that the identification of such applications prior to the construction of an HRExpertext document's header skeleton will be highly desirable, if not necessary. It may be very difficult to adapt an HRExpertext document after its production to an unanticipated application if this requires that the header skeleton has to be modified. This is similar to the classic discovery of Clancy (1979; 1983; Clancy and Letsinger, 1981) with the GUIDON tutorial expert system, which was based on MYCIN/NEOMYCIN, that a considerable amount of additional effort is required to turn an advisory system into a tutorial one - GUIDON required over 200 additional rules (Alty and Coombs, 1984) and Coombs and Alty (1984) say that:

> "... it was found that much of the knowledge required by a person attempting to learn how to problem-solve within the subject area ... proved to be implicit within the diagnostic rules, and so not available for inspection. It thus proved necessary to augment substantially the knowledge-base, including new information about subject primitives, the structure of concepts and suitable learning strategies".

Similarly, to convert an existing software engineering HRExpertext document into one able to act as tutorial text is likely to require additional headed records as well as possible modifications to the header skeleton itself if this application was not initially anticipated.

8.6   FUTURE HREXPERTEXT DEVELOPMENTS

Perhaps the most important result from the HRExpertext simulation was that a very large number of different documents could be generated using a very simple header representation of the record contents. This finding deserves to be pursued as the construction of headers of this type should be relatively easy for authors, whereas if a more sophisticated header form is used, for example, in the style of PROLOG-like rules, then this is likely to be considerably more difficult and time consuming for authors, and some authors may not be able to do it at all. Furthermore, the simple type of header representation proposed should also be reasonably easy to understand by users, who are not authors, of an HRExpertext system

Considerable work has now been done on expertext and HRExpertext and this technology is surely now ready to be prototyped in a real application. Such a prototype will need to be for a non-trivial application as there is still a range of problems that require further investigation, most notably, the style and impact of more complex or larger headers. Such investigations within a small application are likely to be of only limited value as there is a long history of computer technologies that appear satisfactory and useful when initially tested but fail in large, real world applications.

APPENDIX A

Executive Summary:

Knowledge Acquisition in Perspective

D. Diaper

University of Liverpool

Knowledge acquisition is one of the stages in knowledge engineering and can, for the purposes of review and for structuring this paper, be broken down into three perspectives:

1. the stages

2. the personnel

3. the technologies

Each stage in knowledge acquisition has associated with it a form of knowledge representation. Knowledge elicitation works with domain experts' psychological representations. The representation stage involves making domain experts' knowledge public as an intermediate or mediating representation; and the encoding stage involves coding this explicit representation in an E/KBS.

The encoding processes involve the coding of the intermediate or mediating representation into an E/KBS. The technologies involved are thus more computer orientated than those associated with the knowledge elicitation processes. Knowledge Engineering tools such as KEATS, KEE, etc. have been most successfully developed to support many of the encoding processes.

The famous bottle neck of Hayes-Roth *et al.* (1983) in knowledge acquisition is actually one connected with the knowledge elicitation processes, rather than those of encoding. This is hardly surprising given the psychological nature of the knowledge elicitation processes. It remains the case that there has been too little research on the efficacy of different approaches to knowledge elicitation and even Cordingley's comprehensive review of the techniques does not offer a set of selection criteria for matching knowledge elicitation techniques to: the type of knowledge to be elicited; the representational form of the intermediate or mediating representation; the time and circumstances available for knowledge elicitation; and the interaction of the personality traits of the domain expert and the knowledge engineer.

The two processes associated with knowledge elicitation and knowledge encoding have very different technologies associated with them. Crudely, the former is people orientated and the latter is E/KBS orientated. Until adequate forms of mediating representation are developed there will remain a set of analytical processes that need to bridge the difference between these anthropocentric and computer-centric perspectives.

The encoding technologies associated with encoding an intermediate or mediating representation in an E/KBS are, in theory, fully automatable and as Cordingley (1989) says "there is no particular role for a human elicitor in a fully automated knowledge acquisition process itself.".

Bell and Hardiman's (1989) list of roles for the knowledge engineer include:

- management of the knowledge engineering process;

- primary interviewer - normally one of the knowledge engineers, but may occasionally be the user or the expert interviewing each other and facilitated by the knowledge engineer;

- notetaker, or back-up interviewer - a function which needs filling in any interview and is best rotated between two knowledge engineers;

- knowledge analyser - primarily the task of the knowledge engineers, but the experts and users can do it to the advantage of themselves and the knowledge engineers;

- system coder - the knowledge engineer again if   he or she has the skill. Otherwise it can be   delegated. The knowledge engineer should not   be selected merely for programming skill.

They say that these "five roles may well fall to one over-burdened knowledge engineer, which illustrates why we stress the importance of partnership of two people for this job, preferably with complimentary skills."

APPENDIX B

Executive Summary:

Knowledge Acquisition Personnel in Perspective

D. Diaper

University of Liverpool

Knowledge acquisition is one of the stages in knowledge engineering and can, for the purposes of review and for structuring this paper, be broken down into three perspectives:

1. the stages

2. the personnel

3. the technologies

Even the limited intelligence of all current E/KBS has a consequence with respect to their impact on purchasing organizations and their personnel that is greater than for other information technology systems. Diaper (1989 - in press) has suggested that great care needs to be taken when considering all the many people in an E/KBS purchasing organization who will be either directly or indirectly affected by a new system as only a single group or just a few individuals, and not necessarily readily identifiable key ones, can cause the system not to be fully accepted.

Bell and Hardiman (1989), for example, have identified ten different roles in knowledge engineering, equally spilt between roles in the client organization and in the knowledge engineering team, and their list is almost certainly not exhaustive.

Bell and Hardiman (1989) identified the following five general roles within an E/KBS client organization:

- representative(s) of the users;

- supplier(s) of the knowledge - experts;

- management of the target function (user's   managers);

- system maintainer - to keep the system up to date once it is in use;

- auditor - whose concern is the trustworthiness of the process, and therefore the validity of the resulting process.

Of course, these roles may be further divided and individuals may inhabit more than one role, although usually not at the same point in the knowledge engineering process. (Diaper 1989 - in press). Furthermore, the list is incomplete in at least two ways. First, senior management are not listed and their support for a project is usually, if not always, crucial to its commercial success (Trimble, 1989). Second, in any organization but the smallest there will be personnel who never use the new E/KBS but who are affected by both its input and output and by the changes in working practice that are caused by its the introduction.

Bell and Hardiman's (1989) list of roles for the knowledge engineer include:

- Management of the knowledge engineering process;

- Primary interviewer - normally one of the knowledge engineers, but may occasionally be the user or the expert interviewing each other and facilitated by the knowledge engineer;

- Notetaker, or back-up interviewer - a function which needs filling in any interview and is best rotated between two knowledge engineers;

- Knowledge Analyser - primarily the task of the knowledge engineers, but the experts and users can do it to the advantage of themselves and the knowledge engineers;

- System coder - the knowledge engineer again if he or she has the skill. Otherwise it can be delegated. The knowledge engineer should not be selected merely for programming skill.

They say that these five roles may well fall to one over-burdened knowledge engineer, which illustrates why we stress the importance of partnership of two people for this job, preferably with complimentary skills.

One of the least understood aspects of software engineering, and even more so in knowledge engineering, is the understanding of the impact that a very large range of people can have on the commercial success of a new computer system. An understanding of the direct end users (operators), while essential and still not always done adequately, is clearly not sufficient (e.g. Diaper, 1987; 1989 - in press).

REFERENCES

Alty, J.L. and Coombs, M.J. (1984) *Expert Systems: Concepts and Examples*, NCC Publications, Manchester, UK.

Barlow, J., Beer, M., Bench-Capon, T., Diaper, D., Dunne, P.E.S. and Rada, R. (1989) Expertext: Hypertext-expert system theory, synergy and potential applications in *Research and Development in Expert Systems VI*, (ed. Shadbolt, N.) Cambridge University Press, Cambridge, UK, pp. 116-127.

Bench-Capon, T.J.M. and Dunne, P.E.D. (1989) "Consistent Graph Modification Systems for Some Classes of Electronic Document". Report *CS/CSCW/1/89*, Department of Computer Science, University of Liverpool, U.K.

Cawsey, A. (1989) Explanatory dialogues. *Interacting with Computers*, 1, 69-92.

Chandrasekaran, B., Tanner, M.C. and Josephson, J.R. (1988) Explanation: the role of control strategies and deep models, in *Expert Systems: The User Interface*, (ed. Hendler, J.A.). Ablex, Norwood, New Jersey, USA, pp.219-248.

Clancy, W.J. (1979) Tutoring rules for guiding a case method dialogue, *International Journal of Man-Machine Studies*, 11, 25-49.

Clancy, W.J. (1983) The epistemology of a rule-based expert system, *Artificial Intelligence*, 20, 215-251.

Clancy, W.J. and Letsinger, R. (1981) NEOMYCIN: Reconfiguring a rule-based expert system for application to teaching, *IJCAI-7*, 829-836.

Coombs, M. and Alty, J. (1984) Expert systems: an alternative paradigm, in *Developments in Expert Systems*, (ed. Coombs, M.J.) Academic Press, London, UK, pp.135-158.

Czuchry, A.J. Jr. and Harris, D.R. (1988) KBRA: A new paradigm for requirements engineering, *IEEE Expert,* 21-35.

Daniels, P.J., Brooks, H.M. and Belkin, N.J. (1985) Using problem structures for driving human-computer dialogues in *Actes of the Conference: Recherche d'Informations Assistee par Ordinateur.* IMAG, Grenoble, France.

Diaper, D. (1989a) Designing expert systems: from dan to beersheba in *Knowledge Elicitation: Principles, Techniques and Applications*, (ed. Diaper, D.) Ellis Horwood, Chichester, UK, pp. 15-46.

.Diaper, D. (1989b) Knowledge acquisition in perspective in *Proceedings of the Conference on Knowledge Acquisition for Knowledge Based Systems.* IBC Technical Services, London, UK.

Duncan, E.B. (1989) Structuring knowledge bases for designers of learning materials. *Hypermedia*, 1, 20-33.

Fischer, G., McCall, R. and Morch, A. (1989) *JANUS: Integrating hypertext with a knowledge-based design environment.* Department of Computer Science, University of Colarado, Boulder, Colorado, USA.

France, R.K. and Fox, E.A. (1986) Knowledge structures for information retrieval: representation in the CODER project, in *Proceedings of the IEEE Expert Systems in Government Conference.* IEEE Computer Society Press, Washington, DC, USA, pp 135-141.

Fox, E.A. (1987) Development of the CODER system: a testbed for artificial intelligence methods in information retrieval. *Information Processing and Management,* 23, 341-366.

Hahn, U., Jarke, M., Kreplin, K., Farusi, M. and Pimpinelli, F. (1989) CoAUTHOR: A hypermedia group authoring environment, in *Proceedings of the First European Conference on Computer Supported Cooperative Work*, 226-244.

Johnson-Laird, P.N. (1983) *Mental Models: Towards a Cognitive Science of Language, Inference and Consciousness*. Cambridge University Press, Cambridge, UK.

Koo, R. (1989) A model for electronic documents. *ACM SIGOIS Bulletin*, 10, 23-33.

Monk, A.F., Walsh, P. and Dix, A.J. (1988) A comparison of hypertext, scrolling and folding as mechanisms for program browsing in *People and Computers IV*, (eds. D.M. Jones and R. Winder), Cambridge University Press, Cambridge, UK, pp 421-436.

Morton, J. and Bekerian, D. (1986) Three ways of looking at memory, in *Advances in Cognitive Science*, (ed. N.E. Sharkey) Ellis Horwood, Chichester, UK, pp 43-71.

Motta, E., Eisenstadt, M., West, M., Pitman, K. and Everstz, R. (1986) KEATS: The knowledge engineer's assistant - final project report. *Technical Report No. 20,* Human Cognition Research Laboratory, The Open University, Milton Keynes, UK.

Narula, I.S. (1989) A prototype hyperdocument on anaemia using the GUIDE professional hypertext system. Unpublished M.Sc. thesis, School of Tropical Medicine, University of Liverpool, UK.

Newell, A. and Simon, H.A. (1972) *Human Problem Solving*. Prentice Hall, Englewood Cliffs, NJ, USA.

Puncello, P.P., Torrigiani, P. Pietri, F., Burlon, R., Bruno, C. and Conti, M. (1988) ASPIS: A knowledge based case environment, *IEEE Software*, 58-65.

Rada, R. and Martin, B. (1987) Augmenting thesauri for information systems *ACM Transactions on Office Information Systems*, 5, 378-392.

Rada, R. and Barlow, J. (1989a) Expert Systems and Hypertext. *Knowledge Engineering Review*, 3, 285-301.

Rada, R. and Barlow, J. (1989b) Expertext: Expert Systems and Hypertext in *Proceedings of EXSYS 89*, IITT-International, Paris.

Rada, R. and Diaper, D. (1989) Converting text to hypertext and vice versa in *Proceedings of the Conference on Hypermedia/Hypertext and Object Oriented Databases*. Unicom Seminars Ltd., Uxbridge, UK. (reproduced in this book).

Rada, R. (in prep.) *Hypertext*.

Schank, R.C. (1986) *Explanation Patterns: Understanding Mechanically and Creatively,*. Lawrence Erlbaum Associates, Hillsdale, NJ, USA.

Stelzner, M. and Williams, M.D. (1988) The evolution of interface requirements for expert systems, in *Expert Systems: The User Interface,* (ed. J.A. Hendler) Ablex, Norwood, NJ, USA, pp 285-306.

Thompson, R.H. and Croft, W.B. (1985) An expert system for document retrieval, in *Proceedings of the Expert Systems in Government Symposium*. IEEE Computer Society Press, Washington, DC, USA pp 448-456.

Tong, R., Shapiro, D., Dean, J. and McCune, B. (1983) A comparison of uncertainty calculi in an expert system for information retrieval, in *Proceedings of the International Joint Conference on Artificial Intelligence*, pp 194-197.

Tong, R., Askman, V. and Cunningham, J. (1984) RUBRIC: An artificial intelligence approach to information retrieval, in *Proceedings of the First International Workshop on Expert Database Systems*.

Part Three

Data Models and Structures

9. CONVERTING TEXT TO HYPERTEXT AND VICE VERSA

R. Rada and D. Diaper

University of Liverpool

9.1 INTRODUCTION

Text is a rather loosely defined term that refers to a cohesive body of natural language. Text may be arbitrarily long or short. The term applies equally well to messages, mail, recipes, reports, papers, books, and software documentation. Electronic text can be broadly construed as any collection of information stored in the computer that might be retrieved by content description. Text may also include pictures. In practice, the two terms "text" and "document" are often used interchangeably. As hypertext is an extension of text, the proper study of hypertext requires an appreciation of the relationship between text and hypertext. To understand text it is necessary to understand the writing process and the impact that different technologies make on this process. Such an understanding leads to an appreciation of document structure, which is crucial to the process of converting text to hypertext (hyperization) and hypertext to text (linearization).

9.2 WRITING

Writing models can be traced over 2000 years. The interest in computerized writing aids has, however, fostered a new perspective on the analysis of what occurs when people write. It has been shown that the importance of moving freely between various forms of organization, such as notes and outlines and prose.

9.2.1 Modelling the writing process

Aristotle wrote that the number of parts of a speech was basically two: stating the case and proving it. But he was willing to recognize the role of an introduction and epilogue. The introduction should show what is the aim of the speech. The epilogue may be used to secure the good disposition of the audience and refresh the audience's memories (Magill and McGreal, 1961).

Many models of writing and schemes for teaching writing have recently been elaborated.upon (Young, Becker and Pike, 1970). In one view, written text is seen as a product of the cognitive processes of writing which is constrained by goal and audience (see fig. 9.1) (Frederiksen and Dominic, 1981). The author is guided by a goal (by wanting to change the audience) but is constrained by what the audience is prepared to accept.

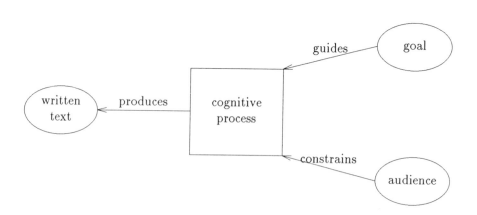

Fig. 9.1   Environment of cognitive writing process

In a broad sense two prominent writing styles are the Mozartian and the Beethovian. The Mozartian creates detailed plans before creating text. The poor Mozartian writer has isolated milestones that don't adequately guide the translation from plans to text (Sharples, 1985). The Beethovian creates text in order to think. As the text emerges it stimulates further searches of memory retrieval and constrains subsequent text translation. The author must be able to deftly reorganize the first draft.

The writing process consists of acquiring and organizing knowledge and viewing it from multiple perspectives in order to find the one that best suits the audience. People restructure ideas to fit patterns that are already familiar or drop ideas that are difficult to assimilate to familiar patterns (Barttlett, 1932). The relationship between topic-specific knowledge and quality in expository writing suggests that the degree of organization of knowledge is directly related to a writer's success (Langer, 1984). Novices find writing a tedious chore of translating what they already know onto paper, whereas experts have a good reader model and continually adjust what they have to say after feeding it through their reader model (Scardamalia and Bereiter, 1987).

In one view, the process of writing a document is divided into three phases: exploring, organizing and encoding. The exploration phase includes brainstorming and making unstructured notes. The organization phase includes organizing the unstructured notes and ideas into an outline or hierarchy. The encoding phase includes writing the prose for the final document (see fig. 9.2) (Smith et al., 1986). Some writers progress through this model of the writing process in a linear fashion, going from rough notes to outline to prose. Other writers may begin in the middle of the process and write an outline before making any notes. The writing process not only varies from one author to another, but the sequence of events may also vary from time to time for a single author. In order to create a useful collaborative writing environment, each of these three phases of the writing process should be supported.

Authors should be allowed to move freely from one phase to another and back again. The difference between the Mozartian and Beethovian styles may be characterized by where the author commences in the flowchart of fig. 9.2.

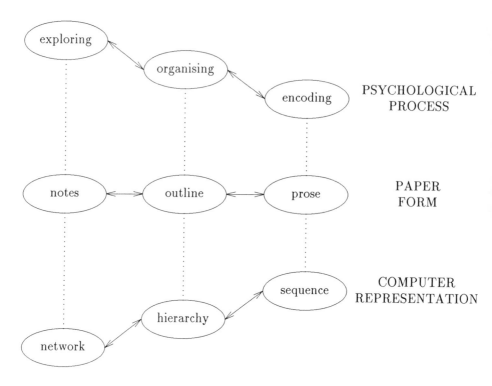

Fig. 9.2   The top row shows the sequence of cognitive processes through which a person writes a document. The paper items in the middle row reflect the activity in the top row, while the underlying structural representation is given in the bottom row.

9.2.2 Writing tools

The standard writing tools are pen and paper. These do not lend themselves to the revision of text on a large scale. Word processors offer a flexibility in the revision process, an opportunity to bring pieces of previous documents into play readily, and a sophisticated printing capability. Under some circumstances students who write with word processors have been shown to get higher grades for their writing products than students who don't use word processors (Griffey, 1986).

(a)   Editors

Text-editors are closely tied to computer input/output hardware. Each generation of input/output hardware has brought a corresponding generation of editors (batch editors, line editors, screen-oriented editors, and integrated text-editor/document formatters).

EMACS is an advanced, self-documenting, customizable, extensible, real-time display editor (Stallman, 1981). As a display editor the text being edited is visible on the screen and is updated automatically as one types commands. Usually after each character or pair of characters that the user types, the display is updated this makes the system real-time. EMACS is advanced because it provides facilities that go beyond simple insertion and deletion. Filling of text; automatic indentation of programs; viewing two files at once; and dealing with sentences and paragraphs as units are some of the advanced features of EMACS. Self-documenting means that at any time one can type a special character, the "Help" key, and learn about the options. The meaning of any command can also be discovered through the Help key. Customizable means that one can change the definition of EMACS commands in little ways. For example, if the user wants to change the keys which are associated with the up, down, left and right motions, the user can easily do that. Extensible means that one can go beyond simple customization and write new commands. Furthermore, EMACS is online extensible, which means that EMACS is divided into functions that call each other, any of which can be redefined in the middle of an editing session.

The Andrew System is being developed by the Information Technology Center at Carnegie Mellon University as part of a joint effort between CMU and IBM. Andrew is a set of tools that one can use to write and edit multimedia documents, send and receive multimedia mail, write programs, and do other activities (Grantham *et al.*, 1987). Andrew uses Unix and the X window system.

The translation between the source file form of a document (for example, created in Emacs) and its final layout is sometimes a complex one which the author has trouble visualizing. Some editors allow changing of the structure of the document but also facilitate viewing of the current, formatted layout of the document. An editor which allows the author to immediately see the final layout is called a "What You See Is What You Get" (WYSIWYG) editor.

(b)   Desktop publishing

One of the fastest-growing application areas in automated office systems is desktop publishing. Many organizations can now produce their own publications. A step-by-step procedure for desktop publishing is:

- prepare text and graphics;

- use the page makeup program to develop the format of each page. The video screen becomes an electronic pasteup board with rulers, column guides, and other page design aids;

- merge the text and graphics into the page formats. The page makeup software will automatically move excess text to another page, help size headings, and such;

- when the pages look correct on the screen, they can be stored on the disk and/or printed on the laser printer.

Desktop publishing merges writing, graphic design, art, instructional text design, and publication production.

Desktop publishing system trainees tend to overuse visual devices that make information prominent, such as typeface variations and boxes. Student writers do not adequately plan their work. Those with little computer experience have problems with the basic computer tasks, such as saving text. Those who view the system as something that they will use occasionally have more persistent problems than any other group (Sullivan, 1988).] Training for desktop publishing, as for other computer systems, must recognize the diversity of trainee needs.

(c)   Structure Editors

Structure-based editors for English text usually provide two capabilities. First, they provide a diagram of the structure of the document - a hierarchical table of contents - to help readers and writers visualize the structure. Second, they provide a set of commands that exploit the structure; for example, a command to move the text cursor to the beginning of the next section.

An outline processor is an instance of a structure editor. Most outline processors are programs designed for personal computers. The first of these was ThinkTank released in 1984 which has been followed by many others including MaxThink, Executive Writer/Executive Filer, Thor, Kamas, Freestyle, and PC-Outline. It is debatable whether these programs constitute hypertext systems, as they don't provide general-purpose linking mechanisms nor explicit, mouse driven link icons. Only a few provide windows for nodes. However, each treats text blocks as objects and supports manipulation of text which coincides with some cognitive models of how one manages ideas. In this respect, they reflect the idea processing of hypertext.

9.3   DOCUMENT STRUCTURE

Specification of a document requires specification of the content of the document and of the structure of the document; this is the abstract specification. To convert the abstract form into a readable version the author needs a formatting language that converts the document into a physical representation.

9.3.1   Physical document structure

An uncomplicated, physically-oriented document abstract structure may be found in the WYSIWYG document preparation systems such as MacWrite. The primary structure is a character. Characters are composed into words and lines where the lines are interspersed with rulers. Inserted material, for example graphics, is inserted into the structure as if it were a line. A document-formatting language like troff or TEX can be directly translated into a physical representation. The physical abstract structure provided by troff is oriented to the structures that will appear in the physical page.

9.3.2   Logical document structure

The Unix Document Workbench builds onto troff with macros that may control logical structure. The macro facility permits definition of new commands based on the facilities provided by the primitively-defined commands. This permits the implementation of a document representation that more closely resembles the classification of logically-structured documents than physically-structured documents. Similarly TEX provides another physical abstract structure and, LATEX atop TEX creates a logical structure.

Document processing systems that logically structure a document include Interleaf's Technical Publishing Software, and Xerox's Tioga. In all cases the minimum addressable unit associated with the primary structure is the paragraph. What distinguishes the representations from one another are the higher-level structures that tie the components together. Imagine a document which looks on the page as in fig. 9.3.

1. Section 1's title

Section 1 text
    * list element 1
    * list element 2

More section 1 text

1.1 Subsection 1.1's title

Subsection 1.1's text

Fig. 9.3 Document structure

Interleaf represents this document by tagging each object with the name of its class: section heading, list item, or paragraph. A linear order to the items suggests their relationships. Tioga uses a tree representation, and the document's data is contained entirely in the leaves of the tree (see fig. 9.4). The internal nodes of the tree are not distinguished from each other.

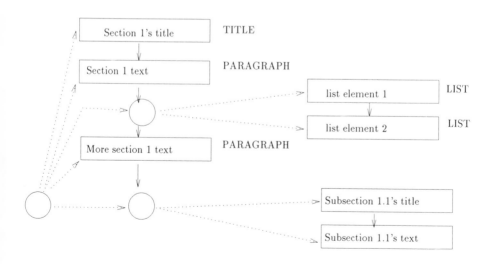

Fig.9.4 Hierarchical logical document representation as it might be seen in Tioga.(Furuta, 1988)

(a)   SGML

To make electronic information more exchangeable standards of logical document structure are useful. The Standard Generalized Markup Language (SGML) is an international standard for publishing (ISO, 1989). It is based on the generic markup of the structural elements of a document without regard to their presentation, which is regarded as a separate issue. SGML is based on the principles of the generic encoding of documents and marks up a document's logical structure and not the document's manner of presentation. SGML contrasts to typographic markup, as with SGML the font and style are not considered when marking up the document. Formatting and all the other detailed information normally contained in a style sheet are thought of as being at another level.

SGML applications include:

- computer-assisted publishing where the final product is a typeset document (hard copy),

- electronic publishing where the document appears on the screen (soft copy),

- database publishing where document elements are retrieved in combination with other elements.

Many types of publications are targeted. The language is device-independent, as the house style is applied later. Graphics and scanned images may be included.

(b)   Office Document Architecture

The Office Document Architecture (ODA) (ISO,1988) provides a detailed tree-like, object-oriented document architecture. The ODA representation simultaneously applies two abstract representations to a document's content. A logical structure that defines the composition of document objects into successively larger logical components and a layout structure that defines the composition of document objects

(Furuta, 1988). The structure of a document is given by the shape of the tree, while the content is stored in the leaves. Attributes provide information about the objects in the tree. For instance, one attribute allows character, raster graphics, and geometric graphics. The logical structure divides the content for the document into logical objects that mean something to the reader. The layout structure is concerned with a visible representation of the contents.

In the logical structure each non-leaf object has an attribute called "generator for subordinates" that describes how the object may be made from subordinate objects. These indicate that subordinate objects may be optional, required, or repeated and that a group of objects may occur in a given sequence order, in any order, or as a choice where only one of the groups occurs. The layout structure divides the content into page sets, pages, and rectangular areas within pages.

For interactive viewing the basic problem with ODA is the focus on sequential and page based layout. Additional desirable features would be:

- an outline facility for displaying selected levels of the outline,

- pop-up displays for the temporary display of additional information,

- folding to hide sections behind a button,

- a linkage facility to enable users to follow links automatically.

With these features a hypertext system like Guide could be implemented in the extended ODA (Brown and Cole, 1989).

9.4 CONVERTING TEXT TO HYPERTEXT

As enthusiasm for hypertext increases there is a great desire to convert existing documents into hypertext (Glushko, 1989). Documents prepared on standard word-processing equipment have formatting commands that do such diverse things as mark headings of sections and render the literature references. A program can accept as input a document with heading commands and produce a hypertext browser of the document's hierarchical structure. Such a program could also find citation keys in the document and then insert links or buttons that would allow the reader to easily jump from the main body of the text to a complete citation.

To map a flat-text file onto a set of hypertext cards or frames, one might first decide how much text to place on a card. If the text is various brief email messages, then each message may go onto a card. For normal documents some more clever breakdown is required. Two distinct classes of links are important. Structural links enforce the mapping between the conventional document and the hypertext skeleton. These links may be automatically generated from a formatted document. The second class give non-sequential and non-hierarchical paths.

If the underlying structure of a document contains many relatively short pieces that cross-reference each other then there is a strong possibility that automatic importation of the document with automatic construction of the links is possible. A straightforward translation of a document into a hypertext will not result in a good product in the absence of careful attention to the design of the hypertext.

9.4.1 Directory-like text to Hypertext

Directory-like text has substantial structure. Examples of directory-like text include technical manuals, dictionaries, encyclopedias, course catalogues, and bibliographies. The embedded commands in the electronic versions of these texts can be automatically translated into a form that a hypertext system exploits. The Prototype Electronic Encyclopedia was developed in the early 1980s as a hypertext system for browsing encyclopedias. From tapes which contained the typeset for the encyclopedia, the hypertext was semi-automatically derived. The markup language of the encyclopedia was exploited (Weyer and Borning, 1985). Other examples are described below.

(a) Manual

The documentation for the operating system Unix is formatted with the document structuring language nroff, which is a subset of troff. Unix has its own housestyle for user manuals so that pages are stored online. These manual pages can be viewed both on paper and on the computer screen. To take advantage of the existing Unix manual pages a pre-processor has been developed to convert manual pages to the hypertext format of Guide (Brown and Russell, 1987). The pre-processor converts each section heading within the manual page into a Guide replace-button. The new structure is represented in a syntax identical to nroff requests. For example, a note-button begins with ".Bu" and ends with ".bU"

.Bu

node

.bU

If requests such as ".Bu" are embedded in a manual page and the manual page is passed to Guide, then Guide converts the text into hypertext. If the manual page is passed to nroff rather than to Guide, then nroff will ignore all the Guide structuring.

(b) Dictionary

The Oxford English Dictionary (OED) is the largest and most scholarly dictionary of written English. It has one quarter of a million entries and about two million quotations. Each entry details the historical development of a given word. The different senses of a word are each catalogued in the dictionary. The OED can be treated as a text database to which formal queries are posed. An electronic version exists which users can enter via string searches. Readers also want to browse in a way that hypertext links might support. Work is ongoing to standardize the structure in the OED and to convert the OED into hypertext (Raymond and Tompa, 1988).

(c) Catalogues

A stereotype example of a course catalogue contains titles and descriptions for each course, plus references to prerequisite, co-requisite, related, and follow-on courses. The logical components of the input that correspond to components in the hypertext can be described with a template or simple grammar. A parser then extracts the components and creates the hypertext database. The NCR Management College Course Catalogue includes abstracts for all courses offered under the aegis of the NCR Management College. In one experiment, each course description was converted into a separate Hyperties article (Furuta, *et al.* 1989). After the semi-automatic conversion, links were added to the database based on term matches.

The University of Maryland Institute for Advanced Computer Studies publishes an extensive series of technical reports. Annual catalogues are produced which give the identifying information of each report as well as a summary. This catalogue is prepared with troff commands. A parser was developed which would translate the catalogue into Hyperties (Furuta, *et al.* 1989). Since troff is more of a layout language than a logical structure language, some additional structure was inferred from the words, such as "author". The description of regular expressions was incorporated into a finite state automaton with each expression being a label on an arc of the automaton. Actions were associated with the transitions of the automaton such that articles could be entered into Hyperties.

9.4.2   Electronic Yellow Pages

The market place for electronic directories has witnessed a wide variety of products over the past few years. The Electronic Yellow Pages is a prominent example of such an electronic directory. There are several different Electronic Yellow Pages systems EYP currently being used and several others are in varying stages of development

(LINK Resources, 1987). In France, the government has taken a leading role in making electronic information services more readily available to the average person. An EYP is accessible to all customers of the French Minitel System (Stoner, 1988). British Telecom has installed an EYP for London. Use of the system requires a personal computer or terminal and a modem.

The Yellow Pages is rarely read from cover to cover but constitutes itself a kind of large reference document from which the smaller documents about one product or service are retrieved. The information overlying the Yellow Pages, such as a classification of businesses and a map of locations, lends itself to graphical, hypertext browsing. To properly convert the Yellow Pages into hypertext and provide robust browsing tools an augmented indexing scheme is needed.

Yellow Pages currently tend to have rather limited indices. The directory for a city of millions of people may have an index of only a few pages. This index is usually presented as an alphabetically-sorted list of keywords. Occasionally one level of indentation is employed. A small part of an actual Yellow Pages index shows one level of indentation for types of physicians (see fig. 9.5).

Hospitals

Medical Clinics

Nurses

Nursing Homes

Physicians

    Cardiologists

    Infectious Disease Experts

Fig. 9.5   Some health care terms from an actual Yellow Pages index.

A better indexing language for the Yellow Pages would have several more levels than the current indexing languages for Yellow Pages have. Part of the problem is that for paper a small index is in some ways more manageable than a large index. For an electronic index the size of the index is less a factor than is its organization and presentation. Fig. 9.6 illustrates an augmentation of the index in fig. 9.5. New levels have been introduced into the hierarchy. Now a user can find the concept "Health Care" and proceed from there to a breakdown of concepts into "Facility" and "Profession". These three new terms also introduce two new levels in the hierarchy. "AIDS Clinic" has been added as a new leaf in the tree.

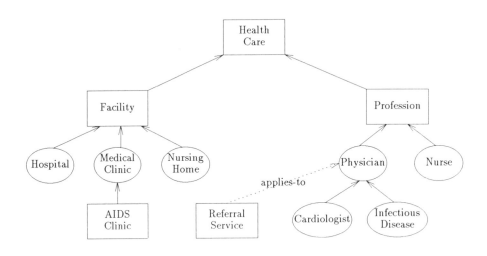

Fig. 9.6 *The concepts in ellipses were present in the original Yellow Pages. The concepts in boxes have been added as a result of the effort to build a more useful index. All the links are is-a links, such as Hospital is-a Facility, except for the link from Referral Service to Physician.*

Fig. 9.6 also illustrates another augmentation which could be made to the index. Non-hierarchical relations might be useful. For instance, a "referral service" to direct patients to appropriate physicians would be important for some users of the Yellow Pages. Referral service could be explicitly connected to the term "physicians" via the non-hierarchical link "applies-to".

9.4.3   Low-structure conversion

Low-structure text refers to text whose explicit logical structure is minimal. The extreme case is an essay which has no subdivisions or other logical decomposition. A novel likewise may often be an extended stream of consciousness for which the logical structure is not determined in the layout of the document and is not indicated by the markup language which may have been used on the computer. To translate low-structure text into hypertext requires that substantial effort be invested in characterizing the abstract structure of the document and the various relations among components of the document.

The July 1988 Communications of the Association of Computing Machinery had eight papers about hypertext. The papers were independently written for journal publication - in linear form with minimal cross-referencing across papers. Those papers were converted into several hypertext products, including Hyperties. The Hyperties effort illustrates the complexity of the task. The eight papers were first cut into 86 Hyperties articles, 38 figures, and 120 references. An overview was added that offered a set of links to topics that were covered in several papers, because the papers didn't provide the links. Simply cleaning up the formatting and putting the papers in Hyperties required part-time effort over six weeks from two people. While some portions of the conversion could be automated, it seems likely that conversion of a similar collection of scientific papers would require a similar amount of overall effort.

9.4.4   Text to Hypertext tools

In converting text to hypertext software tools may be applied to restructuring the source document, to facilitating the loading, and to polishing the target database. However, intervention may be required at various points. By analogy, while there is no single automatic tool for turning raw resources into a house, there are tools for cutting wood, assembling a window, and painting a room.

Some relations which might be encoded in hypertext are not apparent in documents prepared with markup languages that target only publication on paper. "Secondary" authors might read these documents and annotate them with hypertext links. The Thumb system took existing documents and made them appear as hypertext to the user (Price, 1982). The text was represented by a passage tree and a passage-dependent network. The passage tree was inferred from the source document formatting commands and thus captured, among other things, the hierarchical outline of the document. An expert in the domain of the document read the document and interacted with Thumb in the course of building the passage-dependent network which included links which couldn't be inferred from the formatting commands in the document.

Folio Views has characteristics of text retrieval, hypertext linking, word processing, directory management, and electronic publishing systems (Allen, 1989). It can be used to help translate general text into hypertext. Folio Views indexes every word of a text file. A logical view is defined by a logical query of arbitrary terms which are then found in the text. Each logical piece of information in a view is called a folio. Typically each paragraph in a document is a folio. The user can create multiple windows on the screen with a different view in each window. Links can be created among folios which can subsequently be followed in a browsing fashion.

The SuperBook software takes as input a text document prepared for a standard formatting package such as Troff or Scribe and produces an enhanced delivery mode for the document (Remde, Gomez and Landauer, ?). It analyses the words and heading structure of the text and creates a data structure that allows pieces of text to be presented in a print-like format in one or more arbitrary-sized windows which can be scrolled. The hierarchy in which the text is embedded appears at the top of each window in which text occurs and is changed as the text is scrolled. Appearing in a separate window is a Table of Contents. This Table is automatically constructed by SuperBook based on the formatting commands in the marked-up document. The Table is dynamic as the user can specify various fisheye views of it. From the Table the user can also select headings and see the associated full text.

Words and phrases from a book are automatically indexed in SuperBook. Call these words and phrases "terms". The reader can search on any Boolean combination of terms. Furthermore, as the reader finds that some parts of the document don't use the terms which the reader would use, the reader can add synonyms to the index. For example, a seven volume document produced by Bell Communications has been placed into SuperBook. If a user enters the term "phone company" into the term search window but later notices that the term TelCo is used in the book as a synonym for phone company, the reader can add TelCo next to the phrase "phone company" in the phrase index and subsequent searches for phone company will find document portions indexed under either phone company or TelCo.

Tools can be used to automatically convert existing text into hypertext, when the text structure is explicit. If the text structure is only implicit, then substantial human effort may be required to add hypertext links.

9.5   CREATING HYPERTEXT AND THEN TEXT

Tools for writing that encourage the author to make abstract relations explicit are a direct way to create hypertext. The writing tool may support the production of linear text but provides in the first instance of kind of hypertext authoring device.

Automatically translating hypertext to text is a difficult problem which has been addressed in different ways in the three projects (APT, MUCH, and Writer's Assistant) which are discussed in the following three sub-sections.

9.5.1   APT

Instructors of beginning programmers often tell their students that writing a good program is like writing a good essay. A topic must be carefully defined and the material must be grouped into small, manageable sections. APT is an attempt to provide writers with the power to generate structurally sound outlines by casting ideas in a quasi-mathematical or quasi-logical abstractions (Wayner, 1988). The APT compiler takes these abstractions and converts them into an outline. The APT compiler requires the author to define all the ideas at the beginning and carefully connect them in equations.

APT requests the author to enter Ideas, Connectors, and Connections. The Ideas segment contains the principal ideas of the paper, each followed by a semi-colon. The Connectors segment defines various words that will join two ideas. There are three different types of connectors. Ordinary ones place no restrictions on the order the two ideas will take in the outline, while left and right connectors force the compiler to develop either the left or the right side of the equation first. Connections draw together ideas in pairs of connectors.

The APT compiler tries to create an outline by using the basic ideas and the connections that must be made between them. It starts by selecting one of the clauses in the Connections segment and stepping through the ideas one by one. The ideas that should be joined are placed one after another. Then the connection between two ideas is inserted into the outline immediately after the ideas are defined.

The APT outline generator performs its work by creating an acyclic graph. A different node represents each idea. The program adds each connection by generating a new node with pointers to the two nodes it connects. This new node is said to be "higher" than the two nodes it connects. The connections are shown as two lines from the connector pointing downward to the ideas that are joined. Consider the following Ideas, Connectors, and Connections.

Ideas

Marie; Jean-Philipe; Francois

Connectors

Loves; is married to; doesn't know that

Connections

Marie loves Francois;

Marie is married to Jean-Phillipe;

Jean-Philipe doesn't know that (Marie loves Francois);

Francois doesn't know that

(Marie is married to Jean-Phillipe);

APT would diagram these Ideas, Connectors, and Connections as in fig. 9.7.

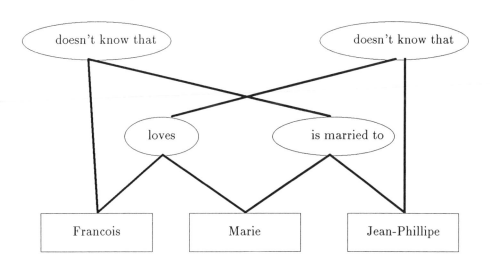

Fig. 9.7 Boxes are Ideas. Ellipses contain Connectors. Graph structure depicts Connections.

The APT outliner traverses the graph in generating an outline which the author is then asked to complete. In the example, if the program starts at the root of "doesn't know that", the program proceeds downward from that root till two Ideas are located. The program then backtracks as it combines the Ideas via the Connectors. The guides to the author would then be:

> Describe: Marie
>
> Describe: Jean-Phillipe
>
> Show how: Marie is married to Jean-Phillipe
>
> Describe: Francois
>
> Show how: Francois doen't know that
>
> (Marie is married to Jean-Phillipe)

APT forces the writer to think more clearly about the logical structure of the document. Yet, the writer can be as colloquial or as proper as he wishes. Users of APT have reported that prior to use of APT their outlines were lists of ideas without firm connections between them. The creator of APT believes that it frees the author from worrying about the overall structure because the machine does the organizing.

9.5.2   MUCH System

The MUCH (Multiple User's Creating Hyperdocuments) system is a prototype collaborative writing environment. It is being developed on a network of graphical workstations to provide an environment where multiple authors can collaboratively create hyperdocuments. Users create a semantic net and link it to textual objects (paragraphs). MUCH uses the semantic net to process text, graphics, figures, tables, and references into a linear document. The semantic net can also be used as a guide for hypertext browsing.

(a) System Characteristics

Semantic nets are supposedly much closer to peoples' internal representations of the world than is prose. However, people get little or no training in the building or reading of semantic nets and generally find that developing a semantic net is a very difficult task. Building a semantic net for a book is like developing a very sophisticated index for that book. The indexing activity is an extremely arduous task. Tools to facilitate collaborative development of the index would be helpful.

Currently the MUCH system prototype is being developed on a network of graphical workstations using public domain software tools including Xwindows, Unix, Emacs, Unix Document Workbench, Xdvi, and Xpic. Xwindows provides a quick and easy means of developing a mouse-driven user interface. Unix is a powerful operating system which supports Xwindows and allows for the creation of complex sets of procedures. Emacs is an extensible text editor that includes a LISP-like programming language for text and document manipulation. The Unix Document Workbench provides a means of incorporating proportional text, figures, tables and graphics in a formatted document. Xdvi is a screen driver which allows typeset text and graphics to be viewed on the user's computer screen. Xpic is a drawing program supported by Xwindows.

In the MUCH system the semantic net comprises of a series of node definitions. Each node has a series of links associated with it. Links are used to describe how nodes are connected. It is these links that form the basis of the semantic net. The MUCH system supports links which can be either hierarchical or non-hierarchical. In practice a mix of both types of link will be used. Each link has a name associated with it to describe its type. Example link types are "extend", "implies", and "uses".

When specifying a node in the MUCH system a series of paragraphs may be associated with each of the links from that node. Paragraphs are associated with links rather than the frame as a whole. The definition of a node is called a frame. Frames are defined in a lisp list of the following form:

> (node_name (link1) (link2) ... (linkN))

where each link is a list of the following form:

> (link_type destination_node paragraph_list)

A typical node definition would look like this:

> (software_engineering_systems
>
>> (begin preview* 06082028rr 01020006rr 061718jmz 01021539rr)
>>
>> (compose software 01012234rr 01012317rr)
>>
>> (require information_technology_management)
>>
>> (include software_life_cycle)
>>
>> (support CASE)
>
>)

There are several things to note about the way a node is defined which are shown in this example. The first is the fact that the paragraph list is optional. It is also of variable length. The second item of interest is the asterisk after the link to the preview node. This is an author inserted feature and provides information to automated traversal utilities.

In practice the paragraph names are more complicated and provide information for the system. They generally contain the date and time of creation and the initials of the author. The need to create paragraph names this way was a result of not using a conventional database to store the text.

(b) Linearization Strategy

The MUCH system uses an independent semantic net to represent an abstraction of the hypertext. When a MUCH document is printed in linear form, the paragraphs associated with an edge in the semantic net are printed as the edge is traversed in a modified depth-first search of the graph. In the following example of the semantic net relevant to "software_engineering" the links to three other nodes are indicated.

software_engineering has software_engineering_definition 01021539rr
software_engineering need information_technology_management 01021736rr
software_engineering include software_life_cycle

The section on software_engineering_definition will begin with paragraph 01021539rr which contains a definition of software engineering. The system will then look for a branch from the software_engineering_definition frame. Given that there are no other paragraphs about this definition, the system next prints paragraph 01021736rr about "software engineering needing information technology management", the second relationship in the software engineering frame. The linear document is created using such a modified depth-first search of the semantic network.

The outline-generation guarantees that every node in the graph is visited once and once only:

```
generate_outline ( starting_node )
        visit ( starting_node )
        mark starting_node as visited
        store all children of starting_node in a list
        while there are children in the list
                {
                if child marked with a '*'
                then insert in the outline but do not visit
                else if child has already been visited
                then insert in the outline but do not visit
                else generate_outline ( child )
```

```
                    remove child from list
                    }

visit (node)
            insert node in outline
            identify all children of node
            return the children
```

The algorithm begins at the node the user declares as the starting node. The algorithm maintains a variable which holds the current level of recursion. This variable is used to calculate the indentation of entries in the outline. The algorithm is slightly different from the one used to produce a linear version of the document. None of the paragraphs of text are retrieved in this algorithm, although the retrieval of text follows the same lines.

9.5.3   Sharples Prototype

Sharples and O'Malley (1988) have specified basic features of a writer's assistant and then prototyped the assistant. The requirements include allowing the writer to specify constraints, to switch easily among writing strategies, and to generate linearizations of networked text.

(a)   System Features

In the network version of the document every node is a note with an arbitrary amount of text. Notes can have direct links to other notes and may be collected into bins. The linear view is a traversal of network. A sample screen is shown in fig. 9.8. As each note is created, it appears in the network window as a box with a title and any links to other notes. To the left of the screen is a set of icons that indicate some of the available operations. On selecting the "history" icon, the user is given the network of notes in the chronological order in which they were created. The "layout" icon activates a formatting of the text according to the layout rules in the attributes of the nodes.

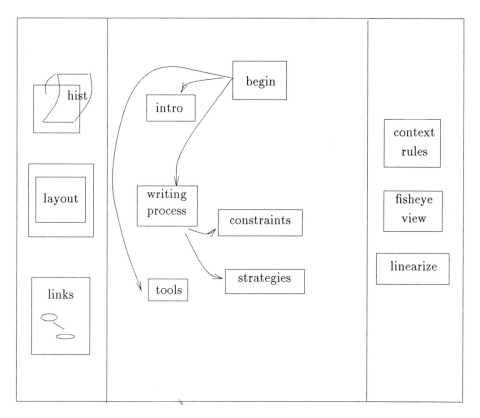

Fig. 9.8   Mock screen display for possible Writer's Assistant of Sharples and O'Malley (1988). Function of icons and other options are explained in text.

The techniques for writing operate within constraints. These constraints evolve from the task, the knowledge in the author's head and otherwise available to the author, and the material thus far generated in the writing process. The constraints themselves can be viewed as those due to content and those due to form. The author's knowledge and the cohesiveness of the text he or she is generating constitute content constraints. An example of a form constraint is that the document contains a title, author, abstract, and body.

To implement constraints in an object-oriented writing tool, every object has attributes and context rules. A context rule is a "demon" with a condition and procedure part. The condition is a pattern that is matched against the object's own properties; the procedure is run whenever the condition is satisfied. A simple example might be a rule within a sentence object to notify the user of repeated adjacent words: $word sub 1$ adjacent $word sub 1 ~ -$ tell_user.

(b) Linearization Strategy

The Writing Assistant algorithm for linearization generates a sequential perspective on a network. The algorithm follows:

1.   Order the link types. The highest value links will be those that form the backbone of the text.

2.   Choose a start node.

3.   Perform a depth-first search of the network, expanding the link with the highest value first. If two links of the same value emerge from a node, then use a heuristic that picks the "shallowest" branch first.

The depth-first search avoids loops by keeping a record of visited nodes and not revisiting a node.

To illustrate the linearization algorithm the semantic net in fig. 9.9 is used. Before the net is translated into linear form the edges are given the following ordering on values: value(cause) > value(explain) > value(part-of) > value(has-part). In the second step of the algorithm a start node is chosen and say for this example that the start node is "hypertext". The depth-first search which is initiated from there follows the link "explain" to the node "new opportunity" and then makes an arbitrary choice between the two links exiting from "new opportunity".

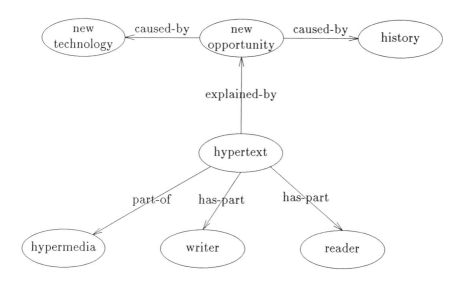

Fig. 9.9   Semantic net used to illustrate linearization algorithm.

The final traversal presented as node-link-node triples is:

> hypertext explained-by new opportunity
>
> new opportunity caused-by new technology
>
> new opportunity caused-by history
>
> hypertext part-of hypermedia
>
> hypertext has-part writer
>
> hypertext has-part reader

To print the document associated with the network another algorithm would select the blocks of text associated with the network and place them in sequence according to the sequence determined by the traversal of the network.

9.6   EPILOGUE

The writing process involves representations of network and hierarchical organizations of thought which might not be directly reflected in the final text. The notation for the general hierarchical structure of a document into sections and paragraphs has been formalized in international standards. Such hierarchical structures facilitate the conversion of text into hypertext and thus allow ready browsing across these structures. Several commercial companies now have computer systems for translating text into hypertext - these systems exploit the standard mark-up commands in the text. Taking a text and converting it into a hypertext with rich, non-hierarchical network structure is, however, very difficult because the re-enactment of the early authoring steps must occur. No computer systems exist which satisfactorily translate text into a "network-rich" hypertext.

The new computer authoring tools are claimed to bring the computer representation closer to the author's internal representation. Rather than being expected to type line after line of text, the author is expected to diagram thoughts and sketch segments of text.   The system subsequently helps the author complete a standard, linear text. The intermediate stage in this process is a network of concepts and text which if linearized might be a standard document. Some computer systems, such as the MUCH system, provide programs for automatically translating the intermediate stage into a standard document. The program includes facilities for elegantly formatting the final text.   Experience with the system suggests that the network of concepts in the intermediate stage must be carefully fashioned in order to support the subsequent automatic generation of a cohesive document.

Easy-to-follow guidelines are needed for the creation of the networks so that the generation of text from hypertext works. No one has yet convincingly provided or demonstrated such guidelines.

REFERENCES

Allen, D. (July 1989) Text retrieval with a twist. *Byte,* pp 201-257.

Barttlett, F.C. (1932) *Remembering*, Cambridge University Press.

Brown, H. and Cole, F. (1989) ODA and Interactive Documents, in, *Interactive Documents: Today and Tomorrow,* BCS, UK, pp. 1-10.

Brown, P.J. and Russell, M.T. (1988) *Converting Help Systems to Hypertext. Software - Practice and experience, 18(2)*, 163-5.

Frederiksen, C.H. and Dominic, J.F. (1981) Introduction: perspectives on the activity of writing, in *Writing: the Nature Development and Teaching of Written Communication,* vol 2, (ed. J F Dominic), Laurence Erlbaum Associates, New Jersey, USA, pp. 1-20.

Furuta, R. (1988) An object-oriented taxonomy for abstract structure in document models. *Technical Report,* Dept. of Computer Science, University of Maryland, College Park, Maryland, USA.

Furuta, R., Plaisant C. and Shneiderman, B. (May 1989) A spectrum of automatic hypertext constructions, *CS-TR-2253,* Computer Science Dept., University of Maryland College Park, Maryland, USA.

Glushko, R.K. (May, 1989) Transforming text into hypertext for a compact disk encyclopedia, *Proceedings of CHI'89*, pp 293-298, Association of Computing Machinery, New York, USA.

Grantham, D., Robertson, J., Subsaic K. and Langston, D. (1987) *A Guide to Andrew Information Technology Center,* Carnegie Mellon University, Pittsburg, Pennsylvania, USA.

Griffey, Q. (September 1986) Word processing for LD college students, *Academic Therapy,* 22, 2, 61-67.

Langer, J.A. (February 1984) The effects of available information on responses to school writing tasks, *Research in the Teaching of English*, 18, 1, 27-44.

Magill, F. and McGreal, I. (1961) Aristotle's rhetoric, in masterpieces of world philosophy in *Summary Form,* Harper & Row, New York, USA, pp. 169-179.

International Standards Organization, Information Processing-Text and Office Systems (1988) *Office Document Architecture (ODA) and Interchange Format,* Parts 1,2,4-8,ISO 8613, Geneva, Switzerland.

International Standards Organization, Information Processing-Text and Office Systems (15 October 1989) *Standard Generalized Markup Language (SGML),* ISO 8879, Geneva, Switzerland.

Price, L.A. (March/April 1982) Thumb: An interactive tool for accessing and maintaining ext. *IEEE Transactions on Systems, Man and Cybernetics,* 12, 2, 155-161.

Raymond, D. and Tompa, F. (July, 1988) Hypertext and the Oxford English Dictionary, *Comms of the A C M,* 31, 7, 871-879.

Remde, J.R., Gomez, J.M. and Landauer, T.K. *Super-Book: An Automatic Tool for Information Exploration-Hypertext?*

LINK Resources, Electronic Directories, (September 1987) *Research Report LINK #0184,* LINK Resources Corporation, 79 Fifth Avenue, New York, NY 10003.

Scardamalia, M. and Bereiter, C. (1987) Knowledge telling and knowledge transforming in written composition, in *Advances in Applied Psycholinguistics*, (ed. S. Rosenberg), Cambridge University Press, Cambridge, England, pp. 142-175.

Sharples, M. (1985) *Cognition, Computers, and Creative Writing,* Ellis Horwood, Chichester, U.K.

Sharples, M. and O'Malley, C.E. (1988) A framework for the design of a writer's assistant, in *Artificial Intelligence and Human Learning: Intelligent Computer-Aided Instruction*, (ed. J. Self), Chapman and Hall, London.

Smith, J.B., Weiss, S.F., Ferguson, G.F., Bolter, J.D., Lansman, M. and Beard, D.V. (August 1986) WE: A writing environment for professionals, *Technical Report TR86-025*, Dapartment of Computer Science, University of North Carolina, USA.

Stallman, R. (October 1981) EMACS manual for TWENEX users, *AI Memo 555,* MIT AI Lab, Cambridge, Massachusetts, USA.

Stoner, M. (March 1988) French connections with minitel: the future has arrived in France. *Online,* 12, 2, 67-70.

Sullivan, P. (1988) Writers as total desktop publishers, in *Text, ConText, and HyperText,* (ed. E. Barrett), pp. 265-278, MIT Press, Cambridge Massachusetts, USA.

Wayner, P. (November 1988) It's APT to write. *Byte,* 375-384.

Weyer, S.A. and Borning, A.H. (1985) A Prototype Electronic Encyclopedia. *ACM Transactions on Office Information Systems,* 3,1, 63-88.

Young, R.E., Becker, A. and Pike, K. (1970) *Phetoric: Discovery and Change*, Harcourt, Brace, and World, New York, USA.

10. HYPERMEDIA FOR MULTI-USER TECHNICAL DOCUMENTATION

Ian Williams

Office Workstations Limited

10.1 THE EVOLUTION OF HYPERMEDIA

The term "hypertext" was coined by Ted Nelson in 1965, but Nelson attributes the underlying concepts to Vannevar Bush who presented his ideas in a classic article on Memex (Bush, 1945).

A number of experimental systems have been developed. Douglas Englebart's Memex-like NLS implementation at Stanford is also known for the introduction of the mouse, multiple windows, and other innovations familiar to workstation users. Xerox PARC have developed a system called NoteCards (Halasz, Moran and Trigg, 1987). In addition to Nelson's ambitious Xanadu project (Nelson, 1981), there is Intermedia at Brown University (Meyrowitz, 1986), and Guide at the University of Kent (Brown, 1986). Conklin's survey (Conklin, 1987) gives details of these developments.

The work on Guide by Peter Brown, led in 1986 to the first commercial implementation of a hypertext system for personal computers by Office Workstations

Ltd - first on Apple Macintosh, and then on IBM and compatible computers. Apple Computer themselves have released a product called HyperCard, which is quite similar to Xerox NoteCards.

The basic design goal of hypertext software is that users should be able to explore information freely, in multiple parallel paths, instead of being confined to a fixed path or structure.

Guide can be described as a system in which the reader is provided with a friendly interface to screen-based documentation. Guide does not attempt to imitate the linear structures of paper-based information. Rather it presents an hierarchical view of information, allowing the user to read only those parts of the documents in which he or she is interested. The reader simply points to a text highlight (called a button) with a mouse driven cursor, clicks the mouse, and displays a detailed expansion. In addition to text, Guide supports high resolution graphics, and graphical objects can also be made into buttons. Similar point/click actions on other types of button cause reference points in the same document or in other documents to be displayed, or cause pop-up notes to appear. Navigation within and between documents is simple and intuitive. Another important feature of the software is that the author's view of documents is identical to that of the reader.

This family of products has grown, and now includes read only versions of Guide; Guidance, which is designed for interaction with other software systems; and IDEX, a document management and delivery system for technical documentation. These products share the use of powerful PC-based technology, high-resolution screens, and easy-to-use graphical interfaces.

The idea of hypertext has broadened to incorporate the notion of displaying graphics and audio data, and we increasingly use the term hypermedia to describe a set of characteristic software. Other hypermedia products or products with hypermedia features are appearing, and increased interest in this technology is evidenced by regular conferences and exhibitions devoted to hypertext and hypermedia in both Europe and North America. Table 10.1 outlines a range of systems showing considerable diversity in application objectives, and product features. This rich diversity makes it difficult to define hypermedia precisely.

Table 10.1. Hypermedia applications and systems

Application	Systems
Universal	Memex/Xanadu
Collaborative work	NLS
Ideas organization	NoteCards
Education	Intermedia
Software engineering	Neptune
Documentation	Guide/IDEX
Programming interface	HyperCard

10.2 REQUIREMENTS OF TECHNICAL DOCUMENTATION SYSTEMS

Although Guide was initially developed as a retail product for single users, its applicability to documentation was recognized at an early stage. A number of systems based on it have been designed for application to large technical documentation systems in the engineering industry. These systems are quite diverse: they include CD-ROM based manuals for automotive repair and catalogues of car parts; standards documents for design and production engineering in the aviation industry; the production of user documentation by computer manufacturers; and operation and maintenance manuals in nuclear power generation.

Despite the diversity of these applications, there are a number of requirements which are common to all the systems described. There are significant differences in the design problems posed by networks on the one hand and CD-ROM based systems on the other. For the most part this paper refers to network implementations, though there are very close similarities, especially in the requirements of authors, in both cases.

The outstanding feature of all these applications is that the number of documents is very large. The very size of these collections requires the provision of tools which technical authors can use to manage the collection prior to publication. Readers require help to find the documents they wish to consult.

This has led to the design of a network environment known as IDEX, incorporating a Document Manager, and supporting a number of processes:

- document conversion;
- indexing and retrieval;
- document style management.

and system-wide hypermedia documents:

- tables of contents;
- list of illustrations;
- glossaries and citations;
- help facilities.

in addition to those basic applications needed to Author and Read documents.

10.3.   SYSTEM ORGANIZATION

The general structure of IDEX is layered, such that we can readily substitute comparable processes for those implemented as standard features. For example, there is no difficulty installing entirely different printing or retrieval engines. Small changes in the user interface, and the replacement of an interpreter are all that is required.

This is an important feature when the need for connectivity to other systems is so obvious. So is the use of a standard network product, which we expect to be directly replaced with enhanced functionality by OS/2 LAN resources.

10.3.1 Use of standards

Adherence to a number of standards can bring long term benefits. IDEX has been designed around three important standards relating to networks, database access, and user interface.

Large collections of documents can be shared quite efficiently over a local area network in which a host computer supports a file server containing a document store. A typical configuration includes a DEC VAX host running VMS services for MS-DOS or a similar implementation of MS-Net. IBM PC/ATs or compatible microcomputers are connected to the network over an Ethernet, and run the hypermedia process locally.

The initial version of IDEX has been built around a proprietary database; however the intention has always been to adopt a standard access method which leaves a great deal of independence of the nature of the database being used to catalog the Document Collection. Structured Query Language (SQL) appears to be the best candidate in this area with opportunities for unifying support for database access mechanisms and networking solutions with the advent of OS/2.

Running under Microsoft Windows version 2, IDEX benefits from the tools that the environment provides towards adherence to the Systems Application Architecture (SAA) standard. It also ensures a smooth migration to OS/2 systems in the near future.

10.3.2   The Document Collection

IDEX supports many collections in a system, each one being associated with a single MS-DOS volume. This allows the system manager to segment the collection for different work groups, and attach CD-ROM volumes to individual machines.

10.3.3   Document type

The next level of organization is associated with the concept of document type. Document type is user defined and can be any convenient system of classification such as: design standard, specification, production tool drawing, operation flow chart, parts list, etc.

Typing determines a variety of attributes, including how a document is indexed, and how it is styled in the screen display or how it appears if it is printed. The document manager creates a directory for each type and its associated style files.

Those of you who have used MS-DOS will know how unhelpful the filename and pathname conventions can be. The task of keeping track of this unwieldy nomenclature, and of such things as unique document references is handled by the Document Manager. The user sees only full document titles.

10.3.4   Document status

Document status (draft, approved, issued etc), describes the stage reached in the document "life cycle", and is used to control the publication process, and (with other controls) to limit user access privileges.

The Document Manager application provides a formalized mechanism for changes in document status allowing full control of the progress of a document towards publication. Draft documents can be edited by authors, and read by editors; only approved documents can be issued; and only issued documents can be viewed by readers.

10.3.5 Catalogue card

Being maintained in a database, Documents can be represented to users of the system in terms of their attributes, including document status described above. These attributes are shown through a Catalogue Card interface, familiar to the vast majority of users. Each Catalogue Card can be brought into view when the appropriate document is being browsed.

10.3.6 Application structure

An Indexer module provides services to each application: whether this be the Reader, Author or Document Manager. This allows a consistency of interface across the whole application suite. In addition, the structure of the Indexer module allows all other applications in the suite to call on the hypertext component to present related information, whether this is online help, example material or any other context-sensitive information.

10.4 FINDING DOCUMENTS

In keeping with the design goal of providing a variety of paths through the collection, there should be several ways of finding documents.

Most users of technical documents know their system well, and clearly prefer to use conventional access paths such as tables of contents and lists of illustrations. At the top level there may be a number of contents tables which consist largely of reference buttons linked to documents concerned. Clicking on the button opens the required document.

Selected fields in the cards are inverted in a multi-key index. The user can search the indexes by writing search scripts with a context sensitive editor, and can name and save commonly used scripts as Queries.

In some cases it is useful for a reader to search for a subset of documents defined by criteria like document type, subject, or date. This is implemented by creating an entry for each document in a file of "Catalogue Cards". Cards for different document types can contain appropriate field combinations, thus allowing (for example) a design standard to be indexed by part number, and a drawing by scale, while sharing common fields such as author and issue number.

The output of the search process is either a filtered list of document titles which can be displayed in a list box in an "open" dialogue or a view of the Catalogue Cards (fig. 10.1). The results of such searches can be combined into Worklists which can also be saved for future reference. These sets of documents can be presented to the more naive users of the system, typically the readers, removing them entirely from the complexities of the search process. Queries are also used to define document sets for batch processing by the system manager.

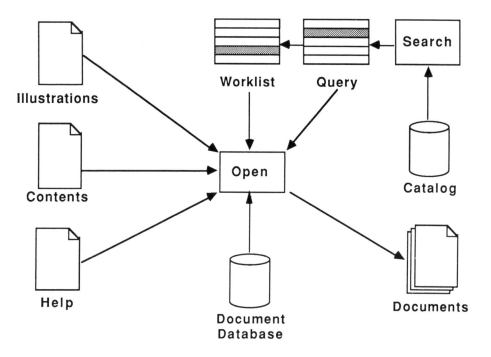

Fig. 10.1   A search of the catalogue first produces a "hit list" of cards; the user then opens the required document.

10.5 MAINTAINING HOUSE STYLE

For any publishing organization a consistent house style is very important. Layout and typography are valuable signposts to readers. Screen-based documentation is no exception to this rule.

10.5.1 On screen

We have found that hypermedia structure can be used somewhat like generalized markup. Information required for screen display: typographical style, indentation, window size and position etc., is stored at shell level. Consistency across sets of documents is maintained by editing style files for each Document type. As a document is displayed the application refers to the style file for the necessary display parameters. This approach allows both the distinctive styling of documents which the authors wish to appear different, and the easy modification of style by accessing a single display template.

10.5.2 In print

Since there will always be internal and external users who do not have access to terminals, printed versions of the hypertext documents are required. An identical approach to that used to style screen display has been used for printed output, where each document type has a page layout, and print style templates.

The Page Template Editor accessed through the Document Manager allows the user to lay out the format of the printed page: not only the position of the area to receive document text and graphics, but also static information such as the Document Title, page number, and any Catalogue Card attribute. These areas are formatted on demand during the printing process.

Despite the generally good quality of fonts now available for high resolution screens, it is clear that fonts that are easy to read on the screen are not the best for printed text. Unfortunately only a few fonts designed to meet the needs of both media, like Lucida, are available (Bigelow and Holmes, 1986). The solution is usually to totally re-style the document for print.

10.6 SHELL DOCUMENTS AND FUNCTIONS

Shell documents have special purposes, such as holding contents information, lists of illustrations, a citations list and a glossary. The use of contents tables and of lists of illustrations has been mentioned above, and the others deserve a brief mention.

Citation documents contain descriptions of documents outside the hypertext collection. Citation references in other documents point to individual entries, and are linked like any other cross reference. Each entry can contain structures allowing the reader to obtain more detail about a title by expanding the document.

Glossaries contain the definitions of note buttons in IDEX documents. However, the definitions are global to the collection and distinct from those that are local to an individual document. Like local definitions, glossaries can contain both text and graphics.

An important category are the Help files. It is appropriate for a hypertext system to be self-documenting. Help documents may contain internal indexes which allow context-sensitivity to be provided to any application in the IDEX suite. Context messages are passed by any relevant application to the Indexer module and are used to find a specific point in the Help file when help is invoked by the user.

There is also a special, hidden "scrapbook" document at shell level. Authors can use it to name and save fragments of structure in it which can be combined in new, arbitrarily complex structures in any other document. Scrapbook objects have proved to be invaluable in the repetitive construction of such structures as flow charts, and complex graphics. If required, structure templates for entire documents can be stored in this way.

10.7 DOCUMENT CONVERSION

Unless it is possible to automate the conversion of data to electronic format, the investment in research, design and authoring required to build a hypermedia application will make only a few applications viable. Further, data which has been converted to hypermedia in the way described should ideally be suitable for distribution to end users with little or no manual authoring.

The problem is simplified by the emergence of standards used in many publishing systems today. For example CALS requires the data exchange formats in Table 10.2 to be supported for compliance.

Table 10.2 CALS standard formats

Data	Format	Standard
Text		SGML
Graphics	Vector	IGES, CGM
	Bitmap	Group 4 Fax

10.7.1 SGML and Hypermedia

In most cases existing documents contain some accessible text structure. If the documents exist in machine-readable form they usually contain embedded markup used by the word processor on which they were prepared, or (more rarely) full encoding in a general markup language like Standard Generalized Markup Language (SGML)(ISO, 1986).

If no machine-readable version is available, there are alternatives. With typeset texts, scanning devices using intelligent character recognition techniques and markup systems can be used to substitute the coding implied by the typographic content.

Both Guide and IDEX use a mapping of tagged text input on to hypertext objects to achieve a highly efficient construction from source text. In most cases, existing source documents contain some accessible text structure. If the documents exist in machine-readable form, they usually contain embedded formatting used by the word processor on which they were prepared or, better still, a structured markup language like SGML.

Because application designers can expect to deal with a wide variety of non-SGML source files, a two-stage approach is used. First, a source document is converted to an SGML-compatible intermediate format. Standard utilities then interpret this intermediate format to generate hypermedia structure in the second part of the conversion process. A markup definition file maps any user-defined document type definition (DTD) onto the intermediate format.

Conversion tools are packaged in two ways. In the IDEX Author, single documents are converted using the hypermedia DTD. Alternatively, an application programming interface to a set of object code libraries is available. This gives the application designer more freedom in the manner that the conversion is implemented.

10.7.2   Graphics

We have seen that graphical objects can be linked both to text and other graphical objects and that these links can represent expansions in detail, cross references, notes, and user-defined extensions. Alternatively, readers can narrow the scope of browsing by searching for graphics attributes of the documents.

In large paper-based information systems it is common for graphics to be used redundantly. But this is unnecessary in hypermedia systems. Consider a system in which a graphic is used to illustrate maintenance manuals in 12 languages; only one instance of the graphic need be held, and displayed at runtime. Often this can be done without any change to the existing file format. Graphics identifiers in the SGML document can be converted into external graphic references in IDEX, and format-specific processors are used to display the images.

10.8 CD-ROM VARIATIONS

The early acceptance of an industry-standard solution for CD-ROM (the High Sierra data format) has made it possible for publishers to issue documents on optical discs, in the certainty that users of the information can use devices from a wide range of manufacturers. Up to 550Mbytes of data can be distributed on a single disc at a very low cost, especially if there are a large number of users.

Since data transfer rates from CD-ROM are rather slow, it makes sense to have document index structures that are optimized for such systems, or to use an external system to address the disc.

In the first case our approach has been to work with established retrieval mechanisms developed by third parties. An interesting example of the second case is in a service bay diagnostics system built for Ford Motor Corporation. The implementation is for a Hewlett Packard Vectra computer.

The system provides for a connection to an on-board diagnostic computer in a vehicle. Expert system technology provides diagnostic support, and is linked to the documentation, largely held on CD-ROM. This information is supplemented from a remote database connected to the diagnostic system over a dial-up circuit. The expert system contains embedded references to CD-ROM based documents, which can also be accessed through tables of contents as described earlier. If the user wishes to read documents held on the database, they are converted to hypermedia at run-time by routines similar to those used for batch process text file conversion. The interface to the three subsystems is designed to be transparent. A simple combination of pointing and scrolling, allows the user to select a mode and a sub-set of documents. Regardless of the source format, documents are displayed in a consistent manner.

One of the more interesting interface modifications for this diagnostic system is the replacement of the cursor/mouse interface with one for use with a touch screen.

Service mechanics are generally unfamiliar with computers, and there is no scope in the service bay environment for a mouse and keyboard. The constraints of the touch screen display made it necessary to confine display to a single document at a time, to alter the scroll interface, and to replace menu commands with action buttons.

10.9 FUTURE DEVELOPMENTS

Hypermedia is rapidly moving from being a novel and exciting single application to the status of a user interface in which many cooperating applications are integrated by sophisticated object management controls. The potential is illustrated by developments in two key areas.

10.9.1 Graphics and video

An important development for technical documentation will be toward documents containing complex, composite images in different formats called by external reference. Each format will require a distinct process to manage the display of that graphic data. Very large vector images will be displayed in separate windows, scrolling in both coordinates, with optional scaling facilities. This makes it possible to display complex information such as cad-originated electronic circuit diagrams in the hypermedia context. Objects in such diagrams can be associated with link tables, providing the reader with powerful access tools.

One of the more interesting recent developments is the incorporation of video images in hypermedia. Hardware support which locks the video signal to the computer display is required. Typically, an extension to the link commands is developed to support calls to a video disk player. Sequences are defined by authors and played back by readers by action on the command objects. Image display technology is moving very rapidly and we can expect the performance of hardware to improve dramatically, with an increasing number of video cards and device drivers providing co-processor technology. Software development systems are also evolving to support hypermedia software with interfaces for event synchronization and object manipulation. The most promising development is in the Digital Video Interactive (DVI) standard. Companies like Intel, IBM and Microsoft, are working together to deliver hardware and software that will decompress digitally recorded video at run time.

10.9.2 Databases

We have seen how database techniques are used to record and index document attributes. Standards like SQL have made it possible to package development tools that will access any database system conforming to the standard. It is now quite straightforward to link hypermedia objects in documents to powerful retrieval engines.

A hypermedia document may contain multiple images. These images are displayed in diagram frames which may themselves contain many graphical elements. It is possible to develop a hierarchy of images; for example a car parts explosion. The reader clicks on a model, then on a sub-system, and eventually reaches a parts illustration. Each callout on the illustration is linked to further data in the parts database and dynamic information is retrieved from a remote host using programable extensions.

10.10 CONCLUSIONS

Large, screen-based documentation systems demand innovative designs which are consistent with the overall design goals of hypermedia software. The solutions are not always obvious, for there are few useful precedents from the world of paper-based documentation.

Authors are engaged with the problems of how best to present information clearly, concisely and attractively. They need powerful tools that ease the task of converting existing documents to new formats, and which enable the management of the entire system.

Hypertext systems have been applied in a variety of documentation applications, and some common design problems have emerged. We can now offer generic development platforms which can be used with confidence by designers wishing to make the best use of this exciting new technology.

REFERENCES

Bigelow, C. and Holmes, K. (1986) The design of Lucida: an integrated family of types for electronic literacy, in *Text Processing And Document Manipulation*. Cambridge University Press, Cambridge, UK.

Brown, P. J. (1986) A simple mechanism for authorship of dynamic documents, in *Text Processing and Document Manipulation*. Cambridge University Press, Cambridge, UK.

Bush, V. (July 1945) As we may think. *Atlantic Monthly.*

Conklin, J. (1987) Hypertext: a survey and introduction. *IEEE Computer*, 20, 9.

Halasz, F. G., Moran, T. P. and Trigg, R. H. (1987) Notecards in a nutshell, *Proceedings of the ACM CHI + GI Conference,* Toronto, Canada.

ISO 8879 (1986) Standard Generalized Markup Language (SGML), Geneva, Switzerland.

Meyrowitz, N. (1986) The architecture and construction of an object-oriented hypermedia system and applications framework. *OOPSLA '86 Conference Proceedings.* New York, USA.

Nelson, T. (1981) *Literary Machine,.* San Antonio, USA.

11. EXTENDING SOFTWARE INTO THE FUTURE

L. Bottaci and A. Stewart

University of Hull

11.1 INTRODUCTION

We begin by briefly introducing the general idea of a hypertext and go on to emphasize those aspects which we believe are most relevant for our needs. Clearly, hypertext is a very powerful and general concept which is widely applicable and so an important part of our research effort is concerned with identifying those aspects that are potentially most useful and developing and refining them to the stage where they can be given concrete realization in a real application. To test the usefulness of hypertext we are building a programming and documentation tool.

One aspect of hypertext which we think has considerable relevance for software development tools is the notion of an active link and the consequent scripting language in which activities are defined. We illustrate the usefulness of active links by considering how they can be used to support consistency checking during the process of writing or modifying software and its documentation.

11.1.2 Background

Although the term "hypertext" was coined by Theodore Nelson some twenty years ago, while Nelson was at the University of Harvard, one of the earliest references to the concept   of hypertext is the paper by Vannevar Bush (1945), in the section entitled "Memex". A Memex is

> "a device in which an individual stores his books, records and communications, and which is mechanised so that it may be consulted with exceeding speed and flexibility. It is an enlarged intimate supplement to his memory."

In the eyes of Bush, a Memex system was an essentially personal thing; a user would interact with his (or her) memex system to store notes. Hypertext depends critically upon reference by association,   not by pre-defined connections. Barrett (1988) remarks:

> "The user is presented with a collage of contingencies - information, not necessarily understanding. This tangle of linkages becomes an even more critical limitation to the user when navigation in hypertext is unmediated by an instructor or experienced guide. A user may just glance over the surface of a body of knowledge without integrating it into a personal knowing. *And if pathways are too firmly established, then the point of Hypertext is lost* ."

(our italics)   In other words, a hypertext is intrinsically a dynamic medium that can grow indefinitely and change its structure over time. Any attempt to constrain a hypertext in such a way that it expresses a limited range of concepts and associations raises serious hermeneutic questions as well as violating the principles of hypertext that were laid down by Theodor Nelson (1987).

Hypertext systems have evolved a great deal during the intervening 40 years since the paper by Bush, and there have been a number of casualties; the concept of free association between items of information has, for the most part, been lost; largely as a result of implementation issues. With the exception of the StrathTutor system, (Mayes *et al.*, 1988) hypertext systems are largely constructed in such a way that the links between the texts must be static, and sometimes even pre-defined. Even with StrathTutor, there is a responsibility upon the author to construct the set of keywords from which associations are derived.

One of the most interesting hypertext proposals to emerge is the Xanadu proposal put forward by Ted Nelson (1987). Xanadu is unusual, in that it seeks to provide an architecture upon which almost any existing hypertext system could be built; it is unusual in that it does not seek to provide an interface to a hypertext system, but a server that is capable of providing hypertext functions to any application via a defined set of protocols. It is based around a highly secret and proprietary file structure (referred to in Nelson (1987) as "enfilades"), a linkage structure and a numbering scheme based around segmented integers which can grow to arbitrary size[1]. The essence of the Xanadu storage system is that it is capable of dealing with a collection of interlinked texts which may be distributed amongst a large group of machines and whose size may be many thousands of megabytes without loss of speed or efficiency.

A good overview of the current state of the art in hypertext is presented by Conklin (1987).

---

1   The numbering scheme devised by project Xanadu is similar to Dewey Decimal notation, but has some interesting mathematical properties. The authors recommend a study of Chapter 4 in Nelson (1987) for further information.

11.2 IMPORTANT ASPECTS OF HYPERTEXT

There is an enormous variety in the hypertext systems that have been developed to date. This is not surprising given the power and generality of the hypertext concept. In this section we consider those aspects of hypertext that would appear to be particularly relevant to writing and maintaining software systems.

11.2.1 Multiple Readings

One of the aspects of hypertext that the authors wish to emphasize is that it offers support for documents that are structured, whilst being an essentially literary medium, if one considers literature as being a body of interlinked texts; a significant proportion of the meaning of a hypertext lies in the structure and pattern of the links and not simply in the contents of the texts. (Indeed, if literature is to survive as a highly flexible medium of expression this must be so.) As a result, a hypertext is subject to a variety of interpretations.

It is important that this variety of possible interpretations is allowable by the texts that make up a software system and its documentation. Such texts have many different kinds of readers who each expect to gain something different from the text. Obviously, the various possible interpretations must be consistent with each other so that the documentation is not ambiguous. An important advantage of using a hypertext system for documentation is the support it can provide in maintaining consistency.

11.2.2 Multiple Authors

One of the most powerful facilities offered by hypertext is user annotation ; allowing the user to augment or modify the links between the sections of the hypertext; these modifications will be only be visible to the user that creates them. This implies that a hypertext can be divided into two sections: firstly, the texts and links that are fundamental to a particular hypertext and, secondly, the links between texts that are of importance to a particular user or group of users.

Hypertext can therefore, in principle, provide a vehicle for co-operative systems design. If a hypertext is shared between a group of users, all of whom have read and write access to the hypertext, a document can evolve by progressive stages of amendment and revision. Of particular importance is the fact that the hypertext can contain individual documents (or complex hypertexts) which explain why certain decisions were made. These "motive" documents can then be attached to the documents that they inspired. An example of this approach to design, where a book is produced by collaboration, is presented in Trigg and Sichman's paper (1989).

11.2.3 Version Control

In general, hypertext can offer support for version control of both texts and links. If a hypertext system provides version control, the user can decide which version of a document he (or she) wishes to link to; the user can also decide whether to make a link to a particular version of a document or the most recent version of a document.

One consequence of the document numbering system in Xanadu is version control; each document is issued with a unique identification number and a user modifies the original document by storing modifications to the original document. The Xanadu designers claim that any version of any document can be retrieved in approximately the same time as a result of the enfilade and linkage structures. If this is so, document version control becomes a relatively trivial operation.

11.2.4 Active Links

Since much of the information in a hypertext lies in the connections between texts, it seems natural therefore to attach behaviour to a link so that the link may perform some action in addition to establishing an association between two texts.

The concept of an *active link* has recently been given life with the arrival of the HyperCard system (Goodman, 1987) which has an embedded programming language called "HyperTalk" (HyperTalk Programming, 1988). The HyperTalk language allows an application to be active (and interactive) in a way that conventional, static, hypertext cannot provide.

In the simplest case, an active link may simply consist of a script describing a connection between two texts; when a HyperCard designer creates a link between two items (from one **card** or **stack** to another), the HyperCard system creates a HyperTalk script that is attached to the button that invokes the connection. In a more sophisticated case, a HyperTalk script can make a button or a text field visible or invisible, play some music, activate an external device (such as a video disk or CD-ROM), or perform almost any other task that the programmer might desire. The HyperTalk language is easily readable and intuitive; a script connecting two cards together may simply consist of:

```
on mouseUp
    visual effect zoom open
    goto card "Introduction" of stack "hello"
end mouseUp
```

HyperTalk provides a simple programming model that allows the sophisticated user of HyperCard to construct quite advanced applications. (One of the authors' colleagues has constructed a tutorial on natural language parsing written entirely in HyperTalk, including the routines to draw the parse tree.) HyperTalk suffers, to some degree, by being an interpreted embedded command language and like virtually all such languages it has the following problems discussed below.

(a) Efficiency

An interpreted language, by definition, cannot be as efficient as a compiled language, although modern software methods (such as threaded interpreters) can make an interpreter extremely fast.

(b) Transparency

If the basic set of operations provided by an interpreter is not sufficiently powerful or efficient, the programmer will become aware of the boundary around the interpreter; it will be necessary for the programmer to step out of the interpreter into the surrounding environment to implement a function that HyperTalk does not provide, or cannot implement efficiently. (This problem is being corrected in the more recent versions of HyperCard; HyperTalk is being converted into a compiled language.) Stepping out from HyperTalk into Pascal or C can be a considerable effort, since these languages are very different from HyperTalk and are much more difficult to use effectively. In addition, the applications become non-portable.

If a hypertext system were to include an extensible "scripting language" that could be incrementally compiled to make full use of the underlying machine, that is, a script would be treated in exactly the same way as a computer program in any other compiled language, the power of the resulting system could be considerable. Since the scripting language could be both sufficiently expressive and efficient, the programmer would no longer need to be aware of a restricting boundary between the hypertext environment and the rest of the system,

The authors believe that the ideal base for such a scripting language is an obbject-oriented programming language supported by an interactive programming environment. The major benefit of object-oriented languages such as Smalltalk-80 or Lingo (the language that is being used by the authors) lies in their ability to raise, with ease, the level of abstraction at which the programmer can work, the result being more powerful software without additional complexity.

11.3   OBJECT-ORIENTED DATABASES

For the purpose of this discussion, the authors are adopting the definition of an object-oriented database that is presented in the papers by Beech (1987) and Linsjorn and Sjoberg (1988). Unlike a conventional database, which is primarily intended to represent items of information and their relationship to other items, an object-oriented database is primarily intended to represent persistent "entities" and their states. These entities can be real (having a corresponding physical model) or abstract (having no physical model). In a conventional database system, the semantics of an item of data are defined in a schema ; in an object-oriented database, the semantics of an object are defined by the class of the object. Each object in the database will have a class. An object-oriented database can also provide support for applications to be held as items in the database.

One of the interesting aspects of an object-oriented database is that objects can be either passive or active. A passive object is one which is held in the database and waits for a message to be sent, at which point it undertakes a task. An active object is one that can invoke itself in order to perform a task; an example of an active object would be a calendar or diary object which wakes up when an appointment is due and dispatches a message.

One application for an object-oriented database which the authors are investigating is as a vehicle for a computer-aided software engineering system. This is being pursued in a collaborative project with Paisley College of Technology, Linn Smart Computing of Glasgow and AI Ltd. of Watford [2] to develop a distributed database based around the Rekursiv[3], a computer designed to support object-oriented systems. It is the intention of the authors to design a hypermedia browsing system for the database and to study computer-aided software engineering as an application area.

---

2   This project is funded by the Systems Engineering section of the Information Engineering Directorate.

3   A product of Linn Smart Computing Ltd.

11.4   THE NATURE OF DOCUMENTATION AND THE NEED FOR HYPERTEXT

In the previous section we considered hypertext, in general, and identified some aspects likely to be important for the development and maintenance of a software system and its documentation. However, if we are to evaluate in detail the applicability of hypertext we must now consider the nature of software and its documentation.

11.4.1   Different Kinds of Reader

The novel by Roald Dahl, *Charlie and the Chocolate Factory*, is written for two very different kinds of reader. On the one hand it is written for children who appreciate it as a comical and rather fantastical adventure story. On the other hand it is also a shrewdly satirical novel, a politically sophisticated comment on capitalist society and hence also written for adults. The one text accommodates the two kinds of reader by allowing two interpretations which although distinct are not inconsistent. Indeed, the two interpretations may overlap in that occasionally the young reader will sympathise with the "unfair treatment" of Willy in the factory and the adult reader will laugh at some of the slapstick humour. Consistency is maintained by ensuring that the humour is such that it never detracts from the political message and vice versa.

In common with Dahl's novel, software documentation is written for a number of different kinds of reader. Software engineers involved in the construction and maintenance of the system require precise and detailed descriptions of its operation, but there is a difference between the documentation required by those involved in the construction of the system and those involved in its maintenance; the former are concerned with the system as it is and will be, whereas the latter are looking at the system with a view to exploiting new arrangements that may not have been anticipated by the developers. Furthermore, the needs of project leaders are different from those of the software engineer and the documentation must allow for interpretations suitable for them. Support engineers, application builders, users, etc., all require different interpretations.

Although documentors and novelists may share a similar objective in writing for more than one kind of reader, the structure of the texts they produce are radically different. Documentors are not obliged to overload a single document with the various required interpretations, which in any case would be difficult. Typically, different documents are produced for different kinds of reader. Documentation is structured, therefore, as a number of "parallel" and consistent documents.

11.4.2 The Importance of References

This simple "parallel" structure is adequate only for the most basic forms of documentation. The variety of interpretation required of the documentation reflects the separation of concerns that forms the basis of the software life cycle and modular system design. However, in practice, a clean separation of concerns may not be achievable and it is often the case that one needs access to more than one interpretation. For example, in examining a code change it may be necessary to know the reason for the change which means that the requirements and design documents will need to be inspected. Not only must the documentation provide a number of interpretations, it must also allow a reader to move conveniently between them as required. Typically, this is done by following a reference from an item in one document to some other related item in another document. Notice that the reference is crucial in directing the reader immediately to the relevant item in the other document. Without the reference the reader would need to search through the document.

The structure of documentation must reflect the fact that the majority of readers will not read it in its entirety or in a single prescribed order, instead the reader is expected to select and order relevant portions of the documentation. Indeed, the term "browsing" is used to describe the special style of reading appropriate to documentation. Efficient browsing is possible only if the documentation contains adequate references.

The reference is central to the structure of documentation. A reference need not be explicit, but is present whenever in some portion of text, an item is mentioned and there exists further documentation, in some other portion of text. In traditional (non-hypertext) forms of documentation, the item concerned is either explicitly annotated with details of the reference or the reference is implicit and made by looking up the item in an index.

The references present in documentation perform a number of different functions. A characteristic they all have in common, however, is that they allow the reader to move to some other part of the document and encounter an item of text, possibly out of context in that the reader may not have read the preceding text. If references are to be effective then there must be an efficient way in which the reader can find the necessary context. A simple reading of the preceding text is not necessarily adequate. The required context depends on the item of text, the knowledge possessed by the reader and the task in hand. It follows that not all readers require the same context and a variety must be available. Each reader must explore the document to locate a suitable context and again references are particularly useful here. Typically, the reader follows references, "spiralling" outwards, to build up the necessary context.

We can see that the textual structure of documentation is logically a hypertext and so, clearly, there are advantages in having a hypertext as the concrete realization of the documentation. References, for example, can be located with a single command. The convenience with which references can be followed naturally makes browsing more convenient. It is essential, of course, to use of a bit mapped display which allows several pages of a document to be simultaneously accessible. A hypertext system for browsing and documenting software which make extensive use of references between code and documentation is described by Fletton (1989) ; Bigelow's article (1988) also deals with hypertext and software engineering.

11.4.3 Support for Reading

Convenient reference following only begins to exploit the power of a hypertext system. The complex structure of documentation invariably leads to navigation problems for the reader. If the documentation is held in hypertext form, navigation problems are likely to be exacerbated since the reader is denied contextual cues such as page markers, distance into the book, and so on. Hypertext however, can also provide support for navigation. A number of systems, including Intermedia (Yankelovich *et al.*, 1985) and NoteCards, provide a graphical map of the nodes and connecting links. A history or audit trail allows the reader to easily backtrack. NoteCards has a Guided Tour facility which guides the reader between "clusters" of cards.

Hypertext, unlike paper, is an active medium allowing documents to be modified dynamically to suit the needs of a particular reader at a given time. References can be generated dynamically on the basis of search criteria provided by the reader (StrathTutor). These potentially very powerful hypertext features, navigation support and dynamic references, are still being researched but it is clear that any mechanisms that are developed will involve extensive computation over the hypertext. This highlights our concern for developing an expressive and efficient "scripting language".

11.4.4 Support for Writing

In addition to the support that hypertext can provide for browsing, there are also important advantages in using hypertext for writing, where the special structure of documentation poses significant problems. Given the presence of extensive references, considerable care is needed to ensure that when a change is made to one part of the document, some other part which references it does not become outdated.

This problem is compounded if a number of authors are involved in the writing of the documentation.

The fact that references are implemented as hypertext links can be exploited in maintaining consistency. Active links, which are sensitive to changes to the text at either end, can be used; this approach is adopted in the IPSEN system (Lewerentz, 1988). A simple approach would involve time stamping all documents and equating consistency between a document A which depends on a document B with the time of writing of A being later than the time of writing of B. It is not sufficient in general however, to simply detect that a document has been changed, a change may or may not lead to inconsistency. The introduction of inconsistency depends on the nature of the relation between the two documents and the nature of the change.

In the SOFTLIB system (Sommerville et al., 1986), a number of different types of modification are recognized. Some changes are inconsequential (e.g. formatting) and are termed cosmetic. Code changes are changes to the implementation of a module but not to the specification, hence only the implementation documentation needs modification. There are also design changes and interface changes, each with their own implications for maintaining consistency. In the SOFTLIB system, the software engineer is responsible for identifying the type of change being made.

One particular approach to maintaining consistency which is applicable in some special cases is shared or included text. In a number of situations, there is a need for several documents to contain a common item of text. If a single copy of this common item is shared amongst the several documents then any changes to the common item are automatically reflected in the item as it appears in the various documents. A typical example of this technique is the include file, usually containing common declarations, which is included into a number of program texts. In this situation the included text is included always in its entirety and without modification.

The mechanism of shared text is easily implemented in a hypertext and works well providing all the including documents require the same identical copy of the common item. More often however, only a part of the common text needs to be included in a particular document and different documents should include different parts. This is essentially the mechanism termed transclusion in the Xanadu system. In some cases, there is a need for part of the the common text to be modified before it is included into another document. For example, if the common text is a formal specification for a software component, part of it may be translated into English and included in a document for managers. Again different inclusions would be modified in different ways.

In this situation, each inclusion is potentially different from any other. Clearly, we would not want to store different versions of the common item since this would nullify the advantages of shared text. Different versions however, in certain cases, could be generated automatically. The various versions might be generated by filtering a single common text in different ways and applying simple transformations. The responsibility for generating each inclusion would lie with a procedure attached to the link (an active link) between the common text and the including document. Here is yet another use for the scripting language.

Note that shared text solves the problem of consistency among the including documents, in that they all contain suitable versions of the common item. However, there still remains the problem of consistency between the including document and the inclusion, the common item. If any of the including text is modified, it may become inconsistent with the included text. This form of inconsistency is isolated to a single document. In the opposite situation, where the included text is modified, it is necessary to check that the new version is suitable for inclusion in each of the including texts.

Active links can be used to signal the need to check consistency. This is important in situations where there are many, perhaps successive, inclusions. If document A is included into B and B is included into C

$$A \ -> \ B \ -> \ C$$

then a change to A must signal the need for consistency checks with both B and C. Clearly, there is a need to structure the documentation to avoid the situation where a change to any one text causes consistency check signals to be propagated to all (or almost all) the other texts.

The question arises as to whether it is possible to automatically detect actual inconsistencies as opposed to potential inconsistencies. Unfortunately, automatic inconsistency detection seems very unlikely since in practice consistency is determined by arbitrary semantic relations. Even if we consider the simpler case in which all documents are written in a formal language with a well-defined semantics, consistency in general remains undecideable. We believe the most promising approach is to allow user defined consistency relations between arbitrary portions of text, documentation or code, which are semantically related. Once again, there are implications for the scripting language here in that it will need to be sufficiently expressive to allow the definition of the required consistency relations.

11.5   CONCLUSION

We have argued that there is considerable potential for exploiting hypertext and object oriented databases for the writing and maintenance of software and its documentation. The task, as we see it, is to adapt a powerful and general concept with a host of features in a way that is appropriate for the application in hand. In this paper, through lack of space, we have concentrated on the utility of active links and the scripting language in tackling the problem of maintaining consistent documentation. Clearly, there are other important considerations to be addressed; access to documents will need to be controlled by a protection system, any software engineering tool must be flexible enough to be tailored for the particular working practices of the organisation adopting it and the user interface is vitally important. However, our adoption of object oriented programming and object oriented databases is designed to facilitate the integration of future systems which tackle these problems.

REFERENCES

Barrett, E. (1988) Introduction: A new paradigm for writing with and for the computer, in *Text, Context and Hypertext.* (ed. E. Barrett) MIT Press.

Beech, D. (1987) Groundwork for an object database model, in *Research Directions in Object-Oriented Programming*, MIT Press.

Bigelow, J. (March 1988) Hypertext and CASE. *IEEE Software*, 5,2,:23-27.

Bush, V. (1945) As we may think. *The Atlantic Monthly,* 176,101-108.

Conklin, J. (1987) Hypertext: An introduction and survey. *IEEE Computer*, 20,9,17-41.

Fletton, N.T. (1989) A hypertext approach to browsing and documentation software, in *Proceedings of the Hypertext II meeting of the Alvey HCI Club Interactive Learning Systems SIG.* Currently unpublished.

Goodman, D. (1987) *The Complete Hypercard Handbook,* Bantam Computer Books.

Hypertalk Programming. (1988) Hayden Books.

Nelson, T.H. (1987) *Literary Machines*, Published by the author.

Lindsjorn, V. and Sjoberg, D. (1988) Database concepts discussed in an object oriented perspective, in *European Conference on Object Oriented Programming,* . Springer Verlag.

Trigg, R.H. and Sichman, L.A. (1989) Collaborative writing in NoteCards, in *Proceedings of the Hypertext II meeting of the Alvey HCI Club Interective Learning Systems SIG,* Currently unpublished.

FURTHER READING

Lewerentz, C. (1988) Extended programming in the large in a software development environment. *ACM SIGSOFT/SIGPLAN Software Engineering Symposium on Practical Software Development Environments,* pp. 173-182.

Mayes, J.T. Kibby, M.R. and Watson, H. (1988) Strathtutor: The development and evaluation of a learning by browsing system on the Macintosh. *Computers and Education,* 12,221-229.

Sommerville, I., Welland, R., Bennett, I. and Thomson, R. (1986) Softlibadocumentation management system. *Software-Practice and Experience,* 16,2,131-143.

Yankelovich, N. , Meyrowitz, N. and A. van Dam. (October1985) Reading and writing the electronic book. *IEEE Computer,* 15-30.

12. THE OFFICE DOCUMENT ARCHITECTURE AND HYPERMEDIA

H. Brown and F. Cole

University of Kent

12.1 STRUCTURES FOR DOCUMENTS AND HYPERTEXT

The concept of underlying document structure has existed in document preparation systems for many years. It has appeared in many diverse forms, but most recent developments have been based on the work of (Alan Shaw, 1980) and have lead to the development of structured document editors like GRIF (Quint and Vatton, 1986) and Interleaf (Morris, 1987). There is no agreement yet on the form such structures should take, but a number of trends can be identified. In particular, the structures are almost always hierarchical, object-oriented, and provide a framework for multimedia documents. Other common features include keeping details of layout separate from the document structure and content (thus allowing different 'views' of the document to be produced relatively easily) and a mechanism for defining generic document styles.

These structures have been developed for interactive document preparation systems whose primary goal is to produce a printed document. The document may be created, edited, and previewed online, but there is an implicit assumption that it will eventually be read from paper. This constrains the material to be organized in a sequential fashion, though it may be embellished with cross-references and footnotes.

The document structure is designed to provide intelligent editing and updating aids for the author, such as automatic renumbering of sections or checking that the document conforms to a required style.

For truly interactive documents and hypertext, the emphasis is on providing a structured body of objects with links connecting related objects. There may be a complex 'web' of objects tied together by a large number of links. Users browse through the information online by following links from object to object. In this case the structure is designed specifically to help readers navigate around the information.

Systems based on paper documents provide traditional, rather rigid, forms. They contain additional features to assist interactive editing, but do not exploit the truly interactive nature of the electronic medium. Hypertext goes to the other extreme with highly interconnected structures. Users are allowed so much freedom to follow links that they can lose all sense of context and get lost and confused. This is such a well-known problem that many hypertext systems impose (or advise) a hierarchical arrangement of information. This helps readers to maintain a sense of position, and provides well-defined 'primary' routes through the information without imposing a sequential ordering. Furuta et al. (1988) distinguish between the primary structure of a document and its secondary structure.

The primary structure is the predominating hierarchical structure that defines how objects are combined into higher-level objects, while the secondary structure represents additional relationships between objects. Hypertext systems clearly emphasize secondary structure, but have demonstrated that users become confused without a well-defined primary structure. The Office Document Architecture (ODA) (ISO8613 1988) provides a detailed 'document architecture' that is hierarchical, object-oriented, and conforms to all the other trends described at the beginning of this section. Although ODA is designed mainly to support paper-based documents, it includes a general 'bindings' mechanism that can be used to specify arbitrary links between objects. It thus provides the basic primary and secondary structures needed for interactive document editing and hypertext.

This paper looks at the problems and possibilities of using ODA as a standard for interactive documents and hypertext. To do this, it first introduces the main features of the ODA document structures and layout process, and then shows how ODA can represent the structures used by two very different hypertext systems. Some minor extensions to the ODA model are introduced.

12.2   ODA DOCUMENT ARCHITECTURE

ODA provides a tree-like model of a document. The structure of the document is given by the shape of the tree, while the content is stored entirely in the leaf objects. Attributes provide information about the objects in the tree. A few of the most important attributes are introduced in the examples and discussion below. Only one needs to be mentioned at this stage. This is the *content architecture* attribute that defines the type of content for each leaf object and thus allows different types of content to co-exist within the document. Currently ODA defines three types of content (character, raster graphics, and geometric graphics) but definitions for further types (including sound) are expected.

An ODA document is described by two structures. The logical structure divides and subdivides the content of the document into logical objects that mean something to the human author or reader. A logical object may be a general item like a section, title, paragraph or reference. Alternatively it may be a specialized item like a telephone number or price, or a collection of related information like a list of companies selling a particular product. Only the lowest level objects, such as titles or prices, have content.

The layout structure is concerned with a visible representation of the content. It divides and subdivides the content into page sets, pages, and rectangular areas within pages. Rectangular areas with nested areas defined within them are known as frames. The lowest level areas are known as blocks and, by definition, are the only areas to have content associated with them. A frame might be used to represent a column of text, for example, with nested blocks for the content of individual paragraphs.

Each document has its own specific logical and specific layout structure, but their creation is guided and controlled by generic document structures for that particular class or 'style' of document. These are sets of object type definitions (one set for logical objects and one for layout objects) that specify the types and combinations of objects allowed. In ODA terminology the definitions constitute the generic logical and generic layout structures for a document class.

12.3 EXAMPLES OF ODA STRUCTURES

This section illustrates the structures introduced above by presenting snippets of the generic structures that might be used for a journal containing technical papers. It also introduces a few important attributes.

The generic definition for each non-leaf object has an attribute called **generator for subordinates** that describes how the object may be made up from subordinate objects. These indicate that subordinate objects may be optional (OPT), required (REQ), repeated (REP), or optional and repeated (OPT REP), and that a group of objects may occur in a given sequence order (SEQ), in any order (AGG), or as a choice where only one of the group occurs (CHO). The information given in these attributes provides a simple grammar for the primary structure of the document class.

Fig. 12.1 shows the generic logical structure for a single technical paper in the journal. It indicates that the paper consists of a compulsory title, followed by a compulsory author's name, followed by an optional abstract, followed by one or more sections. If the abstract is present it consists of one or more paragraphs. Each section begins with a subtitle. The 'REP CHO' construct indicates that the subtitle is followed by a series of paragraphs or lists occurring in any order. Lists consist of one or more list items. (In practice, a more complex structure catering for items like footnotes and diagrams would be needed.)

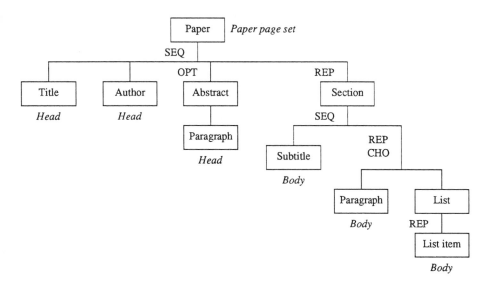

Fig 12.1   Generic logical structure

The corresponding generic layout structure might define one page style for the first page of the paper, and a different style for all subsequent pages. Fig. 12.2 shows the top level of such a structure. The 'Title page' contains a 'Header frame' representing an area set aside for the title, author's name and abstract, and a 'Body frame' for the start of the first section. The 'Continuation pages' contain 'Continuation body frames' to hold the rest of the sections. (Again, in practice, further frames would be needed for items like running titles.) Blocks are not included in the generic layout structure but are assigned to pages and frames during the layout process as outlined below.

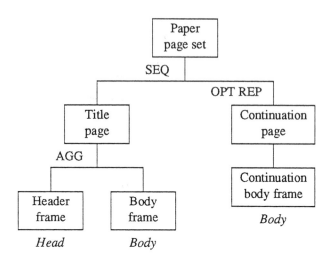

Fig. 12.2 Generic layout structure

ODA's layout process decides exactly where each item of the document is to be placed. It uses the specific logical structure, the generic structures, and the content architectures to create the specific layout structure. It works at two levels

- *Content layout* takes portions of content and lays them out into blocks. This stage is dependent on the content architectures involved and on sets of attributes known as *presentation styles*.

- *Document layout* places blocks in frames or pages. This stage is dependent on sets of attributes known as *layout styles*.

The content layout process thus deals with character sets and the fine positioning of items within blocks, while the higher level document layout process decides how to place the blocks within pages and frames.

The document layout process is guided by three attributes whose values are shown in italics in figs. 12.1 and 12.2. *Layout object class* is normally used to indicate that a major logical division of the document should be directed into a particular page or page set. In the example the logical 'Paper' has its layout object class defined as 'Paper page set'. This dictates that each paper must be laid out in a single instance of the page set shown in fig. 12.2.

Within a layout object class, the attributes *layout category* and *permitted categories* can be used to direct logical objects into different frames. If a leaf logical object is given a layout category name, it can only be laid out in a frame that has the same name as one of its permitted categories. In the example the only category names used are 'Head' and 'Body'. When the layout process tries to place the blocks corresponding to the title, author's name, and abstract (if present), it will look for a frame with 'Head' as a permitted category, and will therefore create a 'Header page' and place them in the 'Header frame'. But when it reaches the blocks corresponding to the contents of the sections it looks for frames with 'Body' as a permitted category, so it uses the 'Body frame' until that is full and then creates 'Body pages' as necessary in order to use the 'Continuation body frames'.

When the specific layout structure has been created, it associates the document content with pages, frames and blocks. The two specific structures are related and come together at the level of the content. Figure 12.3 shows a fragment of the specific structures for the beginning of a paper. It assumes the paper has no abstract and that the first section begins with three paragraphs, only one of which fits onto the title page. Figure 12.3 shows a neat one-to-one correspondence between logical objects and layout objects. This often occurs, but not always. Logical content portions may, for example, be split between blocks (when paragraphs are split over pages) or concatenated into paragraphs occupying a single block.

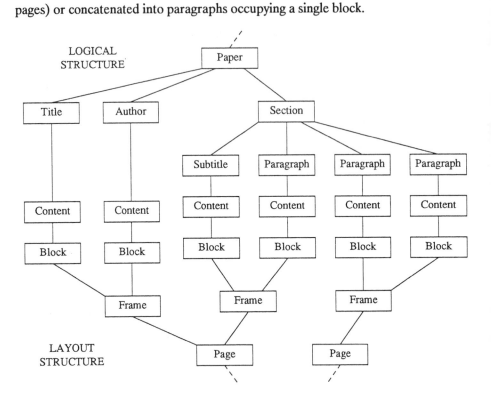

Fig. 12.3   Specific logical and layout structures

12.4 PROVIDING DIFFERENT VIEWS OF AN ODA DOCUMENT

The previous section gave only a brief sketch of the ODA layout process, but it should be sufficient to show that the appearance of a specific logical document can be altered by judicious changes to its generic layout structure. As a simple example, deleting the 'Body frame' from the 'Title page' in fig. 12.2 would cause each paper to be laid out with only the title, author's name and abstract on the first page. There would be no frame on the first page with 'Body' as a permitted category, so the first section would have to start on a new page in a 'Continuation body frame'.

More radical changes to the layout can be achieved by altering the attributes that make up the layout and presentation styles. The attributes in these styles apply to logical objects, but the objects contain only the identifier of the appropriate style. The styles themselves are held separately. This provides a more concise document representation and allows the styles to be changed without changing the logical structures.

The layout styles include the layout object class and layout category attributes (described in the previous section) and other attributes governing the selection of frames and the positioning of blocks within a frame. The same layout object attribute constrains the block containing the logical object to share the same frame as the block containing another specified object, while new layout object constrains the block containing the object to start a new frame. Offset and separation control the minimum spacing between adjacent blocks, and the relative position of blocks is dictated by fill order which allows normal top-to-bottom positioning or traditional footnote positioning.

The presentation styles guide the lower-level content layout process and thus affect the appearance of content within individual blocks. They contain different attributes for different content architectures. For character content, for example, they include attributes affecting the indentation of the first line, the distance between lines, and the initial font size.

Changing the generic layout structure and the styles can lead to significantly different views of the same logical document. Page and margin sizes can vary, single or double column layout can be used, and paragraph spacing and font size can change. In particular, it is possible to cater for different 'house styles' by this means and to provide different styles for interactive editing and the final printed version.

12.5   EXTENSIONS TO ODA FOR INTERACTIVE DOCUMENTS

ODA allows a measure of flexibility in the layout and presentation of documents, but different views are not a substitute for proper interactive facilities. The basic problem is that the ODA layout process is sequential and page based and several attributes reflect this. Any form of online editing requires extensions to the layout process to make it incremental and to allow the user to scroll around the document, but some more ambitious features desirable for screen-based documents are:

1.   An outline facility: to display selected (usually high level) items, such as chapter and section headings, and ignore other items.

2.   Pop-up displays: to allow the temporary display of additional information on demand. These can be used for the equivalent of footnotes, marginal notes, and glossary entries in paper documents.

3.   Folding: to allow sections of a document to be hidden behind a 'button' on the screen and revealed on request. Folding should be allowed to any level, so hidden sections can contain further buttons.

4.   A linkage facility: to enable users to follow links or cross-references automatically.

For items 1 and 2 it would be sufficient to extend the document layout process to recognize and act on two special layout categories called, say, 'invisible' and 'pop-up'. Different layout styles could then provide online versions with pop-up notes and varying levels of outlining, as well as a standard version with footnotes and other appropriate embellishments.

Item 3 demands a more significant change. The layout process needs be able to display either the button or the item(s) folded behind the button. One way to do this is to allow non-leaf logical objects to have content (the representation of the button) and additional attributes to tell the layout process whether to display this or the content of the object's subordinates (the folded information). Combining this with the pop-up layout category would allow a general button mechanism where the hidden content could replace the button as part of the main flow of the content, or it could appear as a temporary pop-up display.

Item 4 again needs additional intelligence in the layout process. The actual linkage can be represented using ODA's binding mechanism. A binding is a user-defined attribute consisting of a binding identifier and a binding value. The value can be an integer, a character string, or a pointer to another object. It can thus represent a user-defined link to a remote object, and the layout process could 'follow' such a link on request. This could be done in several ways depending on the type of link. Three possibilities are:

- Move the current point of display to the target object.

- Display the target object (or subtree) as a temporary pop-up item.

- Include the target object (or subtree) at this point in the document.

One current restriction in ODA is the limited way attributes and bindings can be specified. Their values are normally derived from generic object definitions or inherited from attributes called *default value lists* (held higher up the structure). In most cases the value is given by a single item, but for bindings (and a few other attributes) the value can be calculated from an attribute expression. Space does not allow a full description of these expressions but arithmetic operations, for example, are limited to incrementing and decrementing integer values by one, and the only attribute values that can be referenced are binding values.

A valuable extension to ODA, for paper-based documents as well as interactive ones, would be to allow all attribute values to be derived from general expressions with a full range of operators (including conditional operators) and operands (including attribute values and content portions). This would provide much needed flexibility and allow relative sizes and other constraints to be expressed properly. (This extension is already used in the Fortune documentation system for software engineers [Mullin 1988].)

12.6 MODELLING GUIDE BUTTONS IN ODA

Guide (Brown 1986a and 1986b) is a hypertext system that supports a hierarchical model of a document and also allows cross-linking of information. A typical Guide document presents the reader with a summary consisting mainly of buttons. These can then be selected to reveal greater levels of detail as required. Buttons may be nested many levels deep. The reader selects only the buttons he is interested in, and if he finds he is not interested in the information revealed he can 'undo' the selection and fold the information back behind the button again. Guide is also a WYSIWYG editor. It allows the reader to edit the contents of the document and to add or delete buttons, thus becoming an author as well. The emphasis is on allowing the reader to tailor the document to his own requirements.

The overall Guide model is similar to ODA's hierarchical model, but with the added concepts of:

1.   folding logical items behind buttons,

2.   allowing more than one button to access the same logical items.

Guide's layout model is of a single long scrollable frame holding all content except temporary pop-up items. Using an ODA framework could enrich the Guide layout model.

To show how the Guide model fits with ODA, we shall introduce two different types of Guide button and explain how they might be represented. (The examples use the Unix version of Guide, which is similar to the version marketed by OWL for the Apple Macintosh (OWL 1986) but differs in some details.)

The commonest type of button is the **replacement-button**. When a replacement-button is selected, the button itself disappears and is replaced by information that may in turn contain further buttons. The replacement is in line, so surrounding text may be reformatted or scrolled out of the way to make room for the replacement.

2.3.2 Content portion descriptions

2.3.3 Object descriptions

2.3.4 Object class descriptions

2.3.5 Styles

2.3.6 Document profile

2.3.7 Document class descriptions

(a) Summary containing unexpanded buttons only

2.3.2 Content portion descriptions

2.3.3 Object descriptions

    Each object within a structure is characterised by a set of attributes called an *object description*.

    Each attribute has a value and may represent one of the following **More**

2.3.4 Object class descriptions

(b) Result of selecting 'Object Descriptions' button

Fig. 12.4   Guide document showing (a) button and (b) expanded button

Figure 12.4 shows two different views of a Guide version of part of the ODA standard. In fig. 12.4(a) the visible text is made up entirely of buttons giving section headings. (By convention, Guide buttons appear in a distinctive font - typically in bold; so that readers can recognize them.) Figure 12.4(b) shows the result of selecting the 'Object Descriptions' button. Two further buttons are shown within the replacement. The 'More' button is another replacement-button for the user to select if he or she requires more detail. The words in italics are a different type of button known as a **glossary-button.** If the reader selects a glossary-button an explanation of the term appears temporarily in a separate window.

To represent Guide buttons in ODA we would not set about defining a special new object type for each type of button. Instead, for replacement-buttons, we would look first at the existing objects in a document class, decide which were appropriate as buttons, and modify the definitions of these objects to turn them into buttons. Replacement-buttons would then have different generator for subordinates attributes depending on their function within the document and would generally allow further buttons as subordinates. We might decide, for example, to turn the 'Section' object of fig. 12.1 into a replacement-button with an abbreviated title as the button contents. The replacement would then automatically consist of the subtitle and the paragraphs and lists making up the section. After modifying existing objects we might also decide to add new button objects similar to paragraphs or strings of text within paragraphs.

The definitions of objects chosen as replacement-buttons would be defined to have contents (to represent the button itself) and the following additional bindings:

- **Button-type** = local, definition or usage (default "local" - see below).

- **Button-state** = not selected or selected (default not selected).

- **Button-level** = integer value (default value given by an attribute expression setting the value to 1 more than the Button-level of the next superior button in the tree).

Button-type and Button-state tell the enhanced layout process how to deal with the button and whether to display the button itself or its subordinates. Button-level could be used to provide different levels of automatic expansion of replacement buttons. As the subordinates represent normal document content, they do not need to be given any special layout category or changed in any way, except perhaps to be turned into buttons themselves.

There are several variations on the basic replacement-button. The simplest form is the **local-button** where the replacement applies only to the button itself. This is the default type described above. Two other forms are the **definition-button** and **usage-button**. For definition-buttons the replacement applies not only to the button itself but also to usage-buttons with the same 'name'. (Guide provides a mechanism for attaching names to the buttons.) In ODA we could provide these variations on the local-button by setting the appropriate Button-type value and adding a further **Button-name** attribute. A usage-button effectively refers to replacement content held elsewhere, so it would be a leaf object with no generator for subordinates.

Although the use of the **Button-name** binding reflects Guide's own naming mechanism, it demands a high degree of knowledge from the layout process. It might be more efficient to mirror this in ODA by providing usage-buttons with a binding that contained a pointer to the appropriate definition-button object. This then becomes a general mechanism for attaching the subtree containing the replacement content to several places in the document.

Glossary-buttons are like footnotes, annotations, glossary entries, or other embellishments to the main document. Unlike replacement-buttons their replacement is not part of the main document, instead it is typically a short piece of pop-up text. We could represent glossary-buttons in ODA by defining a new 'Glossary-button' generic object with a generator for subordinates specifying a single 'Glossary-text' item. A 'Glossary-button' would have contents (to represent the button itself) and the following bindings:

- **Button-type** = glossary

- **Button-state** = not selected or selected (default value = not selected)

'Glossary-text' would be defined as a leaf object with character content (to represent the explanation text) and a default layout category of 'pop-up'. Glossary-buttons are intended to provide the same explanation for each reference to a term or item throughout the document, so it is attractive to think in terms of two variations, similar to the definition-button and the usage-button, to avoid holding multiple copies of the explanation text.

12.7 MODELLING KMS FRAMES IN ODA

KMS (Akscyn, McCracken and Yoder, 1988) supports a data model based on workspaces known as frames. Frames may contain text, graphics and image items, and individual items within frames can be linked to other frames. There is no built-in notion of hierarchical organization and no concept of a linear ordering of information. Information is divided into frame-sized chunks and one chunk is displayed in each window on the screen. The reader follows links to view different frames.

In spite of this very general model, strong conventions have evolved for the format of frames and for distinguishing between hierarchical links and other links. Figure 12.5 shows the overall layout of a conventional KMS frame. (To avoid confusion this section will use 'KMS frame' and 'ODA frame' to distinguish the different meanings.)

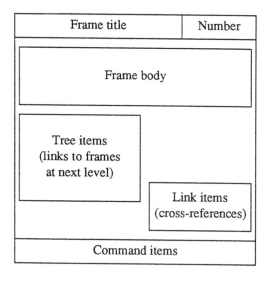

Fig. 12.5 Layout of typical KMS frame.

The generic logical objects defined to support a standard KMS database would correspond to the KMS frame and the items within the KMS frame. Figure 12.6 shows the top levels of a possible generic logical structure. The generic layout structure for a KMS frame would correspond to an ODA page with ODA frames representing the areas shown within the KMS frame in fig. 12.5. Layout object class would be used to direct each KMS frame into a single instance of this ODA page, and layout category and permitted categories would be used to direct the different logical items into the appropriate ODA frames.

The 'tree' and 'link' items would be set up like the replacement-buttons described for Guide in the previous section. Thus 'tree' items would be like definition-buttons and would have contents (to represent the button text shown in their parent KMS frame) and a subordinate KMS frame (to be shown if the button is selected). The 'link' items would be like usage-buttons. They would also have button contents to be shown in their parent KMS frame, but the linked KMS frame would be identified by a binding instead of being attached as a subordinate. The layout process could be relatively simple as it only needs to display complete KMS frames and to follow the primary and secondary links to further KMS frames given in the 'tree' and 'link' objects.

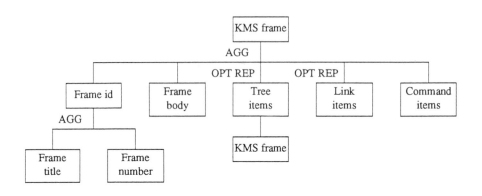

Fig. 12.6 Generic logical structure for a KMS frame.

12.8 CONCLUSIONS

The descriptions above cover only a few of the issues involved, but they indicate that ODA contains a great many of the basic facilities needed for interactive documents and hypertext. The only additional facilities introduced are

- allowing non-leaf items to have content (which may be used or ignored by the layout process).

- a generalization of the method currently used to specify attribute values.

- an enhanced or tailored layout process (which is clearly needed for any form of WYSIWYG editing).

ACKNOWLEDGEMENTS

We would like to thank our colleagues in the Alvey Fortune Consortium for many discussions on ODA and document structures. We would also like to thank the SERC for its support of Fortune and other research projects on document processing.

REFERENCES

Akscyn, R.M., McCracken D.L. and Yoder E.A. (1988) KMS: A distributed hypermedia system for managing knowledge in organizations. *Comm. of the ACM* , 31, 7, pp. 820-835.

Brown, P.J. (1986a) Interactive documentation in *Software - Practice and Experience,* 16, 3, pp. 291-299.

Brown, P.J. (1986b) A simple mechanism for the authorship of dynamic documents, in *Text Processing and Document Manipulation,* (ed. J. C. van Vliet) pp. 34-42, Cambridge University Press.

Furuta, R., Quint V. and Andre, J. (1988) Interactively editing structured documents, in *Electronic Publishing - Origination, Dissemination and Design*, 1, pp. 19-44.

Guide: Hypertext for the Macintosh, (1986) OWL International Inc.

ISO 8613 (1988) Information Processing - Text and Office Systems - Office Document Architecture (ODA) and Interchange Format, Parts 1,2,4 8..

Morris, R.A. (1987) The interleaf user interface, in *PROTEXT III: Proceedings of the Third International Conference on Text Processing Systems*, (ed. J. J. H. Miller) pp. 20-29, Boole Press.

Mullin, D. (1988) Fortune - A documentation support system for software engineers, in *ESEC'87 First European Software Engineering Conference*, (eds. H. K. Nichols and D. Simpson) Springer-Verlag Lecture Notes in Computer Science 289.

Quint, V. and Vatton, I. (1986) Grif: An interactive system for structured document manipulation in *Text Processing and Document Manipulation,* (ed. J. C. van Vliet) pp. 200-213, Cambridge University Press.

Shaw, A.C. (1980) A model for document preparation systems, *Technical Report 80 04 02*, University of Washington, USA.

Part Four

Object-Oriented Databases

13. STRUCTURE AND SCOPE
OF OBJECT-ORIENTED DATABASES

S. Roberts

University of Leeds

13.1 INTRODUCTION

In recent years there has been considerable interest in new types of database systems, including object-oriented, semantic and deductive databases. It is the purpose of this paper to look particularly at object-oriented databases (OODB), and in order to provide some motivation for this I will begin by considering why the need for new types of database has arisen.

Database management systems based on the relational or network data models offer a structured record as the basic unit of modelling; we shall call these traditional database management systems. That these have proved adequate for supporting traditional data processing applications is hardly surprising when one considers that the punched card, and perhaps even the paper records they replaced, conditioned systems designers to the idea that records are necessarily structured, fixed length, comprising a fixed number of fixed length fields. Kent (1978) puts it this way: 'Record technology is such an ingrained habit of thought that most of us fail to see the limitations it forces on us. It didn't matter in the past, because our real business was record processing almost by definition'. In recent years, however, attempts have been made to exploit database technology for the support of other computer applications;

examples are CAD/CAM, geographical information systems, and management of office information and hypermedia. The entities of interest in such applications are generally of a complexity which cannot be easily and directly represented by structured records of data. These applications require drawings, diagrams, free text, maps and combinations of these together with the more familiar structured records.

It was partly in order to support the new structural demands of these applications that semantic data models were proposed (for example, Peckham and Maryanski, 1988) which provide a much richer modelling environment, and which were motivated by concerns shared by researchers in AI Knowledge Representation. At the same time object-oriented programming languages (for example, Smalltalk, Goldberg and Robson, 1983), were being developed, the primary concern being with modelling behaviour. Object-oriented database systems have much in common with both semantic data models and object-oriented programming languages, and there is still a good deal of confusion regarding terminology that has resulted from similar concepts being introduced by researchers in different sub-disciplines. In this paper I shall attempt to describe what object-oriented databases are and to give some idea of applications that might benefit from their use. I shall also consider the availability of OODB software.

13.2 OBJECTS AND OBJECT CLASSES

An object is considered to be a sufficiently general representational tool that data items at all levels of detail, and at all levels of abstraction can be modelled as objects. This contrasts with the relational model, for example, where different constructs are required for different levels of data item detail (attribute value, tuple, relation) and where there is a clear distinction between data and its description (metadata).

The advantage of modelling everything as an object is two-fold. Firstly, it provides for greater uniformity; we do not need to make artificial distinctions, for example, between entities that are represented by a single value, and those represented by some higher level structure. Secondly, it allows us to represent directly real world entities which require a complex data structure to describe them, and to have these as our units of handling within the database.

It is worth noting that the term object is used as short-hand for the more accurate description object representative. It is because there is this close association between real world objects and their database counterparts, that the accepted terminology usually causes no confusion.

An important aspect of any object is that it has identity in the database. This is usually implemented by giving every object a machine-generated surrogate, or unique identifier which does not change during the lifetime of the object, and is not visible to the user. An object can therefore change any of its (visible) properties, but still remain the same object.

13.2.1   Object classes

During database design it is usual to classify together entities which fit a given description into entity-types. The essential thing is that entities classed together have the same attribute-types and (in principle at least) can participate in the same relationships. For example, all entities of type person would be expected to have a forename and a surname, and could participate in a marriage relationship with another person.

In an object-oriented database we are concerned with classifying objects according to their structure, relationships with other objects and also according to their behaviour. For example, the object-type "line" might be defined as:

object-type:	line
attribute:	thickness
relationships:	starts_at xyCoordinate
	finishes at xyCoordinate
operations:	stretch(line, real) - > line
	move(line, xyCoordinate) - > line
	rotate(line, real) - > line

which indicates that any object of type line has the same static (structural) properties, and the same behavioural properties, that is any line can be stretched, moved or rotated. In keeping with the objective to model everything as an object, we note that the distinction between **thickness** as an attribute-name and **starts_at** as a relationship-name is an artificial one. It is better to model them both as relationships or, to choose a more neutral term, properties. A line can then be thought of as being related to a real number (an object of type real) via the thickness property. The description of the line object class then becomes:

object_type:	line
properties:	< thickness: real >
	starts_at: xyCoordinate >
	< finishes at: xyCoordinate >
operations:	stretch(line, real) - > line
	move(line, xyCoordinate) - > line
	rotate(line, real) - > line

Corresponding to this type definition would be the definition of the xyCoordinate type:

object_type:	xyCoordinate
properties:	< x Value: real >
	< yValue: real >
operations:	move(xyCoordinate, real, real) - > xyCoordinate

13.2.2 Encapsulation

In our specification of the object-type line, we have left the behaviour of the operations stretch, move and rotate, to the imagination of the reader (there are of course several interpretations). If the specification is to be of use this behaviour must be well defined (for example, we need to know about which point the line will be rotated), however, provided it is well defined, the user of a line does not need to know the implementation details. This principle of separating the specification from the implementation is known as encapsulation, and is perhaps the most central feature of object-oriented systems. Nierstrasz (1989), in a survey of object-oriented concepts notes that encapsulation is a common feature of all systems considered and that many object-oriented concepts depend ultimately on encapsulation. We say that the operations, stretch, rotate and move form part of the public interface of the object-type line, but the actual implementation will be defined by underlying methods.

It is now possible to argue that the properties of an object-type are best not considered as part of its public interface. Consider a further specification of line viz:

```
properties:   <thickness: real>
              <starts_at: xyCoordinate>     private
              <finishes_at: xyCoordinate>
```

```
operations:   thickness(line) -> real        public
              start(line) -> xyCoordinate
              finish(line) -> xyCoordinate
              stretch(line, real) -> line
              move(line, xyCoordinate) -> line
              rotate(line, real) -> line
```

By hiding the properties in this way, the structure of the object-type could be changed (for example finishes_at could be replaced by two properties: length and direction) and although the methods which implement the various operations would need to be changed, the public interface would remain the same. This clearly provides more uniformity at the public interface, and better data independence. We note, however, that this does require extra work at the data definition stage, and we lose the ability to have a generic "update" operation such as can be applied, for example, to any attribute of a relational database.

13.3. OBJECTS AS MODELLING TOOLS

It is worth pausing to consider whether the object is a better building-block for modelling data than, say, the relation. Many people's reaction to the object-oriented model is that it the network model in disguise. If this is so, and since the network model has been largely usurped by the relational, might not the object-oriented model be a retrograde step?

In answer to this we first note that there is an important feature shared by the network and object-oriented models, namely, the explicit declaration of relationships (via the set construct in network models and via the property construct in the object-oriented model). This contrasts with the relational model where such relationships are implied by value.

The advantage of the relational model is that all relationships which can be implied by value enjoy equal status, whereas with the network model only those which have been predefined can be used to define access paths. However, there is no fundamental reason why access paths have to be restricted to chains of relationships, it just happens that we would expect these to define the most likely needed access paths. Object-oriented database systems will tend to offer navigational style access, but this does not prevent them from offering a relational SQL-like access language as well.

Systems such as ONTOS (formerly Vbase +) (Ontologic, 1988; Roberts and Jenkins, 1988) and Iris (Fishman *etal.*, 1987) have extended the SQL language to an object SQL which combines the power of a relational language with the navigational capability of the object-oriented model.

From the modelling point of view it is, in any case, arguable that the network provides a better representation than the relational (see, for example, Powell (1988) and Kent (1978)), so we should not let the network resemblance put us off the object-oriented model.

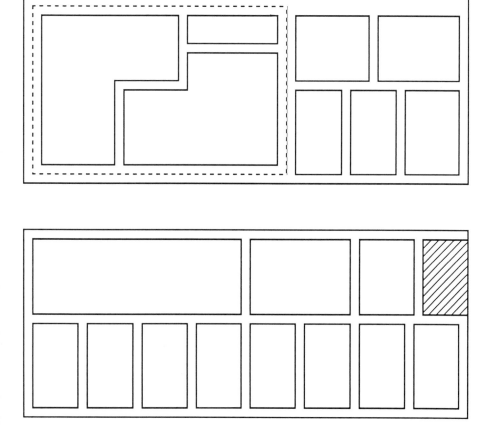

Fig. 13.1 Example cutting-stock patterns.

Let me illustrate this with a simple example. As part of aproduction control system we have developed at Leeds a package to solve a cutting-stock problem, for a local company. The program retrieves from the (relational) database the orders and order-quantities, and the details of the raw material available. During execution it produces cutting patterns which are written back to the database. The orders can be one of three shapes, rectangular, L-shape or J-shape, so the cutting patterns can be quite complex (see fig13.1). The cutting stock problem has been coded in the C programming language, wherein appropriate data structures are defined to represent the raw material, the orders, and the cutting patterns. Mapping these data structures onto the relations in the database is non-trivial; a full description of a cutting pattern requires tuples from seven relations. Had the company an object-oriented database management system (DBMS) in which to store the data, not only could there be a 1:1 correspondence between the application data structures and the database objects, but also the specification of these structures would only need to be done once.

13.4 GENERALIZATION AND AGGREGATION

Encapsulation is the property of object-oriented databases borrowed from object-oriented programming. Generalization, however, owes more to the work on semantic data modelling and knowledge representation. We have already seen how we relate objects by placing them in the same class (i.e. declaring them to be of the same type), and also how we relate objects through the property concept. Smith and Smith (1977), identified two further data abstractions called generalization and aggregation.

Aggregation forms an object by defining a relationship among other objects. For example, "a person borrows a book from a library" is an aggregation which might be named borrowing. An aggregate object of type borrowing can have properties of its own, for example, due-date. In an object-oriented model this aggregate object would be modelled just as any other object, that is there is no special support for it. This conflicts with some interpretations of the aggregate data abstraction, for example, King

(1989) claims that an aggregate object takes it's identity from the identities of its components, whereas Elmasri and Navathe (1989) consider the components to be existence-dependent on the aggregate-object (i.e. delete the aggregate, and all components are deleted with it). Clearly, it depends on an individual application as to which semantics would be most useful.

Generalization forms an object-type by suppressing the differences between other object-types. For example, a type graphical_element might be defined to be a generic type including all lines, polygons and circles. It should be clear that types can form a hierarchy in this way, which may be in the form of a tree, or more generally a lattice, as shown in fig. 13.2.

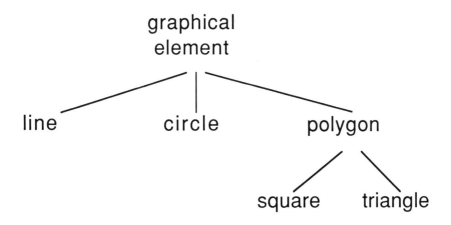

Fig. 13.2 Generalization hierarchy.

The advantage of singling out generalisation as a special type of relationship is that certain aspects of objects or object-types can be inherited from others in the hierarchy.

13.5 INHERITANCE

Let us consider what types of inheritance are possible. First, there is the possibility of both structural and behavioural inheritance among object-types. For the object types in fig. 13.2, for example, correspondence might have among its properties, sender, receiver and date received. These properties would be inherited by each of the sub-types, email, fax and snail-mail (fig. 13.3). In addition, the sub-types might have further properties, for example, email could be further endowed with sender_address and body_of_text. In a similar way, operations can be inherited, for example, an operation age which returned the number of days since the correspondence had been received could be attached to the correspondence object-type and inherited by sub-types.

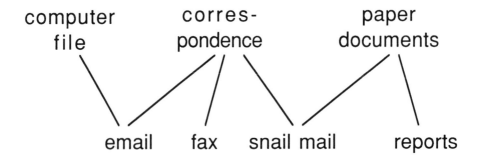

Fig. 13.3 Generalization lattice

Structural and behavioural inheritance is, in fact, of fundamental importance in object-oriented database systems such as ONTOS (Ontologic, (1988)), where every object is (ultimately) of type object. That is, there is a type called object which is at the top of the generalization hierarchy and has properties and operations that are inherited by all other object types. The operations associated with object typically include delete, equal and has_type. In this way the fundamental database operations are available to all object-types which is why, among other things, we do not need separate constructs for entities at different abstract levels, or at different levels of detail.

At the method level it is often necessary to override the behaviour inheritance, for example, the method for moving an xyCoordinate will be different from that which moves a line or a polygon. However at the level of the public interface the move operation can appear the same for all graphical elements. This illustrates again the importance of encapsulation, and allows a user to move a graphical_element without the need to specify what type of graphical element it is.

Two other types of inheritance are worth mentioning. Value inheritance may be provided at the object level. For example, a type named unit_square could be defined to be a subtype of square, with the obvious effect that all objects of this type inherited the value of 1 for the length_of_side property. A further type of inheritance is default inheritance. If we assume all properties of a type can be assigned default values, then it is sensible if sub-types inherit the default values of their parent type. It should be possible, however, for defaults to be defined for a sub-type which override the defaults that would otherwise be inherited. It should be noted that we would not necessarily expect an object-oriented DBMS to provide for all types of inheritance.

13.6 VERSION CONTROL

Because object-oriented databases are particularly suited to design environments, attention has been paid to supporting the concept of having several versions of the same object. This can be thought of as another data abstraction. It is not the same as generalisation, since properties will be inherited by a version at the instance level, with the provision made for them to be overridden. Different object-oriented DBMSs will provide different types of version control. One issue is whether a single version of an object can spawn several, or only one, new version. The advantage of allowing only one is that the concept of the latest version is well defined and can be used as the default version. Another issue is whether early versions are immutable. In principle there is no reason why they should be (at the application level), however it is convenient at the implementation level to represent a version of an object by the changes required to be made to its predecessor, in which case allowing changes to the predecessor would present problems. Another question is how a user should specify the version he or she wishes to work with. ONTOS addresses this last issue by requiring an application to enter a version configuration which ensures that the correct version of any object is retrieved from the database. Objects are not directly versioned, but take on the version of the configuration current at the time they were written to the database.

13.7 PERSISTENCE

It is important when describing the features expected of an object-oriented DBMS, to remember that, above all else, it must be a data management system, distinguishable from an object-oriented programming language. The distinguishing feature is that an object-oriented DBMS manages persistent data, that is, the life of the objects and object-types are allowed to begin before, and persist after, the execution of any application code that uses them. In the foregoing sections of this paper, we have concentrated on the object-oriented aspects of an OODB and have said little about the management of persistent data. In this section we briefly consider the various requirements that any DBMS must meet, and in particular consider what new issues there are if the DBMS is object-oriented.

13.7.1 Concurrent Access

Provision must be made for objects to be altered by concurrent applications without these alterations, or updates, interfering with one another. A common database technique is to introduce the concept of a transaction, and to allow the data item(s) involved in the transaction to be "locked" during the transaction duration. In an object-oriented database there can be three types of hierarchy locking required (see Kim *et al.* 1989), one is the conventional granularity-hierarchy locking which provides a way of minimizing the number of locks to be set whilst maintaining concurrency; a lock placed at any level in the hierarchy causes all objects below it to be locked. The other types of locking requirements are first, extending locks to object-types in the generalization-hierarchy which, through the inheritance mechanisms would be updated if a super-type were updated (required if dynamic schema modification is allowed), and second, allowing a collection of logically related objects to be locked using a single lock, rather than a separate lock for each component.

A further concurrency issue has more to do with the kinds of applications which have led to the development of object-oriented DBMS rather than the object model itself. This is the issue of long transactions in typical design environments. If a database contains a technical report, an engineering drawing or a VLSI design, updating such an object may take hours or even days, during which time the object may well violate some of the integrity constraints in the database. If transactions of this length are allowed to lock other applications from using the objects concerned, the ability to share data is clearly much reduced. A possible solution is to allow two or more such transactions to proceed concurrently without locking, taking the optimistic view that they are unlikely to interfere. If, once each transaction has tried to commit (i.e., to write any changes back to the database), some conflicts are evident, then these must be referred back to the user for resolution.

13.7.2 Backup and Recovery

Little needs to be said on this topic, except that, as is the case for any DBMS, we would expect to have support for transaction logging, database copying and database backup which helps ensure the security of the database against hardware and software failure. Backup and restore should be available at the database level or at the level of smaller units, for example, objects, object-types or closures.

13.7.3 Performance

In order to improve the performance of a database system it is useful to place data items that are often required by the same application(s) together on the disk (e.g. in the same segment). The object-oriented model helps in this organization of physical data; if we assume that instances of a given type are often required together, then these instances can be clustered. Where instances of different types are often required together, the user can specify that instances of the two types are to be clustered.

Whether such a scheme for clustering actually leads to good performance will, of course depend very much on the applications. In particular, it will be interesting to discover how efficiently clustered data can be retrieved via *ad hoc* queries made through a relational-type query language. Some prototype object-oriented DBMS map onto relational structures at a level below the object-level. This would seem to make it difficult to take advantage of clustering based on object semantics.

Maier (1986) makes a good case for predicting that in design environments object-oriented databases will be able to provide acceptable access times where relational databases have been considered to be too slow.

13.8 TYPE LIBRARIES

The persistence of object-types means that an application programmer has access to a type library which can be used for defining program variables whether or not they are to persist. Usually we would expect the object-oriented DBMS to provide an online browser to aid the programmer (or the database designer) in becoming familiar with what types are defined in the database.

As well as types defined by the Database Administrator (DBA) this library will include system-supplied types. These will include meta-types, for example, the top level object or entity type defined as the root of the type-hierarchy. Another important class of system-supplied types are the aggregate types which, in a system such as ONTOS, form a sub-hierarchy, including set, array, list and dictionary. There is a generic iterator which allows iteration through the elements of these aggregates, and one expects there to be object-type completeness, i.e. that any object-type can appear as an aggregate member, including aggregates themselves.

These aggregate types allow complex objects to be built:

object_type:	diagram
properties:	set{ <line_element: line > }
	set{ <polygon_element: polygon > }
	set{ <arc_element: arc > }

They also allow data management, including retrieval, to be set based (or aggregate based) since a set or other aggregate of objects is itself considered to be an object.

13.9 SAMPLE OBJECT-ORIENTED DBMS

During an evaluation of object-oriented DBMSs undertaken at the Universities of Leeds and Glasgow (see Bloor *et al.* 1988), seven packages were selected for evaluation, some of which were less obviously object-oriented than others. These were selected from a list of nineteen object-oriented DBMSs known to Bloor, *et al.* (1988), fourteen of which were being developed in commercial research environments, the remaining five being developed in academic environments.

It is clear that many of these products are at the prototype stage, some will eventually be available as commercial products, whereas others are seen as vehicles for research. Of those evaluated at the University of Leeds, there were two (Generis and Vbase) which appeared most promising. Vbase has since been re-named OB2, and more recently, ONTOS.

There is insufficient space here to describe in detail a range of systems, but it may be useful to consider briefly the two packages, Generis and ONTOS, to give some idea of what is currently available.

Generis is built on the Entity-Relationship data model, and perhaps is more aptly named a semantic DBMS rather than object-oriented. It supports generalisation and aggregation data abstractions, with property and default inheritance. The basic unit of modelling is an Entity, which, structurally is much the same as an object, but the behaviour is defined by rules rather than encapsulated methods. These rules can be used generally to model the behaviour of entities and as a rule-based application language. In the Leeds evaluation (Bloor, *et al.* 1988) they were found to be particularly useful for representing application-dependent constraints. Generis offers a dynamic data dictionary environment in which entity-types can be defined, placed in hierarchies and refined interactively. In this same environment facts and rules can be established and data (both stored and derived) retrieved, via a restricted natural language query syntax. A feature of Generis not usually expected of an object-oriented DBMS is explicit support for textual information with keyword-based retrieval. Generis does not offer aggregate types such as sets and arrays, and does not provide an object-oriented programming language in which database applications can be written.

In contrast with Generis, ONTOS is clearly an object-oriented DBMS. Object-type definitions, methods and application programs are all written in C + + which has been extended by adding a few extra function calls for opening and closing a database, and to activate (retrieve from the database) or deactivate (write back to the database) objects. Object types can be created at run time, although this feature was not available at the time of the evaluation. The advantage of pre-compiling object types is that (application program) compile-time type checking is able to uncover type-mismatches early on. ONTOS provides an exception as a system managed object class which makes for easy and tidy exception handling. Support for version control is provided, as discussed above, by an object-type browser and an Object-SQL interface. Serious criticisms of the early Vbase system were that compilation was slow and that the kernel database required a large amount of disk space. These problems have been addressed, and the new version running at Leeds confirms that compilation times are now acceptable.

13.10 CONCLUSIONS

It is clear that there is now a demand for database management systems to support a large variety of types of application, and it is not surprising that a new generation of DBMSs is emerging to meet this demand. Object-oriented DBMSs are playing a leading role in this new era of database technology and have the advantage that the highly-modular style of object-oriented development is becoming popular through object-oriented programming languages.

Compared with traditional DBMSs object-oriented DBMSs currently demand that more be invested both in terms of learning to use the DBMS and the work involved in implementing a database. However they also promise greater returns. That the learning investment appears large may be due, in part, to the novelty of the concepts involved, and, in part, to the relative immaturity of available products and their languages compared to traditional databases. The extra work required at the implementation stage is due to the need to capture additional structural semantics and object behaviour. This is work which would traditionally have been done (possibly more than once) within the application programs.

The extra returns that are promised by the object-oriented approach are that both data and methods can be shared and managed together, this means that behaviour as well as data can be guaranteed to be consistent. The mapping from the application model to the "schema" should be more straightforward than for traditional DBMSs, with fewer arbitrary degrees of freedom. Finally, for many areas, application development should become much easier, with less code required at the application level.

The question remaining is whether or not object-oriented DBMSs will be able to achieve efficiently all they promise. It would seem to be too early to be give a definite answer to this question, there is need for more evaluation work to be done and systematic comparisons to be made, but for many applications where the traditional approaches have not been considered to be successful, the object-oriented DBMS is looking to be one of the best ways forward.

REFERENCES

Bloor, M.S., Roberts, S.A., Preece, P.E., Atkinson, M.P. and Bailey P. (1988) Engineering database evaluation project, *SERC Project DB22082,* CIM Unit, University of Leeds, UK.

Elmasri, R. and Navathe, S.B (1989), *Fundamentals of Database Systems,* Benjamin Cummings.

Fishman, D.H., Beech, D., Cate, H.P., Chow, E.C., Connors, T., Davis, J.D., Derrett, N., Hoch, C.G., Kent, W., Lyngbaek, P., Mahbod, B., Neimat, M.A., Ryan, T.A. and Shan, M.C. (1987), Iris: An object-oriented database management system, *ACM Trans. on Office Information systems*, 5, 48-69.

Goldberg, A. and Robson, D. (1983) *Smalltalk-80: The Language and its Implementation,* Addison-Wesley, Reading, MA., USA.

Kent, W. (1978) *Data and Reality,* North-Holland, Amsterdam.

Kim, W., Ballou, N., Chou, H.T., Garza, J.F. and Woelk, D. (1989) Features of the ORION object-oriented database, in *Object-Oriented Concepts, Databases, and Applications* (ed. W Kim and FH Lochovsky), ACM Press, New York, USA.

King, R. (1989) My cat is object-oriented, in *Object-Oriented Concepts, Databases, and Applications* (ed. by W Kim and FH Lochovsky) ACM Press, New York, USA.

Maier, D. (1986) Why object-oriented databases can succeed where others have failed, *Proc. of the International Workshop on Object-Oriented database Systems,* September 1986.

Nierstrasz, O. (1989) A survey of object-oriented concepts, in *Object-Oriented Concepts, Databases, and Applications* (ed. by W Kim and FH Lochovsky), ACM Press, New York, USA.

Ontologic (1988) *Vbase+ Object Database for C++: Functional Specification,* Ontologic Inc., USA.

Peckham, J. and Maryanski, F. (1988) Semantic data models. *ACM Computing Surveys,* 20, 153-189.

Powell, M. (1988) Challenging the word of Codd *Computer Weekly*, March 17, 1988.

Roberts, S.A. and Jenkins, T. (1988) Ontologic's VBase - database of the future? *The OOPS Report*, 2, 9-12.

Smith, J.M. and Smith, D.C.P. (1977) Database abstractions: aggregation and generalisation. *ACM Transactions on Database Systems*, 2, 105-133.

14. OBJECT-ORIENTED DATABASES - EVOLUTION OR REVOLUTION?

J. Spiers

Oracle Corporation UK Ltd

14.1 INTRODUCTION

The object-oriented paradigm has proved its value in the areas of program development, artificial intelligence and user interfaces. In the latter area, the object-oriented approach leads naturally to the "direct manipulation paradigm" with user manipulation of objects via screen-based metaphors.

The strength and appeal of the approach derives largely from the close resemblance between the model and the "real world" it seeks to represent. Computer applications can now begin to relate more closely to this "real world", rather than to the nature of the underlying computer hardware and software technology.

Object-oriented techniques are used for encapsulating information, thereby shielding layers of complexity from the user or developer. Complex problems can be resolved into simple reusable components. A systematic approach can be taken to information of all types and at all levels of abstraction. Such techniques offer great promise for dealing with the ever-increasing complexity of computer applications, and can have a significant effect on how this complexity is handled.

This paper identifies the relevance of the object-oriented approach to databases and examines the various overlapping and sometimes conflicting factors propelling database technology in this general direction. The two key aspects of object-oriented DBMSs are discusssed - structural and behavioural. Some of the early evolutionary steps being taken in the world of relational databases are examined, leading to conclusions about the database systems of the 1990s.

14.2   OBJECTS AND OBJECT-ORIENTEDNESS

There are many uses of the word "object" but in general an object encompasses properties (data) and behaviour (procedures). The properties of an object cannot be accessed from outside the object; they are manipulated only by its behaviour. The behaviour of an object can only be invoked by sending messages to the object. The implementation of both properties and behaviour is hidden from the outside world; data and processes are encapsulated within the object.

Unfortunately, the term "object-oriented" is now applied to all kinds of systems, including databases, almost irrespective of their qualities. It is used as a mark of respectability, without which the system would in some sense be seen as rather unfashionable, and lacking in desirable features. The term object-oriented suffers from a wave of imprecise usage, which makes it difficult to distinguish worthwhile developments from simple hype.

Nevertheless, the term object-oriented is much more than a buzzword. Behind the slogans, there is something interesting occurring. Object-oriented development and user-interfaces have established a role for themselves with real benefits in quality and efficiency of development and ease of use.

14.3 THE IMPETUS FOR OBJECT-ORIENTED DATABASES

Applications interfaces and end-user tools for database access have brought both the concept of an object and the intuitive user appeal it can provide to the database community. The word object is now in routine use and misuse in the database world, applied both to internal data structures, procedures, and external items such as reports and displays.

Object-oriented interfaces require object-oriented development techniques; both need to be able to store and retrieve persistent objects. A database provides a logical way to deal with these persistent objects, which after all are really just a variant on the well-worn theme of data.

In addition, Database Management Systems (DBMSs) can seek to exploit the object-oriented approach to simplify applications through encapsulating and sharing behaviour. Furthermore, new applications of DBMSs such as office automation systems, and computer-aided design require data modelling capabilities not readily provided by traditional implementations.

So the requirements for object-oriented databases arise from both the evolution of conventional database applications, and from new requirements based on a new approach to computing.

However the practical directions in object-oriented databases are dictated not only by the requirement to support object-oriented applications, but also by the general direction of databases themselves.

14.4 WHAT IS A DATABASE?

Database Management Systems today lie at the heart of virtually all major information systems, acting as the guardians of the information resource. The information held on computer systems is recognized as a key asset which needs to be maintained, cherished and made available to support both operational requirements and management information needs. There is a continuing requirement to enhance DBMSs in terms of functionality, performance and more particularly intelligence - to make them more useful, to work harder, to further capitalize on the resource with which they are entrusted. At the same time, the focus of users is increasingly turning away from the underlying technology towards exploiting, through tools and applications, the information resources with which DBMSs are entrusted. Most users therefore would hope to be able to embrace new concepts within the scope of their existing DBMS investments.

The DBMSs of today and of the 1990s are expected to be very hard working. The DBMS looks after the physical management of storage space. It is expected to make information available on a 24 hour basis leading to a requirement for online back-up, recovery and administration procedures. It needs to provide efficient access to operational systems, such as payroll, and at the same time make that same information available to end-users for *ad hoc* query and analysis. It needs to guarantee transaction integrity through locking during update operations; to achieve high concurrency will require a locking scheme with fine granularity. Queries should be provided with access to consistent views of the data, even when the underlying information is being continually updated.

Performance requirements which grow year by year need to be met. The database needs to support multiple styles of access, from a variety of front-ends, batch applications, interactive screens and end-user interfaces of all types. The system may involve a variety of machines, with a need to provide both distributed processing and distributed database operations transparently across a range of machines, networks and even DBMSs. Being a DBMS is not an easy life!

Relational databases are increasingly being applied to object-oriented systems which can extend the application of computers into new areas, particularly those which involve a mix of different data types, both structured (e.g. numbers) and "unstructured" (such as text and image). At the same time, object-oriented developments promise easier applications development, simplified database administration and intuitive front-ends.

The quickest mechanism for delivering practical object-oriented databases will surely be by building on top of existing technology, provided it can offer a suitable foundation.

14.5 THE ROLE OF THE DATA DICTIONARY

At the heart of any DBMS lies the data dictionary whose role is to hold information about the structure and content of the underlying data. The dictionary is a central reference point for the database, and without the dictionary the data is no more than a meaningless binary image.

Traditionally, however, the data dictionary has been seen primarily as a means of protecting the DBMS and its data, rather than as a means of enhancing the value of the information held.

Dictionary technology is increasingly seen as central to all aspects of the development and operation of a system, a central reference for virtually everything within the configuration - data, processes, users, configurations, applications requirements and so on.

Imagine a traditional development environment, where an analyst is faced with some new data concept such as a "customer". The user already views "customer" as an object in the real world with some associated behaviour. The developer then goes through a painful process of breaking down the concept of a customer to map it into the normalized relational records that form the basis for physical implementation. Separately, programs must be developed to deal with each aspect of the behaviour of a customer. Each such procedure will probably have to deal with the fact that a single customer is physically implemented as many database records of perhaps many different types. Each such procedure has to concern itself with the semantic structure and integrity of customer information as represented in the physical database.

Note particularly that there may be no single point in the system where the concept of an customer is fully and coherently defined; a customer object is made up of the individual relational records, plus the applications logic for their processing.

Today's CASE (Computer Aided Systems Engineering) tools support a structured approach to the analysis, design and physical implementation of computer systems. Real-life objects are defined and modelled, with details captured in a data dictionary (or repository). Although the dictionary may define real-life objects in some detail, these cannot be fully and directly represented in the physical implementation since this is constrained by the implementation tools available.

Every persistent item dealt with by a system may be considered to be a database object; a database is an object, each table and each record is an object, text files are objects, procedures and programs are objects and so on. A central dictionary which contains all relevant information about objects and their relationships can become the sole source of reference and activity.

The dictionary needs to describe what an object is, how it can be used and by whom. Indeed, in organizations using CASE tools, much of the infrastructure for supporting real-life objects in a physical implementation is already in place. The dictionary already refers to objects; the database needs to directly store and support them.

14.6 OBJECT-ORIENTED DATABASES

An object-oriented database can be simply viewed as a system that provides database functionality - storage, query, update, transactions etc., - for objects, that is encapsulated data and operations. At the very least it is a handy, conceptual umbrella for a range of wide range of directions.

More specifically on object-oriented approach aims to minimise the gap between the realworld and its implementation by supporting higher levels of abstraction. It allows the semantics of the requirement to be represented in database objects rather than in applications programs. It offers a convergence between the programming language and database concepts of an object.

The movements towards object-oriented databases are fuelled by four distinct research directions:

1.   semantically oriented developments, with the focus on more fully representing the structure and meaning of data;

2.   behaviourally oriented developments providing encapsulation of methods and procedures, in addition to conventional data structures;

3.   logic based developments focused on the fusion of artificial intelligence techniques with database technology to provide "expert databases";

4.   enhanced relational developments, which seek to extend the relational framework to include concepts derived from the object-oriented paradigm.

These overlapping directions can be crystallized under two main headings: structural and behavioural developments. A key issue is that of where the structural and behavioural requirements are to be implemented:

●   within the application, the traditional approach;

- within the DBMS, by extending its functionality to embrace the required new concepts;

- in an intermediate layer, bridging applications to conventional data structures.

14.7 DATA STRUCTURE REQUIREMENTS

An object-oriented database needs to address some or all of the following data structure requirements:

complex objects: traditional relational systems have successfully implemented commercial requirements, through a small number of simple data structures. In contrast, however, much information in the real world, for example engineering data, graphical images and the like, and even commonplace commercial concepts such as 'person' or 'order', are much more complex. Although such objects can be simulated in a relational system, the performance may be unacceptable, and integrity and transparency are jeopardized.

data-types: traditional systems provide a small set of built-in data-types and access methods, typically chosen to meet common commercial requirements (for example by inclusion of date/time, currency and similar data types). Many applications may well require specialized data-types, for example, geographical coordinates. Whilst it may be possible to simulate these data-types, the resulting procedures will be unnecessarily verbose and inefficient.

"unstructured" data: databases need to accommodate new categories of information, such as text, sound and graphics. However, simply storing and retrieving such items alongside conventional structured data is only part of the solution. "Unstructured" is really a misnomer since specific mechanisms should be provided, not only for moving such information around a system, but also for dealing intelligently with such information. An obvious example is the ability to combine free text retrieval against an 'unstructured' text item alongside conventional selection criteria against structured fields.

14.8 SEMANTIC DATABASES

Many users and applications are familiar with relational concepts and there are clear advantages in retaining these, if at all possible, as database requirements embrace the object-oriented approach.

Arguably, however, the relational model has abstracted the data structure from both the program and the database to the point of over-abstraction. Practical implementations, which in general have not enforced all the integrity constraints implied by the model, have abstracted it even further.

In response, further developments of the model and alternatives to the relational approach have been proposed.

Semantic databases are concerned primarily with the meaning of data, and reflecting this as fully as possible in the structure and operations supported. Semantic data models attempt to use richer and more expressive concepts to capture more meaning than is provided by the classical data models.

The semantics which we are here considering are essentially the elements of meaning about data which are at the heart of today's structured data analysis techniques. The concepts of classes and sub-classes correspond closely to those of entity type and sub-type in entity-relationship models. Indeed the concept of an entity-relationship database is that it directly implements such models.

While there are many approaches to semantic data structures, there does not appear to be a single approach and a small model which can meet everyones' requirements. In response, probably the best approach would be through a small simple model that was extensible. The "spartan simplicity" of the relational model has proved to be its key strength, the source of its generality. Some have claimed that the baby was thrown out with the bath water when relational databases overtook structured databases. However, it is clear that the rigid navigationally oriented hierarchical and network structures that predated relational systems come nowhere near the richness of function and flexibility required to support the object-oriented direction.

Unnecessary confusion has been created by a growing tendency to refer to semantic models, which are concerned with structural abstraction, as object-oriented. Object-oriented models are derived primarily from developments in programming languages and hence focus on behavioural issues.   Such behavioural issues are concerned not just with the maintenance of semantic integrity, but also with encapsulating the manipulation of data through arbitrary methods and procedures stored with the data structures themselves.

14.9   BEHAVIOURAL DEVELOPMENTS

In an event-driven object-oriented application, the highest level of control is provided by a dispatch loop that responds to all actions of a user.

Similarly, in a database, actions may be triggered solely by events in the realworld. In a complete implementation, the whole of the conventional applications layer will have been absorbed into the database itself which becomes a self-managing system.

The requirements for many systems may be most effectively implemented using alerts and triggers. Triggers can be used to validate data, propagate updates and initiate specific processing according to the rules of the business, for example to recalculate tax tables in response to changes in the rates of taxation. Alerts will send messages based on transaction activity or database conditions. For example, we may wish to alert a stock level which falls below safety level at the point the transaction which takes it past this level is applied to the database. Or we may wish to arrange to send a message to the manager of each and every department which has overspent its budget, at the end of each week.

Of course, both of these activities could be implemented in conventional applications. However, the key point is that triggers and alerts are really associated with data values, and it is much more logical to think of them as part of the database itself. Taking the stock level example, implementation at the application level would require the necessary check to be included in each and every application that might adjust stock levels - unnecessary repetition, and difficult to enforce in evolutionary development.

Rules can be used to represent information that may be dynamic and not well suited to storage as conventional data values: for example "Men over age 59 are invited to retirement planning classes". It will be desirable for a DBMS to not only store such rules, directly or indirectly, but also to apply them without a collection of complex integrity constraints.

14.10 THE ROLE OF SQL AS A STANDARD

SQL originally emerged from IBM's research laboratories in the mid 1970s. Despite its name, Structured Query Language, it is in fact a complete language for all aspects of data definition, data access and data manipulation. SQL was originally conceived as an interactive end-user language for database interaction, but in the light of today's end-user interfaces is now more correctly viewed as a communications protocol. Its key role today is as a standard mechanism for applications of all types to deal with a DBMS. Of course, it suffers from a number of deficiencies, most particularly the lack of a standard applications programming interface (API) to define how SQL statements and data are actually exchanged programmatically, particularly across a network, an issue which is now being addressed by the SQL Access group. The question today is not one of "what is the standard way of accessing data" but of how the standard should best be developed to ensure that its full promise can be delivered.

SQL is undoubtedly the standard which offers the possibility of heterogeneous information systems spanning multiple front-end applications and tools, accessing and sharing data from a range of databases. A formal standard has been defined by ANSI and ISO and is under continuing development. The standard has been widely endorsed, for example by IBM, DEC, the X/Open group, by Microsoft and Ashton-Tate in the PC arena, and by all the independent vendors of portable DBMSs. SQL is the keystone in the aspirations for integrated, heterogeneous computing.

Object-oriented database applications cannot be confined to new information. Existing databases constitute a huge investment, and the information in them a key business asset. To prepare for such developments, organizations need to develop overall architectures which can accommodate such developments. SQL offers the only viable standard in this area, not as a user interface mechanism, but as a key interface between applications of all types and data, including access across distributed environments. The database is probably the optimum point at which to define standards, because it is the point of separation between the specific users, interfaces and applications, and the data itself serving as an integrated shared resource.

An important aspect of the relational model is that a single consistent complete language is used for all aspects of data definition and manipulation; there should be no alternative access mechanisms which could threaten the structure and integrity of the database. SQL's key role is to fully encapsulate the database; as database functionality evolves, so must SQL evolve where necessary if the key benefit of encapsualtion is to be preserved.

14.11   EXPERT SYSTEMS APPLICATIONS

A rule-based expert system requires a knowledge base (database) and an inference engine. The latter contains the logic to make inferences based on the knowledge base which contains a set of rules, which in the simplest of systems may be expressed in "if-then-else" constructs. The two commonest inference methods are forward and backward chaining. Forward chaining processes data by having the inference engine fire the relevant rules to reach a goal or conclusion. Backward chaining attempts to find a value for some goal by seeking values for sub-goals until facts satisfying the search have been found.

The data used by the inference engine may be directly stored in the knowledge base, or derived. SQL provides a wide range of functions for data derivation, for example the ability to select dynamically all values greater than the average value in a set. In other words, a rule may be expressed as a SQL statement.

14.12   SQL AS AN EXPERT SYSTEM SHELL

Standard SQL can be used to emulate forward chaining (but not backward chaining which requires recursion) and hence offers a basis for developing some specific classes of expert systems.

Shepherd *et al.*, (1989) describe a system used for monitoring drug usage built using SQL and a relational database. A clear benefit of using this approach is that the data required for expert systems applications may well already exist in a relational database since it will have been generated by conventional applications, in this case a drug prescription system.

Forward chaining can be illustrated by examining a requirement to identify potential drug interaction problems.

IF a Patient is on cimetidine
    THEN
        IF the Patient is also on theophylline
            THEN
                IF the Patient started theophylline
                    more than 14 days after cimetidine
                    THEN
                        IF the dose of theophylline > 900 mg
                            THEN
                                IF the Patient is over 65
                                  THEN
                                      There is a potential inter-
                                      action of level 8
                                ENDIF
                        ENDIF
                ENDIF
        ENDIF
ENDIF

SQL's set processing capabilities allow this to be accomplished by joining drug prescriptions (ORDER) to other prescriptions for the same patient (identified by PID):

```
SELECT PATIENT.NAME, "Severity Level = 8"
    FROM ORDER A, ORDER B
        WHERE    A.PID = B.PID
        AND      A.PID = PATIENT.PID
        AND      A.DRUG = cimetidine
        AND      B.DRUG = theophylline
        AND      B.STARTDATE -A.STARDATE > 14
        AND      B.DOSE > 900
        AND      PATIENT.AGE > 65;
```

In practice, to make the system more general, a rules table would be used to record each possible interaction and variation (age, doses etc). This rules table can then provide the input to the dynamic creation of SQL statements of the above type at runtime, providing a general purpose implementation.

Under a non-relational system, such a derivation would require complex array processing, or the continual opening and closing of files to achieve the required multiple data passes. SQL's non-procedural set processing capabilities allow the required selection to be expressed directly.

Scroggins (1988) provides a more general discussion of the mechanisms for mapping an expert system to a DBMS. Table driven mapping allows an external expert system shell to dynamically query a conventional database using a predetermined mapping; this approach is adopted by a number of commercially available products offering loose integration with relational data structures. Procedural mapping involves the creation of specific procedural code bound with the expert system shell to transfer data; whilst supremely flexible, this approach can clearly lead to major maintenace issues.

Dynamic generation of SQL queries provides a more general approach. A key strength is the posssibility of isolating the declarative knowledge from the DBMS, and thus for the expert system to gain the ability to make intelligent decisions in formulating complex queries. A major draw-back is the amount of meta-knowledge required to generate the appropriate queries and the practical problems arising from the possible generation of queries of indeterminate length, complexity and execution time.

14.13 EXTENSIONS TO RELATIONAL MODEL

XPL*SQL (Mittermeir and Eder, 1988) proposes extensions to SQL to make it more suitable for knowledge representation. The sound theoretical base of the relational model is identified as a sound base for the use of SQL as a basis for deductive databases and knowledge representation.

Two key areas where extensions to the relational model are required are identified as: constructs for the computation of transitive closure and constructs to manipulate imperfect information.

Drucks (1988) identifies the equivalence of expression in first order predicate logic with relational representation, and of the formal language of predicate logic with SQL, subject to the addition of a mechanism for closure. XPL*SQL uses a FIXPOINT construct to define declaratively the condition for terminating an iteration, and hence a mechanism for supporting backward chaining.

Drucks also discusses the use of fuzzy attributes representing the "degree of membership" of a fuzzy set to provide support for certain classes of uncertainty.

14.14   TEXT EXTENSIONS TO SQL

The ability to physically store unstructured data, for example text, graphics and sound, alongside conventional structured data in relational tables is now increasingly offered by vendors. Although there may be some practical issues involved in dealing with rather unwieldy records, no fundamental changes are required to accomplish this within the scope of standard relational systems.

More useful though, is also to recognise that such "unstructured" data may well have very specific structural properties, albeit of types which are not well provided for by traditional systems, together with a high information content. Document architecture, for example, should be directly reflected in the database, supported by selective structural and content-based retrieval operations.

A development by Oracle, SQL*TextRetrieval, provides full function free text retrieval integrated within the framework of a standard relational database and SQL.

Text retrieval is provided through word lists and location information, both held within standard relational tables. Thesaurus entries are also held in such tables. On top of these structures, it is then possible to execute retrieval operations combining structured and unstructured elements e.g.

```
select name, jobtitle
        from Employees
        where location = London
        and experience contains sales & and French & ;
```

In this example, the "Employees" table includes a textual "experience" field; the selection includes only employees whose "experience" includes both the words "sales" and "French", or synonyms thereof. The only extension to standard SQL is the "contains" clause which introduces retrieval qualifiers to be applied against textual data.

14.15 OBJECT-ORIENTED EXTENSIONS TO SQL

In the same way that the practical impact of object-oriented programming is driven largely through extensions of existing languages, as with C + +, Objective-C and the Common Lisp Object System, there are clear benefits in implementing object-oriented databases on top of the existing relational and SQL systems Indeed Beech (1988), goes so far as to suggest that "it is socially irresponsible to invent new languages if an existing language is a good approximation to what is required".

Beech demonstrates a natural mapping between the relational and object models, evidenced through extensions to standard SQL and the definition of Object

SQL (OSQL). An initial version of OSQL has been implemented for the Iris Object DBMS.

The aims of the OSQL work cover three main areas:

1. to provide a general treatment for objects and their relationships, including efficient retrieval and update

2. to address issues arising from the persistence and sharing of objects, such as evolutionary change, access control and transaction management

3. to increase the semantic content of databases, so that more information can reside in the shared database rather than in the programs; in turn this will allow databases to grow into knowledge bases directly supporting inferential retrieval.

Rather like Chen's entity-relationship model, relationships (which in the relational model are represented through keys in relational tables) are explicitly implemented as functions More generally, functions can be used for navigation and user-defined search predicates, and for specifying the semantics for update operations. A small example illustrates the evolution from standard SQL:

```
create type Person
(       name char (20) required,
        address char(40),
        phone char(14) );

create type Author subtype of Person;

create type Paper
(       title char(50) required,
        papno integer unique required,
        status char(10) required,
        authors set of Author required );
```

In the OSQL given above, "Author" is introduced as a subtype of "person", even though (in this example) it does not have additional properties. The properties of "Paper" include the "authors" property which is set-valued.

A conventional SQL implementation would require the following:

```
CREATE TABLE Person
(       personid INTEGER NOT NULL UNIQUE,
        name CHAR(20) NOT NULL,
        address CHAR(40),
        phone CHAR(14) );
```

```
CREATE TABLE Paper
(       title CHAR(50) NOT NULL,
        papno INTEGER NOT NULL UNIQUE,
        status CHAR(10) NOT NULL );
```

```
CREATE TABLE PaperAuthor
(       papno INTEGER NOT NULL,
        personid INTEGER NOT NULL );
```

To represent the set-valued property "authors" requires an additional table to be created containing valid combinations of "papno" and "personid". In turn, these values must be introduced into the "Person" and "Paper" tables as foreign keys, raising the need to maintain referential integrity.

14.16 PROCEDURAL EXTENSIONS TO SQL

SQL offers the hope of a standard mechanism for accessing data across multiple applications, networks, machines and DBMSs. However, it is now increasingly clear that procedural extensions to SQL will be required to fully realise the benefits of heterogeneous distributed systems.

The execution of arbitrary transactions against a database will typically require procedural logic. In a heterogeneous environment, there will be a need to write procedures which are fully portable, identically implemented across a range of hardware types. In a distributed environment, it may well be more effective and efficient to pass the transaction code dynamically to the data, than to move the data to the code. This in turn requires transactions to be written in a language which can be executed on any machine, and hopefully any DBMS, without recompilation. This has been the initial motivation behind the development of procedural extensions to SQL which are now offered by a number of the vendors of portable DBMS products. PL/SQL from Oracle and TRANSACT- SQL from Sybase are two examples.

However, procedural extensions to SQL can also provide a mechanism for implementing arbitrary operations against a DBMS, for example the enforcement of arbitrary integrity constraints. Declarative (non-procedural) integrity is currently addressed partly by the SQL standard, and the forthcoming SQL 2 standard will offer further extensions. However, such an approach will necessarily be restricted to particular types of generic integrity needs. Procedural extensions to SQL provide the most obvious way of implementing arbitrary behaviour against a DBMS, with procedures being stored in the DBMS where they can be shared on behalf of all relevant applications. Such procedures can also be envisaged operating as triggers, firing off automatically in response to database operations. In this sense, the behaviour of data can be moved out of applications into the database, and its operation guaranteed in all circumstances

A note of caution is however required. Arbitrary procedural behaviour which is invoked automatically can prove to be a very dangerous tool. Triggers may invoke other triggers; triggers may be recursive. The nightmare is of a series of changes propagating themselves through a database without control. A database administrator seeking to correct an atomic value might inadvertently initiate a veritable cascade of operations.

Clearly, the mechanisms for defining, testing and controlling triggers need to be carefully developed. This leads to two conclusions. Firstly, that wherever possible, constraints should be implemented declaratively, through extensions to SQL, rather than through arbitrary (and hence unrestricted) procedures. Secondly, that the application of triggers needs to be coupled to high-level, real-world data objects where behaviour can be defined, rather than to the underlying relational tables. The real-life concept of a person may, in a relational implementation, involve five, ten or more physical tables; much better to be writing constraints at the highest appropriate level of abstraction.

Note also a separate use of triggers to provide active alerts; a trigger might be programmed to send a message to the appropriate manager whenever a stock level drops below a preset safety level.

The concepts of shared database procedures, triggers and alerts all push elements of behaviour into the DBMS, through data which not only actively enforces its own integrity but which can also actively "speak out" - data that bites back!

Stored procedures also provide an approach to the representation and operation of rules within a database. Particularly where rules are subject to frequent change, this approach may well be easier to manage than storing rules as ordinary data and enforcing them through what may become a complex set of integrity constraints. Procedural extensions also provide support for iterative operations which can run until a particular completion condition (possibly "no further effect") is reached.

Although a number of vendors have implemented procedural extensions to SQL, these have not typically taken an object-oriented direction. For full acceptability to the object-oriented community, this deficiency may require correction. In addition interfaces to established object-oriented languages will be required; the lack of a standard or even widely portable object-oriented language is currently a restricting factor.

A further key area of development will require vendors to enhance their support for distributed systems and networks. A distributed environment requires the interchange of objects of a very wide range of types, not just conventional data, but also procedures, messages, software updates, reports and so on.

14.17 POSTGRES

The POSTGRES work (Stonebraker and Rowe, 1987) aims to providing an evolutionary successor to the INGRES system. In terms of data structuring its objectives are to provide:

- better support for complex objects

- extensible data types, operators and access methods

- support for time varying data - versions, snapshots and historical data

- support for active databases (alerts and triggers), iterative queries and rule processing.

A particular design goal was to make as few changes to the relational model as possible.

The design provides new data types for holding unbounded variable length arrays for data such as text, image and sound, and provision for fields of POSTQUEL (containing sequences of data manipulation commands), and arbitrary procedures. Fields of type POSTQUEL and procedure are used to represent shared complex objects. The design also provides for the storage and retrieval of historical data and versions.

The POSTGRES work provides inference through recursively defined rules; backward chaining is supported through virtual data columns for which data is inferred on demand.

It may be noted that since the POSTGRES design, SQL has clearly established its supremacy over QUEL as a standard query language for relational systems. The concepts represented by POSTQUEL are equally applicable to a SQL-based interface.

POSTGRES has now reached version 3 as an unsupported, public domain package.

14.18 THE APPLICATION OF ARTIFICIAL INTELLIGENCE

As complex applications in their own right, relational DBMSs themselves are worthwhile applications areas for the use of AI and object-oriented techniques; current examples include expert tuning tools, intelligent query optimizers, CASE tools of all types and their associated repositories holding increasingly rich and active data structures. Future applications will include intelligent user interfaces able to provide explainations of data organization, smart query processors able to understand both the structure of the database and the intention of a user query, and the ability to deal with incompletely expressed queries.

DBMS vendors developing in these areas will of course build from their own technology base allowing them to deliver a growing set of functionality within the framework of the established relational model.

14.19 APPLICATIONS OF OBJECT-ORIENTED DATABASES

The fabled application backlog has been attacked with fourth generation languages, with CASE tools, with relational databases and with expert systems. Despite this, IT departments are still unable to keep up with demands for newer, more powerful and more complex applications.

The object-oriented paradigm has the potential to reduce, or at least redefine, the applications backlog, by pushing logic concerned with data structures and behaviour out of the application into the database where it can be shared and reused.

The major benefits that an object-oriented approach can offer are as follows:

- an integrated approach to the data and functional aspects of analysis and design, plus a clear mapping from design to implementation;

- semantically rich data structures and shared reusable logic leading to smaller and simpler applications.

The object-oriented paradigm represents an important direction in the development of more functional DBMSs. There are clear advantages to be gained in pursuing this direction from the base of today's established standards. In this way, existing investments in information, applications and expertise can be protected and the benefit gained from the ongoing developments of today's DBMSs.

Today's object-oriented databases lie at about the same stage of development as the relational systems of 1980. Unsurprisingly, the performance and functionality of new object-oriented systems are unable at this stage to match that of established DBMSs.

This paper has illustrated some of the evolutionary directions of the relational approach towards the object-oriented systems of the future.   What we can therefore expect to see is a merging of current developments of enhanced relational systems and object-oriented systems to provide practical implementations during the 1990s.

A recent report by Ovum (Hales and Guilfoyle, 1989) has estimated a growth in the object-oriented sector of the database market from 1% to 10% of the (growing) whole in the period from 1990 to 1995.   Whilst this may realistically estimate the growth in the demand for, and use of, object-oriented capabilities, it assumes that by 1995 it will be possible to identify a separate object-oriented segment of the database market. With the evolutionary path being taken by the established vendors, and a lack of an agreed mechanism for distinguishing an object-oriented database, this estimate is unlikely to be ever tested.

A major constraint on the movement towards object-oriented databases is the lack of widespread agreement on just what it entails.   In contrast, the sound mathematical basis of the relational model has provided a unified sense of direction over many years, and a clear litmus test which could be applied when the relational label was misused and abused.

Without a doubt, the next few years will see a proliferation of object-oriented databases.   Of these some will unarguably be databases, but will not pass more than a superficial test of "object-orientedness"; others will be recognizably object-oriented but will not meet the most basic requirements for a practical DBMS. But hidden amongst them will be some real steps forward in database functionality.

APPENDIX A

COMMERCIAL DEVELOPMENTS

In addition to the directions towards object-oriented databases being taken by relational systems, a number of implementations of semantic and object-oriented systems are now becoming available. This appendix summarizes some of these developments.

The Fact system developed at the University of Strathclyde provides a semantic database, based on Chen's entity-relationship approach (1976). Its commercial derivative is Generis, marketed by Deductive Systems Ltd. Generis is built around an object management system, which in turn is built on a relational model. The relational model is extended to incorporate an understanding of the relationships between the underlying tables, on top of which deductive reasoning can be implemented. Generis also supports keyword retrieval on textual information. No specific object-oriented programming language support is provided.

Unisys's Infoexec provides a commercial implementation of a semantic databases, based on the work of Hammer and McLeod (1981).

Ontologic market a commercial object-oriented database, ONTOS (formerly Vbase + then OB2). Object-type definitions, methods and applications programs are all written in C + + which has been extended to provide calls for opening and closing a database, and for activating (retrieving) and deactivating (writing) persistent objects. Support is also provided for data access using SQL.

ADABAS ENTIRE also implements Chen's entity-relationship approach. ENTIRE runs as an additional layer on top of standard ADABAS data structures, which remain directly accessible in the conventional way; whilst providing an evolutionary approach, this mechanism potentially allows applications to circumvent the integrity constraints enforced by ENTIRE. There are plans to support non-ADABAS data structures under ENTIRE in the future. NATURAL EXPERT provides an expert system development tool with a knowledge base (rules and facts) held within ADABAS ENTIRE.

GemStone, developed by Servio Logic Corporation, takes as its base an object-oriented programming language, OPAL, derived from Smalltalk. The functions of the language are extended to provided data definition and manipulation for persistent objects.

Neuron Data's Nexpert Object approaches object-oriented database requirements with an AI focus. Loose integration with relational structures is provided by bridges to a range of SQL databases. A bridge to ONTOS is also planned.

REFERENCES

Beech, D. (1988) A foundation for evolution from relational to object databases, in *Advances in Database Technology,* Springer Verlag.

Chen, P. (1976) The entity-relationship model - toward a unified view of data. *ACM Trans. on Database Systems*.

Drucks, H.J. (1988) Fuzzy relational knowledge-based systems, in *Proceedings of the 6th European ORACLE User Group Conference*.

Hales, K. and Guilfoyle, C. (1989) *The Future of the Database*. Ovum.

Hammer, M. and McLeod, D. (1981) Database description with SDM: a semantic database model. *ACM Transactions on Database Systems* .

Mittermeir, R.T. and Eder, J. XPL*SQL - Research on new AI languages. *Proceedings of the 6th European ORACLE User Group Conference*.

Scroggins, C. (1988) Expert systems as database applications, in *Proceedings of the Oracle 1988 User Week*

Shepherd, J.C., Pollock, T.A. and Livengood, B. (1989) SQL as an expert system shell, in *Proceedings of the Oracle 1989 User Week*

Stonebraker, M. and Rowe, L.A. (1987) *The Design of POSTGRES.*

FURTHER READING

Cook, S. (1989) Editorial. *The Computer Journal*, 32.

Fishman, D.H. and others, (1989) Overview of the Iris DBMS, in *Object-Oriented Concepts, Databases and Applications,* Addison Wesley.

King, R. (1989) My cat is object-oriented, in *Object-Oriented Concepts, Databases and Applications,* Addison Wesley.

Laenenens, E., Staes, F. and Vermeir, D. (1989) Browsing a la carte in object-oriented databases, in *The Computer Journal*, 32, 4.

Martin, J. (1989) Series on object-oriented techniques, in *PC Week* (UK), 5.

Meersman, R.A. The future of relational database design. *Proceedings of the 6th European ORACLE User Group Conference.*

15. A GRAPHICAL INTERFACE FOR AN OBJECT-ORIENTED DATABASE

G. Kemp and D. Melvin

University of Aberdeen

15.1 INTRODUCTION

An object-oriented database system (OODBS) has been implemented in a combination of Prolog and C. This database, P/FDM (Gray *et al.,* 1988; Paton and Gray, 1988), is a natural extension of Shipman's functional data model (Shipman, 1981), which is itself based on entity-relationship concepts. An OODBS enables intuitive organization of data, in which data about a particular object are clustered with that object. Subclass-superclass hierarchies represent specializations of object classes. Relationships between objects are represented directly, forming a network of related object instances. Queries against the database navigate through this network, following relationship links from one object to others.

As an application, we are using P/FDM to store protein structure data (Gray *et al.,* 1990). At present we are storing approximately 40Mb of data on over 80 experimentally determined protein structures.

In this paper, the features of OODBS mentioned above are illustrated with examples from the protein structure domain. We show how the database can be interrogated using the programming language Prolog and the query language Daplex.

Simple database queries can also be formulated using a prototype graphical interface, which is described. Finally, we compare data organization and searching in our OODBS application with that in traditional hypermedia systems.

15.2   STORING PROTEIN STRUCTURE DATA IN AN OODBS

Proteins are molecules which are found in all living organisms and perform a variety of biochemical functions. The best way of determining a protein's three dimensional structure at present is to use X-ray crystallography. The Brookhaven Protein Data Bank (Bernstein *et al.*, 1977) has become established as the main repository for crystallographically determined protein structure data. The data stored in P/FDM is the cleaned up and extended Brookhaven data produced by the BIPED project (Islam and Sternberg, 1989).

Each class of object (or entity) within the database corresponds to an intuitively recognizable real world object. Properties of a class are represented by functions declared on that class. These functions may be either scalar attributes or relationships in which case the result of the function will be an object class. For example, shown below is the declaration of the class protein, followed by seven scalar functions declared on proteins.

```
declare protein - > > entity
declare protein_name(protein) - >   string
declare protein_code(protein) - > string
declare function(protein) - > string
declare molecular_weight(protein) - > integer
declare resolution(protein) - > float
declare authors(protein) - > string
declare source(protein) - > string
key_of protein is (protein_code)
```

The final line of the declaration indicates which function(s) will form the key for the class (Paton and Gray, 1988).

Each protein structure consists of one or more chains of amino-acid residues. Additionally, crystallography may have located the positions of ligands or solvent molecules. Thus we have a class called protein_component, of which chain is a subclass.

```
declare protein_component  - > > entity
declare component_id(protein_component) - > string
declare component_name(protein_component) - > string
declare component_protein(protein_component) - > protein
key_of protein_component is (key_of(component_protein), component_id)

declare chain - > > protein_component
declare num_copies(chain) - > integer
declare copy_num(chain) - > integer
declare num_residues(chain) - > integer
declare num_segments(chain) - > integer
declare molwt(chain) - > integer
declare accessible_area(chain) - > float
```

Subclasses inherit all functions declared on the superclass and may have additional specialized functions. Subclasses also inherit the key of the superclass.

When a relationship function is declared, an inverse function is declared automatically, thus we have a function called component_protein_inv which is declared on protein and has as its values those protein_component objects from which the protein is configured.

Protein chains fold and often sections of chain adopt regular, stable conformations. These include extended sections of chain, or strands, which lie against each other to form sheets. Helices are another regular structure found. Three kinds of helix are possible and these are classified as alpha, 3/10 or pi, depending on the tightness of twist. These regular structures are connected by loops of polypeptide chain. Thus we can think of each protein chain as consisting of a sequence of strand, helix and loop structures. These are represented directly in the database.

```
declare structure - > > entity
declare structure_chain(structure) - > chain
declare structure_name(structure) - > string
declare start(structure) - > integer
declare end(structure) - > integer
declare first_structure(chain) - > structure
declare follows(structure) - > structure
key_of structure is (key_of(structure_chain), structure_name)

declare loop - > > structure
declare helix - > > structure
declare strand - > > structure

declare threeten - > > helix
declare alpha - > > helix
declare pi - > > helix
```

As well as storing function values in the database, we are also able to derive the values of functions "on-the- fly". For example, rather than storing the length, in amino-acid residues, of each structure in the database, we can define a function which will calculate the length of a structure when this is required. This function can be defined in Daplex (Shipman, 1981).

define length(s in structure) - > integer

end(s) - start(s) + 1;

15.3   ACCESSING DATA USING PROLOG AND DAPLEX

Data in P/FDM can be accessed using the logic programming language Prolog (Clocksin and Mellish, 1984). The Prolog primitive getentity is used to retrieve an instance of a given class. For example:

getentity(protein, P)

returns in P an instance of the class protein. Other instances of the class can be found by backtracking. Additionally, getentity can be used to access a particular instance which has a given key value. For example:

getentity(protein, [p2pab], P)

returns in P the particular protein instance which has the protein_code "p2pab"

The primitive getfnval ("get-function-value") returns the value(s) of a function. For example, given a protein instance, P, the following call will return in C the code of that protein:

getfnval(protein_code, [P], C)

If a function is multi-valued, then other values can be found by backtracking. To illustrate the use of these primitives, consider the following request:

"Find all 3/10 helices which contain exactly five amino-acid residues and for each print the code and name of the protein in which it occurs, the component identifier of the particular chain which it is in, and the position in the sequence of residues at which the helix begins."

This request can be expressed in Prolog as follows:

```
getentity(threeten, T),
getfnval(length, [T], 5),
getfnval(start, [T], Start),
getfnval(structure_chain, [T], C),
getfnval(component_id, [C], Id),
getfnval(component_protein, [C], P),
getfnval(protein_code, [P], Code),
getfnval(protein_name, [P], Name),
write([Code, Name, Id, Position]), nl,
fail.
```

The "fail" causes Prolog to backtrack and to try alternative bindings for the variables.

Prolog is a full programming language and can be used to express arbitrarily complex queries. However users should not have to be experienced Prolog programmers to use the database. Data in P/FDM can also be accessed using the query language Daplex. The request described above can be expressed in Daplex as follows:

```
for each t in threeten such that length(t) = 5
for the c in structure_chain(t)
for the p in component_protein(c)
print(protein_code(p), protein_name(p), component_id(c), start(t));
```

In our system, Daplex commands are parsed and optimized before being translated into Prolog for execution.

Daplex is higher level than Prolog, and easier for non-programmers to learn and use, however it is sometimes necessary to use Prolog for particularly complex requests such as the identification of microdomains in hydrophobic protein cores (Kemp and Gray, 1990).

15.4   GRAPHICAL INTERFACE

Complex queries applied to object-oriented databases can be formulated using the high-level languages Daplex and Prolog. However, the gaining of sufficient familiarity with such languages to enable queries to be formulated requires a considerable learning investment for potential users. Therefore in order to widen access to such databases by non-programmers a graphical interface has been developed whereby queries can be formulated using graphical methods and query templates.

Since the advent of graphical interfaces in the late 1970s, the usefulness of such tools for use with relational databases has become apparent. These systems allow users without experience of comparatively complex query languages (such as SQL) to express queries against databases. QBE (Zloof, 1977) is one such query system which has been developed for use with the relational model. The success of QBE makes it a good pointer for the development of graphical interfaces to other data models.

A graphical interface involves the use of images to convey a description of the underlying process. In the case of our prototype system, the aim was to express pictorially the queries on an object-oriented database. In existing graphical systems such as QBE, the image is a table which is what the user perceives the database to be. It therefore seems sensible, in building a query language for an OODBS, to have pictures to represent entities within the database. In QBE, values could be placed in the columns of the table, in order to specify constraints. In our prototype system we wish to place constraints upon scalar functions and also to specify relationships between entities. It was decided that the most suitable form of graphical representation would be frame-like template windows, into which constraints would be entered.

Therefore a system has been developed which allows a non-programmer to interact with an OODBS using query templates which are capable of being manipulated easily using a mouse to form the query. This mouse driven interface is operated by the user selecting one or more templates from a menu. Items in the menu define the class of template- frame, which relates to the entity class that it will match when the query is run. A template-frame consists of several parts:

1.   A unique label;

2.   Zero or more text entry regions (similar to slots within traditional frame based systems) which represent the scalar functions applicable to that entity type;

3.   A bar for adding relationship links.

These features are shown in fig. 15.1.

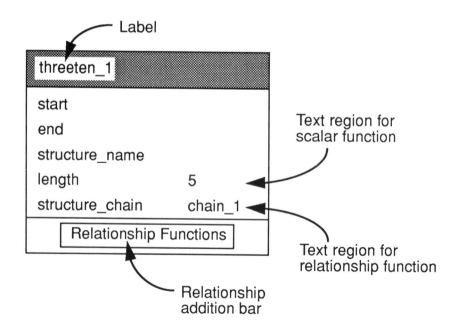

Fig. 15.1 An example of instance template

The unique label is used by the user to refer to a template on the screen when he or she is constructing a relationship constraint (see later). The label consists of a unique integer and the type of entity that the template is intended to match. Since it contains the class name that it will match, the label is used to identify to the user what the template will match.

The text entry regions correspond to scalar functions applicable to the entity class which the template is intended to match. These are used to place constraints upon which of those entities, stored within the database, should be matched to the template and subsequently displayed. In practice this takes the form of the user specifying some value for one or more functions. This restricts the set of possible matching entities to those which satisfy the constraining conditions. The constraining conditions are used to decide if the entity under examination has the correct result when the appropriate function is applied to it.

However constraints are not simply limited to scalar functions since relationships between entities can also be specified. This latter form of constraint is defined by adding a relationship link between two or more templates using the special bar. In this way a link is created between the current template and some destination template. The effect of this is to constrain the template to match only the entities for which the desired relationship link exists within the database.

The Daplex example from the previous section has been successfully carried out using the graphical interface. Queries, as stated earlier, are formulated by selecting templates from a menu. In this particular case a threeten template is first selected to search for threeten entities. Since we wish to narrow the search to threeten helices of length 5 only, a value of 5 is entered for the length constraint. Now the ultimate objective of the query is to obtain information about the protein and the chain containing the threeten helix so protein and chain templates are required to link in some way to the threeten template. The required query thus consists of three entity templates one for each of protein, chain and threeten.

To formulate the example query, the threeten template is linked by means of the structure_chain relationship function to the chain template. This is done by "clicking" the mouse in the special bar at the bottom of the template. When this is done, the user is presented with a menu of possible relationships which the object template may be involved in. Selection from this menu causes a corresponding slot to appear in the template. For the threeten template used in this example one of the possible additions is structure_chain. The user now enters into this slot the label of the chain template. Finally the above process is repeated to link the chain template to the protein template; this time the relationship used is the component_protein relationship. The complete query is shown in fig. 15.2.

With this done, the query can now be submitted to the database system for optimization and conversion into Prolog for execution in a similar way to Daplex queries. The result of the query is to bind an entity instance to each template-frame and to display the results of applying all the scalar functions to that entity instance in their respective text regions. Fig. 15.3 shows an example set of results for the query expressed in fig. 15.2. The user can then choose to continue the search of the database to find whether any other possible bindings are present and, if so, display them in the same way.

Browsing in our system involves a user specifying a pattern of related frames with additional constraints on these and then searching that database for instances which match this pattern. Hypermedia systems also permit browsing through large quantities of data, however browsing in such systems typically takes the form of the user interactively navigating through a network of hypermedia pages, following links from one page to others.

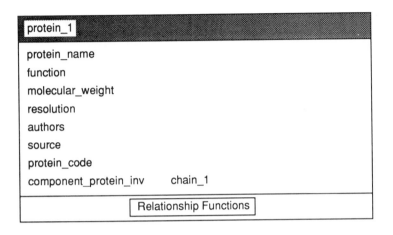

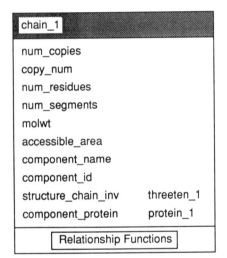

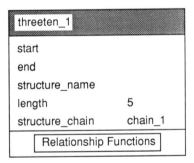

Fig. 15.2   Query to identify 3/10 helices containing five amino-acid residues and their associated chain and protein instances

protein_1

protein_name	CYTOCHROME $C PEROXIDASE
function	OXIREDUCTASE (H2O2(A))
molecular_weight	33536
resolution	1.7
authors	B.C.FINZEL, T.L.POULOS, J.KRAUT
source	BAKER,S YEAST
protein_code	p2cyp
component_protein_inv	chain_1

Relationship Functions

chain_1

num_copies	1
copy_num	1
num_residues	294
num_segments	0
molwt	33536
accessible_area	11933.4
component_name	A
component_id	
structure_chain_inv	threeten_1
component_protein	protein_1

Relationship Functions

threeten_1

start	79
end	83
structure_name	g2
length	5
structure_chain	chain_1

Relationship Functions

Fig. 15.3   *A set of results for the query expressed in fig. 15.2*

The style of browsing and querying in an OODBS is compared with that in conventional hypermedia systems in the following section.

15.5 COMPARISON WITH HYPERMEDIA

Halasz (1988) comments on the similarity, at a high level of abstraction, of the data models presented by hypermedia systems, frame-based systems and object-based systems, since each is "based around the notion of typed, slotted entities that form a network structure via inter-entity references". The correspondence between frame-based systems and object-oriented databases is discussed by Gray (1989), concluding that object-oriented database systems are well suited to the storage of frame-based knowledge representations. Similarly, hypermedia documents can be thought of as frames with links between these, corresponding to objects and relationships in our database, suggesting that an OODBS is also well suited to the direct storage of hypermedia documents.

A typical use of hypermedia systems is the processing (authoring and presentation) of documents (text, graphics, sound, animation). These are generally passive storage and retrieval systems, which are used interactively. Data within conventional hypermedia systems cannot be used conveniently for other applications; it has been structured to enable easy interactive browsing, but is not easily accessible to other applications. Thus a typical hypermedia interface would allow us to browse through the data following the relationship functions, but would not generally allow us to do systematic searching of the kind described above. This is because it provides no way in which the identifiers and attributes of the objects can be used in a piece of application program used to search the data automatically.

When querying an OODBS, we are not just interested in navigating from one object to the next in a linear fashion, but frequently want to identify groups of objects, with particular properties, which are linked to each other by various relationships. This is what Halasz calls "structure search" in hypermedia systems. Querying facilities developed for OODBS make structure search much easier in an OODBS than in conventional hypermedia systems. In our database, subnetworks of related objects can be specified using Prolog, Daplex or the graphical interface described above. Fig. 15.2 shows a template for a simple subnetwork involving three related objects. Groups of instances which match this pattern are found when the query is executed.

The other kind of search mentioned by Halasz is "content search", which involves searching for frames based on the values which they contain. Examples of content search in our database include looking for a protein instance which has a particular code, or those protein instances for which the resolution is less than 2.5 Angstroms. In conventional hypermedia systems content search is limited to string matching to identify frames containing particular words and phrases. For example, KMS (Akscyn *et al.*, 1988) provides a program which can search for text strings within a hierarchy of frames, presenting frames where matches were found for further selection. OODBS allow more general content searching, mainly through the data being more highly structured. Moreover, the ability to interrogate an OODBS using a full programming language such as Prolog enables arbitrarily complex structure and content searches to be performed.

Sometimes hypermedia users know exactly what frame they want, but the querying system does not enable them to specify that frame. In contrast, we can access particular objects directly by specifying a key. For example, if we want information on the protein prealbumin, and we know that the code for prealbumin is "p2pab", then we can access this protein instance directly by specifying the key:

getentity(protein, [p2pab], P)

Since object instances are indexed by key this access is very fast.

15.6   CONCLUSIONS

The similarity between the data models presented by OODBS and hypermedia systems suggest that OODBS are suitable for storing hypermedia documents.

OODBS applications where the nature of the data, and the kind of access required, is different to typical hypermedia applications suggest additional querying requirements which developers of hypermedia systems may find useful to consider.

The prototype interface described demonstrates that even a simple graphical interface can enable some kinds of database query to be expressed easily by non-programmers. This promises benefits from database interfaces with greater functionality which have been developed to have the ease of use found in hypermedia interfaces.

15.7   ACKNOWLEDGEMENTS

The authors would like to thank Norman Paton for help with coupling the graphical interface to P/FDM, and Janet Thornton for supplying the data produced by the BIPED project. This work was supported by the SERC through a grant to one of us (GJLK).

REFERENCES

Akscyn, R.M., McCracken, D.L. and Yoder, E.A. (1988) KMS: A distributed hypermedia system for managing knowledge in organisations. *Comms of the ACM*, 31, 820-835.

Bernstein, F.C., Koetzle, T.F., Williams, G.J.B., Mayer, E.F., Jr., Bryce, M.D., Rodgers, J.R., Kennard, O., Shimanouchi, T. and Tasumi, M. (1977) The protein data bank: a computer-based archival file for macromolecular structures. *J. Mol. Biol.*, 112, 535-542.

Clocksin, W.F. and Mellish, C.S. (1984) *Programming in Prolog.* Springer-Verlag, Germany.

Gray, P.M.D. (1989) Expert systems and object-oriented databases: evolving a new software architecture, in *Research and Development in Expert Systems V,* (eds. Kelly, B. and Rector, A.) Cambridge University Press, pp. 284-295.

Gray, P.M.D., Moffat, D.S. and Paton, N.W. (1988) A prolog interface to a functional data model database, in *Advances in Database Technology - EDBT'88.* (eds. Schmidt, J.W., Ceri, S. and Misskoff, M.) Springer-Verlag, pp 34-48.

Gray, P.M.D., Paton, N.W., Kemp, G.J.L. and Fothergill, J.E. (1990) An object-oriented database for protein structure analysis. *Protein Engineering,* 3, 235-243.

Halasz, F.G. (1988) Reflections on notecards: seven issues for the next generation of hypermedia systems. *Comms of the ACM,* 31, 836-852.

Islam, S.A. and Sternberg, M.J.E. (1989) A relational database of protein structures designed for flexible enquiries about conformation. *Protein Engineering,* B2, 431-442.

Kemp, G.J.L. and Gray, P.M.D. (1990) Finding hydrophobic microdomains using an object-oriented database. *CABIOS,* B6R, 4.

Paton, N.W. and Gray, P.M.D. (1988) Identification of database objects by key, in *Advances in Object-Oriented Database Systems: Proc. OODBS-II,* (ed. Dittrich K.R.) Springer-Verlag, pp. 280-285.

Shipman D.W. (1981) The functional data model and the data language DAPLEX. *ACM TODS,* 6, 140-173.

Zloof, M.M. (1977) Query-by-example: a data base language. *IBM Sys. J.,* 16, 324-343.